Simone de Beauvoir's
Fiction

american
university
studies

Series XXVII
Feminist Studies

Vol. 10

PETER LANG
New York • Washington, D.C./Baltimore • Bern
Frankfurt am Main • Berlin • Brussels • Vienna • Oxford

Simone de Beauvoir's Fiction

Women and Language

Alison T. Holland
and Louise Renée,
Editors

PETER LANG
New York • Washington, D.C./Baltimore • Bern
Frankfurt am Main • Berlin • Brussels • Vienna • Oxford

Library of Congress Cataloging-in-Publication Data

Simone de Beauvoir's fiction: women and language /
Alison T. Holland and Louise Renée, editors.
p. cm. — (American university studies XXVII: Feminist studies; v. 10)
Includes bibliographical references and index.
1. Beauvoir, Simone de, 1908– —Criticism and interpretation.
I. Renée, Louise. II. Holland, Alison. III. Series: American
university studies. Series XXVII, Feminist studies; v. 10.
PQ2603.E362Z884   843.'914—dc22   2005006956
ISBN 0-8204-7085-6
ISSN 1042-5985

Bibliographic information published by **Die Deutsche Bibliothek**.
Die Deutsche Bibliothek lists this publication in the "Deutsche
Nationalbibliografie"; detailed bibliographic data is available
on the Internet at http://dnb.ddb.de/.

The paper in this book meets the guidelines for permanence and durability
of the Committee on Production Guidelines for Book Longevity
of the Council of Library Resources.

© 2005 Peter Lang Publishing, Inc., New York
275 Seventh Avenue, 28th Floor, New York, NY 10001
www.peterlangusa.com

Printed in Germany

To Yolanda Astarita Patterson,
President of the Simone de Beauvoir Society,
for her unwavering support for Beauvoir scholars
at all stages of their careers.

CONTENTS

ACKNOWLEDGMENTS

This book grew over a number of years out of passionate conversations based on a shared enthusiasm for Simone de Beauvoir's ficion. As editors we would like to express our enormous gratitude to all the contributors who have given so generously of their time.

We would like to thank the University of Manitoba, Winnipeg, Canada and the University of Northumbria, Newcastle upon Tyne in the UK for their continuing support. Our thanks also go to the editorial staff at Peter Lang for their patience and advice.

We gratefully acknowledge permission to reuse material from the article by Alison Holland, "Simone de Beauvoir's Writing Practice: Madness, Enumeration and Repetition in *Les Belles Images*", in *Simone de Beauvoir Studies* Vol 15, 1998-1999, 113-125.

Finally, we owe enormous thanks to our families and friends for their unfailing love and support without which this book would not have been possible.

ABBREVIATIONS

AMM	*All Men are Mortal*
ASD	*All Said and Done*
BI	*Les Belles Images (French)*
BO	*The Blood of Others*
DS I	*Le Deuxième Sexe, vol. 1*
DS II	*Le Deuxième Sexe, vol. 2*
FR	*La Femme rompue*
FA	*La Force de l'âge*
FC I	*La Force des choses, vol. 1*
FC II	*La Force des choses, vol. 2*
FC	*Force of Circumstance*
I	*L'Invitée*
LBI	*Les Belles Images (English)*
LM I	*Les Mandarins, vol. 1*
LM II	*Les Mandarins, vol. 2*
M	*The Mandarins*
MJF	*Mémoires d'une jeune fille rangée*
MDD	*Memoirs of a Dutiful Daughter*
PL	*The Prime of Life*
QPS	*Quand Prime le Spirituel*
SA	*Le Sang des autres*
SS	*The Second Sex*
SCS	*She Came to Stay*
TH	*Tous les Hommes sont mortels*
TCF	*Tout Compte fait*
WTS	*When Things of the Spirit Come First*
WD	*The Woman Destroyed*

Quotations are given in the original French and in English. Whenever possible, references are to published translations. The editions used are those listed in the "Works Cited" sections. Unfortunately, it is often the case that the English translations are inaccurate and fail to reproduce the rhetorical impact of Simone de Beauvoir's carefully crafted texts. Readers' attention will be drawn to only the most misleading examples.

Introduction

Alison T. Holland and Louise Renée

Simone de Beauvoir has finally emerged from under Jean-Paul Sartre's shadow as a brilliant and original thinker in her own right. Beginning with Michèle LeDoeuff's ground-breaking *L'Étude et le rouet: Des femmes, de la philosophie, etc.* published in 1989, scholars from all over the world have begun to read Beauvoir's work not just as an extension of Sartre's existentialist thought, but as a radical and original contribution to feminist literature, philosophy and criticism. Sonia Kruks, in her influential article titled "Teaching Sartre about Freedom", argued that Beauvoir developed a concept of freedom that enabled her to denounce oppression, whereas Sartre's ontology, almost devoid of an ethics, could not. Other authors have since emphasized the originality of Beauvoir's thought in relation to Sartre's, and new studies on various aspects of her works continue to appear every year.

These are exciting times for Beauvoir scholars. We are now realizing that her philosophy was very different from Sartre's and far less influenced by it than previously thought. We are also beginning to read her works more seriously than ever before, producing works such as Nancy Bauer's *Simone de Beauvoir, Philosophy and Feminism.* Recent monographs by Eva Lundgrin-Gothlin, Karen Vintges, Debra Bergoffen, Jo-Ann Pilardi, Mariam Fraser, and Joseph Mahon, as well as the collection of philosophical essays edited by Claudia Card, all study aspects of Beauvoir's philosophy, adding invaluable insights into Beauvoir's thinking. Her correspondence and memoirs are also attracting scholars such as Ursula Tidd, author of *Simone de Beauvoir. Gender and Testimony* and Susan Bainbrigge whose book *Writing Against Death: The Autobiographies of Simone de Beauvoir* is forthcoming.

The one area of Beauvoir's work which has been sorely neglected until now, however, is her fiction. This is understandable, since the first task of contemporary Beauvoir scholars was to rescue her from her unfair reputation as Sartre's disciple. But now that this misconception has been corrected, scholars are now turning their attention to her fiction. Her novels are indeed inseparable from her philosophical ideas. However, as she states very clearly in "Littérature et métaphysique," literature is the only genre which allows a writer to convey the rich ambiguity of life. Philosophy can only discuss ideas and abstract concepts. Literature evokes the complexities of lived experience, and grants the reader freedom to work out issues raised by the text. For this reason, Beauvoir considered literature, not philosophy, the most important genre for her.

Early books on Beauvoir's fiction include those of Terry Keefe (1983), Elizabeth Fallaize (1988) and Jane Heath (1989). Two American philosophers have discussed several of Beauvoir's novels: Kristana Arp in *The Bonds of Freedom. Simone de Beauvoir's Existentialist Ethics* (2001), and Eleanor Holveck in *Simone de Beauvoir's Philosophy of Lived Experience* (2002). These authors focus mostly on Beauvoir's philosophy as it is expressed in her fictional works. More recently (2002), Sarah Fishwick has devoted one half of a monograph to the theme of the body in Beauvoir's fiction, whereas Genevieve Shepherd (2003) has studied all of Beauvoir's fiction from a psychoanalytic point of view.

Interest in Beauvoir's fiction in general and in her writing practice in particular is growing. Despite this, there is no recent book on Beauvoir's fiction from the point of view of literary criticism. The misconception about Beauvoir's being Sartre's disciple was a very difficult prejudice to overcome. But there is still one lingering assumption, present even amongst Beauvoir scholars: that Beauvoir did not have a very sophisticated conception of language. This could not be further from the truth. Beauvoir used language not just to express, but to reveal, to challenge, to undermine, to question the very possibilities of language. This is what our collection of essays sets out to demonstrate. Using a variety of approaches in terms of literary theory, our book focuses on Beauvoir's writing practice in her fiction, exploring the extent to which the meaning of her books cannot be separated from the way they are written.

An examination of Beauvoir's attitudes towards language and meaning provides a useful framework for the reading of her fiction. Alison Holland has argued elsewhere that, as Beauvoir struggled with language to make it express her meaning, in a way comparable to the women protagonists in *La Femme rompue,* her writing actually undermines the (patriarchal) ideological assumptions about language and meaning that she, in part, subscribes to.[1]

---

[1] See "Prière d'insérer", where Beauvoir writes of the women protagonists "qui se débattent avec des mots". Reproduced in Ed. Claude Francis and Fernande Gontier, *Les Écrits de Simone de Beauvoir* (Paris: Gallimard, 1979) 231-32. An earlier version of this material relating to Beauvoir's writing practice has appeared in Alison Holland, "Simone de Beauvoir's Writing Practice: Madness, Enumeration and Repetition in *Les Belles Images*", *Simone de Beauvoir Studies* 15 (1998-1999) 113-125.

There is a broad consensus that Beauvoir believes language to be a transparent, unequivocal sign system which allows us to say what we mean. For instance, Toril Moi argues that Beauvoir "relies on Sartre's disastrously simplistic theory of language as a transparent instrument for action", and that for her, language is "the author's most reliable ally; a faithful workhorse that never fails to convey the desired message".[2] Leah D. Hewitt writes:

> For contemporary critics interested in the way writing ("écriture") plays havoc with identity, puts into question the subject of/ in language and disrupts oppositional thought, de Beauvoir's work is perhaps too readable, that is, naive. [...] De Beauvoir assumes with conviction the existence of the coherent ego that attributes meaning and occupies an unassailable position over language. For this powerful subject, unconscious desire has no place.[3]

Whilst it is certainly possible to find support for such judgments in Beauvoir's writing and in interviews she gave, they do not give a complete picture, and Beauvoir's views on language are more complex and contradictory than they suggest.

In *L'Existentialisme et la sagesse des nations,* written in 1948, Beauvoir asserts that "les trahisons du langage [...] empêchent toute communication véritable".[4] In stark contrast, in her contribution to a 1964 debate, *Que Peut la Littérature?*, she argues that true communication is possible and denies that language is a barrier: "Je pense que je dis ce que je dis et qui est ce que vous entendez; il y a là un rapport vrai qui se crée à travers le langage: celui-ci est opacité mais c'est aussi un véhicule de signification commun à tous et accessible à tous".[5] Interestingly, although she contends here that language does not act as a barrier to communication, she nevertheless refers to it as opaque, not transparent. In 1968, in an interview with Ved Solverg Saetre about the *nouveau roman,* speaking about Sollers' *Drame,* Beauvoir seeks to clarify her position on language:

> Il décrit bien l'échec des mots devant la réalité qu'ils prétendent exprimer – c'est cet échec qui est intéressant. Ce thème est essentiel. Je ne l'ai jamais nié:

---

2 Toril Moi, *Simone de Beauvoir: The Making of an Intellectual Woman* (Oxford: Blackwell, 1994) 144, 248.
3 Leah D Hewitt, *Autobiographical Tightropes: Simone de Beauvoir, Nathalie Sarraute, Marguerite Duras, Monique Wittig, and Maryse Condé* (Lincoln: University of Nebraska Press, 1990) 15.
4 "The betrayals of language prevent any true communication." (Editors' translation.) Simone de Beauvoir, *L'Existentialisme et la sagesse des nations* (Paris: Nagel, 1986) 25.
5 "I think that I say what I say and that that is what you hear; there is a real connection created through language: language is opaque but it is also a vehicle of meaning common to all and accessible to all." (Editors' translation.) Simone de Beauvoir, in *Que Peut la Littérature?*, Ed.Yves Buin (Paris: Union Générale d'Éditions, 1965) 78. Sartre's contribution to the same debate appears in the same collection, pp. 107-27. The debate is described in Simone de Beauvoir, *Tout Compte fait* (Paris: Gallimard, 1972) 170-71.

> les mots ne collent pas à la réalité – mais je dis les mots sont notre seul moyen de communication et qu'on doit essayer d'établir une réalité à travers les mots bien que nous sachions quels pièges ils nous tendent.[6]

She argues that although words fit reality imperfectly, they remain our only means of communicating and establishing a reality. In her memoirs, Beauvoir develops these ideas further. She argues that unlike scientific language where there is a clear, transparent link between words and ideas, language in literature operates in a much more complex way. She writes:

> Il n'y a d'oeuvre littéraire que si le langage est en jeu, si le sens se cherche à travers lui, provoquant une invention de la parole même. [...] Une oeuvre qui se réfère au monde ne saurait être une simple transcription, puisqu'il n'est pas doué de parole. Les faits ne déterminent pas leur expression, ils ne dictent rien: celui qui les relate découvre ce qu'il a à en dire, par l'acte de le dire. [...] Qu'il s'agisse d'un roman, d'une autobiographie, d'un essai, d'un ouvrage d'histoire, de n'importe quoi, l'écrivain cherche à établir une communication avec autrui à partir de la singularité de son expérience vécue; son oeuvre doit manifester son existence et porter sa marque: et c'est par son style, son ton, le rythme de son récit qu'il la lui imprime. (TCF 162-63)[7]

Her argument is that language in literature does not transmit a pre-existing meaning or represent reality, but it is involved in a process of signification, of creating meaning. It appears that Beauvoir is always torn between her conviction that she says what she means and that her meaning is unambiguously present in the words she uses and her awareness that meaning is the outcome of a process involving a struggle with language.[8] A close reading of Beauvoir's

---

[6] "He describes very well the failure of words when faced with the reality they claim to express – it is this failure that is interesting. This theme is of vital importance. I have never denied that words don't fit with reality – but I say that words are our only means of communication and we must try to establish a reality through words even though we know what traps they set for us." (Editors' translation) Ved Solverg Saetre, "Interview with Simone de Beauvoir", *Vinduet* 3 (1968) 196-201. Summary and extracts translated from Norwegian in Francis and Gontier, *Écrits* 233.

[7] "A work of literature can only exist if language is involved, if the meaning seeks self-expression by means of language, thus bringing about discovery of the Word itself. [...] No work that has reference to the world can be a mere transcription , since the world has not the power of speech. Facts do not determine their own expression; they dictate nothing. The person who recounts them finds out what he has to say about them through the act of saying it. [...] Whether it is a question of a novel, an autobiography, an essay, an historical work or no matter what, the writer attempts to set up communication with others by means of the uniqueness of his personal experience; his work must make the existence of this experience evident and it must bear the mark of that experience – and it is by means of his style, his tone of voice and his rhythm that he communicates his experience to his work." *All Said and Done*, Trans. Patrick O'Brian (New York: Paragon, 1993, Harmondsworth: Penguin, 1991) 129-30.

[8] Ursula Tidd examines Simone de Beauvoir's disagreement with Sartre about about language, writing and the representation of experience as it is exemplified in a debate they had one day at Saint-Cloud and repeatedly afterwards. She argues that Beauvoir concedes only reluctantly and provisionally to

fiction reveals the extent to which her writing practice undermines patriarchal ideological positions on language and fails to corroborate the view (that she shared to some extent) that language is an unequivocal sign system.

Changes in Beauvoir's views on women and their distinctive relation to language can be traced through comments she made in the 1970s. In 1970, in an interview with Nina Sutton, Beauvoir was categorical: "Une femme écrit-elle autrement qu'un homme? Seulement dans la mesure où sa situation est différente dans notre société actuelle. Un style littéraire ne fait que refléter la situation de l'écrivain et son rapport à sa situation" [9] By 1976, in the preface to Anne Ophir's book, *Regards féminins: condition féminine et création littéraire,* although Beauvoir continued to reject the notion of *écriture féminine* as elitist and esoteric, she nevertheless recognised that patriarchal language holds particular dangers for women: "Je sais que le langage courant est plein de pièges. Prétendant à l'universalité, il porte en fait la marque des mâles qui l'ont élaboré; il reflète leurs valeurs, leurs prétentions, leurs préjugés. Il convient de n'en user qu'avec prudence."[10] Her views on this specific point did not shift. She reiterated her warning in an interview with Alice Jardine in 1977, which was published in 1979. Although we "can't not use this universal instrument", she argues, women must be aware that it incorporates masculine bias and must "enrich their language, clean it up"; "Women simply have to steal the instrument [...] and use it for their own good."[11] She added that language is a universal

---

Sartre's view that in order to « s'approprier les choses [...] il faut saisir leur sens et le fixer dans des phrases » which opposed her own view that « la réalité déborde tout ce qu'on peut en dire; il fallait l'affronter dans son ambiguïté, dans son opacité au lieu de la réduire à des significations qui se laissent exprimer par des mots ». (FA 168) ("I maintained that reality extends beyond anything that can be said about it; that instead of reducing it to symbols capable of verbal expression, we should face it as it is – full of ambiguities, baffling, and impenetrable. I replied that anyone who wished, as we did, to arrange the world in a personal pattern must do something more than observe and react; he must grasp the meaning of phenomena and pin them down in words." (PL 144) See Ursula Tidd, *Simone de Beauvoir: Gender and Testimony* (Cambridge: Cambridge University Press, 1999) 137-43.

[9] "Do women write differently from men? Only in so far as their situation in today's society is different. A literary style is simply the reflection of a writer's situation and their experience of their situation." Nina Sutton, Interview with Simone de Beauvoir, "Sartre and *The Second Sex*", *Guardian* (19 February 1970) 11. Summary and extract in Francis and Gontier, *Écrits* 245.

[10] "I know that everyday language is full of traps. Claimed to be universal, it is in fact marked by the males who made it; it reflects their values, their pretentions, their prejudices. It ought only be used with care." (Editors' translation) Preface to Anne Ophir, *Regards féminins: condition féminine et création littéraire* (Paris: Denoël/ Gontier, 1976) pages not numbered. Preface reproduced in Francis and Gontier, *Écrits* 577-79.

[11] Alice Jardine, "Interview with Simone de Beauvoir", *Signs* (Winter 1979) 230. It is striking that Simone de Beauvoir uses the same verb as Hélène Cixous to describe women's relationship/attitude to language; as Alice Jardine points out, they both use the verb "voler" – Simone de Beauvoir to mean "to steal" and Hélène Cixous in its double meaning, "to steal" and "to fly". See also Beauvoir's comments on language in "Beauvoir elle-même", Interview with Catherine David, *Le Nouvel Observateur* (January 1979) 84-5.

instrument that can be used "in a feminist perspective" and so "find itself
changed in a feminist manner" but rejected the idea that the unconscious
has a role to play in the production of language and that women therefore
have a fundamentally different relation to language. Beauvoir continued to
believe that language is a function of social situation. Yet at this point in the
interview, Beauvoir appeared to flounder as she responded to a question
on the connection between social situation and the unconscious. She told
Alice Jardine: "If the unconscious must express itself it will do so through
the work that you do consciously ... or subconsciously, with words, with
what you have to say".[12] When asked whether there should be a difference
between feminine and masculine discourse, given women's and men's very
different social situations at that historical moment, Beauvoir replied that
on topics common to women and men such as oppression and misery,
women would speak in exactly the same way as men and that women
would speak differently only when speaking of their own personal problems as women. However, a little later in the interview Beauvoir expressed
a somewhat different attitude, noting that on certain topics it would be
impossible to tell the difference between writing by women and men yet
seemingly arguing that women necessarily write differently to men:

> [...] From the moment you involve yourself fully in writing a novel, for
> example, or an essay, then you are involved as a woman, in the same way that
> you can't deny your nationality – you are French, you are a man, you are a
> woman ... all this passes into the writing.[13]

She seemed almost offended at the suggestion that her own books might
have been written by a man.[14]

As we have seen, relatively little critical attention has been given to the
form of Beauvoir's fiction.[15] It also seems to be generally taken for granted

---

[12] Jardine 231.
[13] Jardine 233.
[14] Jardine 233.
[15] Unfortunately, dismissive comments as to the literary merits of Beauvoir's writing by critics who
have barely engaged with the formal aspects of her texts are all too common. See, for instance, Terry
Keefe, *Simone de Beauvoir: A Study of her Writings* (London: Harrap, 1983). Despite his relative lack of
analysis of form, Keefe levels severe criticisms at Simone de Beauvoir's fictional works and concludes
that their aesthetic defects might make us "disinclined even to consider whether they are accomplished
works of art." (p. 229) See also Renée Winegarten, *Simone de Beauvoir: A Critical View* (Oxford: Berg,
1988). Winegarten's starting point is that "basically, [Beauvoir] was not an inventive or highly imagi-
native writer" (p. 3). She neglects to support this assertion by careful analysis of Beauvoir's writing
practice. For example, one page is allotted to *Les Belles Images*; she considers this to be Simone de
Beauvoir's "most accomplished work of fiction in the formal sense" (p. 114) but restricts herself to
summarising the plot.

that Beauvoir herself paid little or no attention to the style of her books. This was not in fact the case. Beauvoir attached a great deal of importance to the artistic reworking of lived experience, the craft of writing. This emerges clearly in "Intermède" in *La Force des choses,* where she describes the long painstaking process of reworking the drafts of her books:

> M'aidant de mon brouillon, je rédige à grands traits un chapitre. Je reprends la première page et arrivée en bas, je la refais phrase par phrase; ensuite je corrige chaque phrase d'après l'ensemble de la page, chaque page d'après le chapitre entier; plus tard, chaque chapitre, chaque page, chaque phrase d'après la totalité du livre. (FC I 294)[16]

Beauvoir believed that attention must be paid to form in order to produce a literary work.[17] In her contribution to the 1964 debate, *Que Peut la Littérature?,* Beauvoir writes:

> En fait, nous accordons beaucoup plus d'importance au langage qu'on ne le dit parfois; il n'y a pas de littérature s'il n'y a pas une voix, donc un langage qui porte la marque de quelqu'un. Il faut un style, un ton, une technique, un art, une invention [...].[18]

She goes on to assert that in literature the distinction between form and meaning is obsolete and that the two cannot be separated ("la distinction entre le fond et la forme est périmée; et les deux sont inseparables").[19] For Beauvoir, literature is an exploration or a search ("une recherche") and style or form plays a crucial role in this exploration: "On ne peut pas séparer la manière de raconter et ce qui est raconté, parce que la manière de raconter c'est le rythme même de la recherche, c'est la manière de la définir, c'est la manière de la vivre."[20] In 1979 in an interview with Catherine David in *Le Nouvel Observateur,* in response to the interviewer's remark that style does not seem to be of great importance to her, Simone de Beauvoir replies:

> Au contraire, j'y attache une grande importance. Je travaille énormément tout ce que j'écris. Vous savez, pour émouvoir, il faut que les choses soient

---

16 "With the help of my rough draft, I sketch the broad outlines of a chapter. I begin again at page one, read it through and rewrite it sentence by sentence; then I correct each sentence so that it will fit into the page as a whole, then each page so that it has its place in the whole chapter; later on, each chapter, each page, each sentence, is revised in relation to the work as a whole." (FC 285)
17 Moi quotes the diary entry in *La Force des choses* where Simone de Beauvoir writes that for the lifeless sentences that transcribe her life to become a real literary work, she would have to pay attention to how she told the story, to 'la façon de raconter'. *Simone de Beauvoir,* 247.
18 *Que Peut la Littérature?* 84.
19 *Que Peut la Littérature?* 84.
20 *Que Peut la Littérature?* 85. "How a story is told cannot be separated from what is told because how a story is told is the rhythm of the exploration, the way to define it, the way to live it."

dites d'une certaine façon, avec un certain ton, des ellipses, des images, des
développements. Ça a toujours beaucoup compté pour moi. [...] Dans mes
romans et mes Mémoires, je fais toujours très attention à la manière dont je
dis les choses. On ne peut évidemment pas séparer la manière du contenu.[21]

Given the importance Beauvoir attached to form and to the craft of
writing, her use of language cannot be regarded as a merely accidental; the
close readings of Beauvoir's fiction which follow reveal the extent to which
the how of the telling is the meaning of the stories told.

In *Que Peut la Littérature?*, Beauvoir tells us that to write is to reveal the
world and so to act and to change the world. For Beauvoir, one of the roles
of literature is to allow us to overcome what separates us from each other
by revealing that what is most personal to us is also shared by others.[22] For
this reason, Beauvoir argues, "il faut parler de l'échec, du scandale, de la
mort, non pas pour désespérer les lecteurs, mais au contraire pour essayer
de les sauver du désespoir".[23]

The essays in this collection focus on Beauvoir's use of language in her
fictional texts, with a particular emphasis on the relationship between
women and language. The contributors approach the texts from a variety
of theoretical positions. The chapters have been ordered chronologically
according to the date of composition of Beauvoir's short stories and novels. Two chapters have been allocated to *Les Mandarins* due to the length
and importance of this novel.

The first chapter by Louise Renée is titled "Gothic Narrative and
Imagery in *Quand Prime le Spirituel*." Beauvoir's first fictional work was
written in 1938 but only published in 1979. Dismissed by the author herself as a rather clumsy book, *Quand Prime le Spirituel* already points to *Le
Deuxième Sexe* in its representation of women's situation and in its insistence on the role that language plays in the conditioning of women. Here,
Beauvoir deconstructs patriarchal discourse by incorporating narrative
strategies typical of Gothic fiction.

Beginning with Michèle Massé's study of modern Gothic fiction as a theoretical framework, Louise Renée argues that Beauvoir uses Gothic narrative

---

[21] David 88–89.

[22] Beauvoir also discusses the role of literature in a lecture she gave in Japan in 1966, when most of her
fiction was already written. "Mon Expérience d'écrivain", Lecture given in Japan, October 1966, in
Francis and Gontier, *Écrits* 455-57.

[23] *Que Peut la Littérature?* 92. "Failure, outrages, death must be spoken of, not to make readers despair,
but on the contrary, to try to save them from despair." (Editors' translation)

and imagery in order to expose the fictions responsible for women's suffering. The bold narrative structure consisting of five interconnected stories is an echoing device where each story is reflected in one or more other stories in the collection, and could be endlessly repeated, thus conveying the idea of woman's common condition. The dark, claustrophobic atmosphere of Gothic novels is created by images of silence and enclosure which symbolize the female characters' sense of imprisonment. A reference to Charlotte Perkins Gilman's *The Yellow Wallpaper* can be found in one of the young woman's fixation on the yellow, rotting wallpaper of a café. Other images, such as corsets and prisons, abound in this novel, pointed reminders of the severe restrictions imposed on the young women of the time.

All of the women in this text yearn for escape through love. The romance plot depicted in Gothic novels and in popular fiction can be construed as a feminist critique of women's oppression because it exposes the ideology that encourages women to deny agency. More than a critique of spiritualism, *Quand Prime le Spirituel* exposes the role that cultural conditioning has on young women, especially romance's mythologizing discourse. The books that are banned, those that the young women are allowed to read, the legends of female martyrs, the emphasis on suffering and masochism in texts, all lead to the Harlequin ideal of the pure heroine conquering a cold and cruel man by the force of her love.

The young women in this novel are trained to memorize and passively regurgitate what they read. Unaware of the destructive and misogynistic messages imbedded in the texts they study, the women not only absorb negative images of women, but more importantly, they deny their own ability to read critically. Thus, they are being trained as Gothic heroines, ready for the subservience that awaits them in marriage. Likewise, the male characters in this text have learned to be cruel or indifferent Gothic heroes who silence, abuse, dominate or neglect their women. But by depicting female suffering, Gothic fiction implicitly calls for Beauvoir's own ideal of reciprocity. In *Quand Prime le Spirituel,* Beauvoir uses language subversively, undermining patriarchal discourse from within, so that women can reject the Gothic script that is still ours to a great extent today.

"Intimacy and Revenge: Language and Power in *L'Invitée*" is the title of Chapter 2 by Alison Holland. Françoise's relationships with Xavière and Élizabeth are inextricably bound with her relationship with language. Françoise fears the power of others to narrate her story. Although she ends up losing faith in language, she nevertheless uses (or abuses) her own narrative power to exact revenge on the two women with whom she has intense relationships.

Holland begins by recalling the two chapters that were originally meant to open *L'Invitée* but which were cut by Gallimard. Here, Françoise's fascination with Élizabeth, Pierre's sister, becomes an unhealthy dependence and desire to merge with the other. In the published version, it is Élizabeth who takes on this slavish admiration for Françoise. She is portrayed negatively, but she is actually Françoise's double, reflecting her darker self – her hate, jealousy, instability, bad faith, and faltering sense of self.

François's sense of self is threatened by her desire for symbiosis with and her ambivalent sexual attraction towards Elisabeth and Xavière. Xavière is represented as a demoniacal persona, with her strange smile and tyrannical presence. She is a hostile consciousness compared to a devouring vagina and associated with slaughter, cannibalism and preying animals. Françoise's emotional reaction to Xavière is reflected in the syntax: the accumulation of clauses, enumeration, repetition, and long uncoordinated sentences communicate a feeling of relentlessness and suffocating enclosure. Françoise sublimates her intense relationship with Xavière by turning to Gerbert, Xavière's lover. The power struggles that entail read as a battle for narrative authority.

Françoise's sense of identity is threatened by others' views of her. She cannot tolerate the idea of someone having a negative image of her in their head, and her distress is reflected in the fragmented syntax. Her survival depends on her gaining narrative supremacy and eliminating Xavière. The use of hyperbole and Gothic excess in her narrative reflect a loss of faith in language. The hallucinatory quality of the murder scene, with the disarticulated and convulsive syntax, the hellish Gothic atmosphere, and the rhythm of broken sobs, ultimately discards the need to justify the murder. "It is Beauvoir's writing", argues Holland, "that succeeds in making everyday life topple over into tragedy". Language therefore becomes at once form, theme and protagonist in Beauvoir's first published novel.

Chapter 3 by Sarah Fishwick is titled "'Ce sera bientôt l'aube': Narration and Lexis in *Le Sang des autres* and *Tous les Hommes sont mortels*". Examining both narrative structure and imagery, Fishwick shows how both novels, published within a year of each other, are marked by circularity and cohesion thanks to patterns that are repeated throughout the texts. Although the main narrators in both texts are men, the female characters not only frame the narratives but play an important role, eventually recognizing the burden of history on the individual. In both novels, the sections focalized by a male narrator take up a far greater portion of each text, but it is nevertheless through Hélène and Régine that their stories are filtered and interpreted.

Repeated motifs associated with the female protagonists punctuate both texts. Each novel is narrated during the course of a long night, and ends with the break of day. In *Le Sang des autres,* Jean Blomart reflects upon the ethics of political action while maintaining a vigil at Hélène's bedside. Fishwick writes: "Night-time represents a period of hesitation and reflection, heralding a pressing search for clarity – the regaining of which will coincide with the symbolic coming of light brought by the dawn" (SA 22). Night also stands for the period preceding death, as various lexemes such as "s'éteindre" and "passer" emphasize. Beauvoir insists on the image of Hélène sleeping in order to highlight the difference between her ebbing life and Jean's guilt-ridden state of consciousness. As the clock ticks away the hours before dawn, Jean feels the full weight of history upon his shoulders. In a similar way, Fosca's long journey through history is marked by images of the route, of walking and of moving forward. Personal story and history become inextricably linked as dawn approaches.

Régine and Hélène are at first associated with images of light, energy, and physical movement. For example, Hélène has a shiny new bicycle, and is always in motion or near sources of heat or light. However as the novel progresses, the images of light and sight become a barometer of her progression towards death. Similarly, Régine is at first depicted in the limelight of the stage, or freely moving through space. But as the novel draws to an end, she becomes more and more immobilized until she stands paralyzed on a threshold, metaphorically nailed to the spot. These images portray women "who become progressively immobilized by their encounters with men" (TH 31). Narrative structure and imagery are deployed to convey the tensions of gender relations in these novels.

Chapter 4 is titled "*Les Mandarins:* The Case of Henri Perron: Writing and Language in Crisis". Here, Susan Bainbrigge examines Henri Perron's relationship to language, which may seem surprising given the subject of this book. Bainbrigge justifies her choice by pointing out not only that Henri is the spokesman for Beauvoir's own experience as a writer, but also that he goes through the same kind of identity crisis as Anne, characterized by otherness and alienation. Bainbrigge explores Henri's development as a character through his reflections on language, discourse, and writing.

Key terms such as "liberté," "bonheur," "vérité," "Histoire" and "histories" reveal the tensions in Henri's private and public life. No longer sure about the meaning of these words, Henri begins to question the values that had shaped his life until then. If words are subject to multiple and contradictory meanings, how can they possibly effect concrete change of any kind? Henri abandons the "roman gai" which was supposed to express who he was because he know longer knows what his reality is. He cannot write about 1935 because that self is dead. Henri's unease about the past is linked to images of enclosure, imprisonment and death. The past, something he cannot escape nor ignore, has an impact on his capacity to write.

Henri's faith in words is further shaken by the various reactions to his play, *Les Survivants*. Just as his novel had been interpreted in contradictory ways, his play cannot capture the truth of his existence if it means completely opposite things to different people. Henri feels that he is on trial and found guilty because he has failed to use language effectively to communicate with others. Dubreuilh eventually convinces him that History and personal stories do indeed have something in common, and that the writer can say things that have universal significance.

Henri's discourse on love further advances the idea that language is an inadequate tool for communication. He does echo dominant patriarchal ideas on women, but he also expresses many of the ideas on female independence found in *Le Deuxième Sexe*. Henri himself is more like a woman in his relationship with Dubrueilh, defining himself in terms of his mentor and seeing himself as intellectually inferior. Like Anne, Henri is deeply involved in analyzing the relationship between language, writing, and self-definition.

A second chapter on *Les Mandarins* by Elizabeth Richardson Viti is titled "A Questionable Balance: Anne Dubreuilh and the Language of Identity Crisis". Here, Richardson Viti examines the various contradictions that expose Anne Dubreuilh's identity crisis. Beauvoir had stated that the whole point of the novel was to express the ambiguities, nuances, and contradictions of experience. Through Anne, Beauvoir explores her own sense of self, as well as every woman's quest for balance in a patriarchal society. The struggle for this balance is expressed in the use of questions, oppositions, and contradictions in Anne's language.

Anne begins and ends the novel asking herself difficult questions. Richardson Viti has counted more than sixty questions in Anne's opening narration, which reveal her uncertainty about her identity. Her relationship with the other characters also underlines her doubt about herself. When she speaks of her husband Robert, she uses an inordinate number of "mais" along with words of attenuation such as "pourtant", "peut-être," "si" as well as the conditional mode. The conditional past mode is used mostly with Henri, emphasizing the sexual undercurrent between them that must be curtailed. Her relationship with other women reveals a blurring of identities through the use of contradictory behavior and speech in both Anne and Nadine. Reacting against the constraints of femininity, Nadine lashes out angrily, yet allows them to limit her life. If at first Paule and Anne seem very different, their identities blend more and more as Anne begins to echo Paule's language when speaking of Lewis. Although Anne uses the future tense when speaking of Paule, ("Tu guériras"), she uses the conditional for herself because she would rather die than lose the feeling she has for Lewis. In an ironic reversal of roles, Paule gives Anne the same advice that Anne had given her.

Anne again makes an inordinate use of the conditional when speaking of Lewis. She hesitates in a balancing act, never able to commit to one position. She is attracted to Lewis partially because he is a contradiction, temperamental, moody and difficult to decipher. When Anne returns to the U.S. for the third time, she vacillates between hope and despair, the future and the conditional. Anne is torn between her physical and emotional needs on the one hand, and her intellectual and professional ones on the other, Lewis and Robert mirroring these two aspects of her identity. Richardson Viti argues that Anne's experience of sexuality rests on a contradiction, recognizing herself both as a subject and an object, which is the case of all women in a patriarchal society. Although she ultimately chooses reason over passion, Anne maintains the dynamic between the two men as long as possible, illustrating, as Beauvoir said in *La Force des choses,* "the spontaneous, whirling quality of existence with its contradictions". Reflecting on her own experience as a woman, Beauvoir successfully represents the contradictions at the heart of the female quest for identity.

In Chapter 6, "*Les Belles Images*: Countering the Refusal of History", Ursula Tidd argues that the mythologizing discourse of patriarchal capitalist ideology creates essences, or abstract notions of real, concrete individuals or groups in order to better subjugate them. She begins by referring to George Perec's *Les Choses,* where human beings become the very objects they are seeking to purchase. In *Les Belles Images* Laurence already has things, and her quest focuses on gaining a sense of identity and an ethical relationship with the world. Laurence is both a gendered subject and a site of struggle and transformation, resisting the glib discourse of technocrats like her husband Jean-Charles and his colleagues. Beauvoir subtly attacks post-structuralist thought, in particular Michel Foucault's *Les Mots et les choses,* because it denies human suffering and especially women's oppression.

Tidd concentrates on two examples of the function of myth and its effects on women. The first is when Laurence's daughter Catherine and her Jewish friend Brigitte are watching a programme on television about young girls putting slices of carrot on herring fillets. Child labour and poverty cannot be brushed aside as the unfortunate but necessary conditions of "progress". The dishonest and morally bankrupt discourse of capitalism is exposed by Brigitte's unblinking questioning of child labour. In the second example, Jean-Charles cannot forgive Laurence's decision to crash the car rather than kill a cyclist. After their argument, he sends her a bouquet of roses, which Laurence correctly identifies as an abuse of romantic discourse: roses are used to silence and subjugate her, to restore the myth of family harmony and conjugal bliss.

Seeking refuge in conjugal and romantic love, Laurence finds nothing but myths that alienate her even more. It is only maternal love, a model of humanity and ethics, which will enable her to rebel against patriarchal bourgeois mythology. Fighting throughout the novel to find the words that might express her emerging sense of self, Laurence had hoped that her father would provide her with the answers. But during their trip to Greece, she realizes that he too has mythologised poverty and is blind to the oppression of women. When she sees a little Greek girl dancing next to her bovine-eyed mother, Laurence realizes that she as a mother can save her own daughters from the oppressive discourse of patriarchy. She rejects psychiatry as an attempt to force her daughter to eliminate her "inappropriate" moral concerns, and stands up for her against everyone else, thus exercising agency for the first time. Her rebellion, although fragile, is against the pressure to be nothing more than a "belle image", which she vows will not happen to her daughters. Female friendship in this novel offers a site of resistance to the oppressive mythologising discourse of patriarchy.

The closing essay is Chapter 7 by Annlaug Bjørsnøs titled "The Rhetoric of Self-Deception: Conflicting Truths and the Undermining of Narratives in *La Femme rompue*". The three short stories that compose *La Femme rompue* are clearly intended to present negative heroines. Bjørsnøs examines how each female protagonist deludes herself, but also searches for truth. Beauvoir examines the relationship between each woman's reality and the ambiguity of language with a view to expose hidden assumptions of patriarchal ideology which have serious negative effects on women.

In "L'Age de discrétion", the unnamed narrator, a woman in her sixties, is at first confident in her views, secure in her marriage and authoritarian towards her son, a doctoral student at the Sorbonne. Her language reflects her faith in linear temporality and coherence. Time, captured in spatial metaphors, repeats itself in a comforting sense of permanence. The vague uneasiness that the narrator feels at the beginning of the story explodes into a full-blown crisis when her son announces that he is giving up his thesis to work for his father-in-law. The new generation challenges the narrator's concept of time, and the narrator begins to review her attitude toward the past, all the more so since her husband sees it as illusory and evanescent. As the story unfolds, her sense of temporality becomes destabilized, and this change is reflected in her language. Whereas at the beginning, her rhetoric evoked security, now her speech is marked by simplicity and hesitancy. She has become more aware of the unpredictability of life and of the loss of meaning and coherence.

In "Monologue", Murielle's disjointed flow of words draws the reader into her version of the facts, but Bjørsnøs points out that monologues are actually distortions that do not admit any corrections or alternate views. Murielle tries to silence opposing opinions and to manipulate the reader's interpretation. Words of neutrality appear like refrains in the text, creating the image of a clear-sighted and lucid observer, when in reality Murielle buries important factual information or makes light of crucial evidence, such as her daughter's suicide note. She attempts to dominate all those around her, and her narcissism and cruelty are only too evident. However her obsession with cleanliness, her jealousy and erotomania also portray the pain of a woman trapped in traditional notions of femininity. The violence of her narrative creates a textual space that leaves no exit. Murielle has internalized myths about womanhood and becomes a prisoner of her own monologue.

"La Femme rompue", the last of the short stories that gives the collection its title, is about Monique, a woman who suffers through a heart-rending crisis when she discovers her husband's infidelity. Bjørsnøs examines the narrative structure of the diary form and argues that it is not conducive to the ironic tone which Beauvoir claims to have used in this story. Although Monique does lie and conceal the truth from herself, she is striving to understand what happened, and she eventually acknowledges her self-deception. On the contrary, Maurice, under a façade of compassion, continues to deceive her and selfishly refuses to take any responsibility for the breakup of the marriage. Monique's suffering is sincere, and her restless and fervent introspection moves the reader in her favor. Thus the ambiguity imbedded in the text works against any ironic interpretation of Monique as the guilty party. Beauvoir denounces traditional patriarchal marriage rather than the weakness of the betrayed wife.

This collection of essays pays homage to Beauvoir's skill as a writer, but much work is yet to be done on her fiction. New theories constantly emerge, as our own experiences never fail to enrich our interpretations, shedding new light on one of the truly great thinkers of our time.

Works Cited

Arp, Kristana. *The Bonds of Freedom: Simone de Beauvoir's Existentialist Ethics*. Chicago: Open Court, 2001.

Bainbrigge, Susan. *Writing Against Death: The Autobiographies of Simone de Beauvoir*. Amsterdam and New York: Rodopi, 2005.

Bauer, Nancy. *Simone de Beauvoir, Philosophy, & Feminism*. New York: Columbia University Press, 2001.

Beauvoir, Simone de. "Mon expérience d'écrivain". Francis and Gontier, *Les Écrits*. 439-57.

_____. "Prière d'insérer". Francis and Gontier. *Les Écrits*. 231-32.

_____. *L'Existentialisme et la sagesse des nations*. Paris: Nagel, 1948.

_____. *La Force de l'âge*. Paris: Gallimard, 1960.

_____. *La Force des choses*. Paris: Gallimard, 1963.

_____. *Force of Circumstance*, Trans. Richard Howard, Harmondsworth: Penguin, 1988.

_____. "Préface". In Anne Ophir. *Regards féminins: condition féminine et création littéraire*, Paris: Denoël/ Gontier, 1976 reprinted in Francis and Gontier, *Les Écrits*. 577-79.

_____. *Tout Compte fait*. Paris: Gallimard, 1972.

_____. 0*Que Peut la Littérature?* ed. Buin,Yves. Paris: Union Générale d'Éditions, 1965. 73-92.

Bergoffen, Debra. *The Philosophy of Simone de Beauvoir: Gendered Phenomenologies, Erotic Generosities*. New York: New York State University Press, 1997.

Card, Claudia, ed. *The Cambridge Companion to Simone de Beauvoir*. Cambridge: Cambridge University Press, 2003.

David, Catherine. "Beauvoir elle-même". Interview, *Le Nouvel Observateur* (22 January 1979): 82-90.

Fallaize, Elizabeth. *The Novels of Simone de Beauvoir*. London: Routledge, 1988.

Fishwick, Sarah. *The Body in the Work of Simone de Beauvoir*. New York: Peter Lang Publishers, 2002.

Francis, Claude and Fernande Gontier, *Les Écrits de Simone de Beauvoir: La vie – L'écriture*. Paris: Gallimard, 1979.

Fraser. Mariam. *Identity without Selfhood: Simone de Beauvoir and Bisexuality*. Cambridge: Cambridge University Press, 1999.

Hewitt, Leah D. *Autobiographical Tightropes: Simone de Beauvoir, Nathalie Sarraute, Marguerite Duras, Monique Wittig, and Maryse Condé*. Lincoln: University of Nebraska Press, 1999.

Holveck, Eleanor. *Simone de Beauvoir's Philosophy of Lived Experience: Literature and Metaphysics*. Oxford: Rowman & Littlefield, 1995.

Holland, Alison T. "Simone de Beauvoir's Writing Practice: Madness, Enumeration and Repetition in *Les Belles Images*." *Simone de Beauvoir Studies* 15 (1998-1999): 113-125.

Jardine, Alice. "Interview with Simone de Beauvoir." *Signs* (Winter 1979): 224-36.

Keefe, Terry. *Simone de Beauvoir: A Study of her Writings*. London: Harrap, 1983.

Kruks, Sonia. "Teaching Sartre about Freedom". In *Sartre Alive,* edited by Ronald Aronson and Adrian van den Hoven. Detroit: Wayne State University Press, 1999. 285-300.

Le Doeuff, Michèle. *L'Étude et le rouet: Des femmes, de la philosophie, etc.* Paris: Seuil, 1989.

Lundgren–Gothlin, Eva. *Sex & Existence. Simone de Beauvoir's 'The Second Sex'.* Translated by Linda Schenck, Hanover: Wesleyan University Press, 1996.

Mahon, Joseph. *Existentialism, Feminism and Simone de Beauvoir.* New York: Palgrave, 1997.

Moi, Toril. *Simone de Beauvoir: The Making of an Intellectual Woman.* Oxford: Blackwell, 1994.

Pilardi, Jo-Ann. *Simone de Beauvoir Writing the Self: Philosophy Becomes Autobiography.* Westport: Praeger Publishers, 1999.

Saetre,Ved Solverg. "Interview with Simone de Beauvoir". *Vinduet* 3 (1968): 196-201.

Shepherd, Genevieve. *Simone de Beauvoir's Fiction: A Psychoanalytic Rereading.* New York: Peter Lang Publishers, 2003.

Sutton, Nina. "Sartre and *The Second Sex.*" Interview, *Guardian* (19 February 1970): 11.

Tidd, Ursula. *Simone de Beauvoir: Gender and Testimony.* Cambridge: Cambridge University Press, 1999.

Vintges, Karen. *Philosophy as Passion: The Thinking of Simone de Beauvoir.* Bloomington: Indiana University Press, 1996.

Winegarten, Renée. *Simone de Beauvoir: A Critical View.* Oxford: Berg, 1988.

1

Gothic Narrative and Imagery in *Quand Prime le Spirituel*

Louise Renée

"Il ne faut pas chercher à être compris tout de suite."[1]

Quand Prime le Spirituel is Simone de Beauvoir's first novel, written in 1938, but only published in 1979. Gallimard and Grasset had rejected the novel on the basis that it lacked originality, as Beauvoir explains in *La Force de l'âge*. She quotes Henry Müller who had said: "le tableau de mœurs que vous avez fait a déjà été, depuis ces vingt dernières années, maintes fois brossé" (FA 375).[2] At the time, Beauvoir was devastated, yet remained convinced that her novel did have something new to say in the subtle psychological portraits that she had attempted to create. Much later in the 1979 preface, she judges her novel harshly: the structure is faulty, the characters lack depth, the story based on Zaza's death is flat, and the satire, although relevant, is timid (QPS vii). Beauvoir adopts the stance of the well-established writer looking back on a clumsy first novel of interest only to her most faithful readers: "[...] c'est, somme toute, sous une forme un peu maladroite, un roman d'apprentissage où s'ébauchent beaucoup des thèmes que j'ai repris par la suite" (QPS viii).[3] Yet just before her death in 1986, she told Deirdre Bair that back in 1938, Sartre had found out the real reason why the book had been turned down:

> [...] Gallimard did not understand books written by women which were about the lives of women of my generation and background and because modern France and French publishing were not yet ready to deal with what women thought and felt and wanted; [...] to publish such a book would brand them a subversive publishing house and they couldn't risk offending all sorts of patrons and critics.[4]

In an article titled "Reading about Reading: *A Jury of Her Peers, The Murders*

---

[1] "One must not seek to be understood right away." (my translation) Simone de Beauvoir, *Carnets de jeunesse,* Holograph manuscript (Paris: Bibliothèque nationale) Sept. 10, 1926.

[2] "[...] the social picture you create has been painted countless times already over the past twenty years." (PL 261)

[3] "After all is said and done, it is a rather clumsy first novel where I sketch out many themes that I developed later on." (my translation) The preface in the translated edition is an extract taken from *The Prime of Life,* and not the one that appears in the 1979 edition.

[4] Deirdre Bair, *Simone de Beauvoir. A Biography* (New York: Summit Books, 1990) 207.

in the Rue Morgue and *The Yellow Wallpaper,*" Judith Fetterley claims that
men equate textuality with masculine point of view and cannot imagine
that women have stories: "Men, controlling the study of literature, define
as great those texts that empower themselves and define reading as an
activity that serves male interests, for regardless of how many actual readers may be women within the academy the presumed reader is male."[5] The
purpose of this chapter is to argue that women indeed have stories to tell,
and in *Quand Prime le Spirituel,* well before *Le Deuxième Sexe,* Beauvoir
deconstructs patriarchal discourse by incorporating narrative strategies
typical of Gothic fiction.[6]

Quand Prime le Spirituel is Beauvoir's most autobiographical novel, with
passages appearing almost intact in *Mémoires d'une jeune fille rangée,* or being
lifted out of her early teenage diaries.[7] This is a novel about the way young
women become socialized, how their minds are mutilated by an insidious
ideology that infiltrates the very core of their being. Ideology, as defined
by Denise Thompson in *Radical Feminism Today,* refers to "systematic
meanings which excuse, permit, legitimate and provide justification for
relations of ruling. [...] Ideological meanings are whatever makes domination palatable or acceptable, or natural, real, unchallengeable."[8] In other
words, ideology, hidden in language, disguises domination.[9] *Quand Prime
le Spirituel* can be read as a series of case studies such as the ones we find in
the early chapters of volume two of *Le Deuxième Sexe.* But this is a novel,
not an essay, and it is through language and literary devices that Beauvoir
brilliantly conveys the damaging effects of patriarchal ideology.

Well versed in English literature, Beauvoir integrates elements of Gothic
narrative and imagery in her first novel with a view to deconstruct the discourses used to oppress women, both in fiction and in real life. In an article

---

[5] Judith Fetterley, "Reading about Reading. *A Jury of Her Peers, The Murder in the Rue Morgue* and *The Yellow Wallpaper,* Ed. Elizabeth A. Flynn and Patrocinio P. Schweickhart, *Gender and Reading. Essays on Readers, Texts, and Contexts* (Baltimore: Johns Hopkins University Press, 1968) 147.

[6] See for example Terry Keefe's *Simone de Beauvoir* (New York: St. Martin's Press, 1998) 22: "It is of particular interest to see Beauvoir, more than ten years before *Le Deuxième Sexe,* exposing the ways in which attempts are made to manipulate daughters by using religion, and by referring to their 'duty' and the social role of women." See also Elizabeth Fallaize's *The Novels of Simone de Beauvoir* (London: Routledge, 1988) 143, where she says that *Quand Prime le Spirituel* was written forty years earlier than *La Femme rompue* but has a "much harsher social critique."

[7] Marguerite's bar adventures (QPS 213-218) closely parallel those recalled by Beauvoir in *Mémoires d'une jeune fille rangée* (376-380).

[8] Denise Thompson, *Radical Feminism Today* (London: Sage Publications, 2001) 22.

[9] Thompson, *Feminism* 36.

titled "Identity and Crisis: The Gothic Textual Space in Beauvoir's *L'Invitée*", Alison Holland has pointed out Gothic elements in Beauvoir's first published novel. Holland studies the Gothic's "writing of excess", and in particular, in Beauvoir's use of syntax to convey the threat to Françoise's sense of self:

> The Gothic symbolic universe she created provided her with the ideal loca-
> tion for her confrontation with pain and the disintegration of identity. [...]
> *L'Invitée* functions as a Gothic text, providing a structure to contain the
> threats to rational and humanist values that it explores.[10]

This chapter will focus on the feminist critique of ideology in *Quand Prime le Spirituel*. According to Michelle Massé, author of *In the Name of Love. Women, Masochism and the Gothic,* the term Gothic refers not just to eighteenth-century horror fiction, but also to contemporary novels. "Gothic is the narrative of the suffering women," she claims, and Gothic fiction exposes and indicts the culture that oppresses women.[11] In "Simone de Beauvoir: Transcending Fictions," Lorna Sage explains that Beauvoir's writing always involves a process of demystification, and that her fiction exposes the fact that we are cultural constructs.[12] In *Quand Prime le Spirituel,* Beauvoir's strategy is to expose the fictions responsible for women's suffering.

Beauvoir begins by using a bold narrative structure: five short stories, with the name of a young woman for each title: "Marcelle", "Chantal", "Lisa", "Anne", "Marguerite." The stories are all interconnected by the characters, and the same events are viewed from different perspectives. This technique creates the impression that one could add endlessly to this list, since so many other similar stories could be evoked. Repetition is a technique commonly used in Gothic fiction in order to insist on the trauma that prohibits female autonomy.[13] In spite of superficial differences, the characters all share similar characteristics; thus, multiplying their stories is a way of confirming a common condition. As Massé puts it, "we need to recognize a community of suffering that extends across place and time."[14]

Beauvoir deliberately creates the dark, claustrophobic atmosphere of Gothic novels. Chantal describes Anne's country home as a Gothic mansion,

---

[10] Alison Holland, "Identity and Crisis: The Gothic Textual Space in Beauvoir's *L'Invitée*," *Modern Language Review* (2003) 334.
[11] Michelle A. Massé, *In the Name of Love. Women, Masochism and the Gothic* (Ithaca and London: Cornell University Press, 1992) 41.
[12] Lorna Sage, "Simone de Beauvoir: Transcending Fictions," Ed. Ruth Evans, *Simone de Beauvoir's The Second Sex. New Interdisciplinary Essays* (Manchester: Manchester University Press, 1998) 99.
[13] Massé 11-12.
[14] Massé 269.

and the old, faded objects are metaphors of the fate that awaits the young women wasting away their lives:

> [...] toutes ces choses mortes qui achevaient lentement de mourir pour la seconde fois: les oiseaux empaillés perdaient leurs plumes, les coquillages s'écaillaient; les papillons épinglés dans des boîtes de verre s'en allaient en poussière; sur des toiles craquelées souriaient de vieilles femmes en coiffe, des hommes à favoris; il régnait dans cette maison couverte de vigne vierge une atmosphère poétique et surannée comme le début d'un vieux roman anglais. (QPS 153)[15]

Images of silence and enclosure, typical of the Gothic tradition, abound. Michelle Massé writes about the "silence, immobility and enclosure that define the perfect wife and the perfect victim in marital Gothic."[16] Beauvoir is careful to emphasize dark, closed spaces symbolizing the young women's mental imprisonment. As a young girl, Marcelle hides behind heavy curtains or under a large desk in the study and later, when she is allowed to visit her aunt's library, she paints a scene fit for a mysterious Gothic drama: "[...] une petite table dans un sombre corridor [...] l'accès des couloirs était interdit aux clients; seule une employée au corsage montant se glissait parfois à pas de souris dans les ténèbres [...] (QPS 4).[17] It is no surprise that Marcelle's brother Pascal is the editor of medieval manuscripts. Chantal, teaching in the small provincial town of Rougement, constantly refers to the Gothic cathedral:

> [...] sur le ciel gris perle se découpent la massive silhouette de la tour Saint-Romain et la flèche de la cathédrale; il me semble être transportée brusquement en plein Moyen Age, tant la vie est silencieuse dans cette ville hérissée d'églises gothiques; l'élan des pierres dentelées crée autour d'elles une telle atmosphère mystique, les toits d'ardoise baignent dans une pénombre si paisible et si ardente, que je me sens un peu l'âme d'une jeune mondaine des temps passés, qui, touchée par la grâce, commencerait une retraite dans la paix d'un cloître. (QPS 47)[18]

---

[15] "[...] all these dead things that were slowly coming to the end of a second death – the stuffed birds were losing their feathers, the shells were crumbling away, the butterflies pinned in the glass-topped cases were disintegrating, old women in mob-caps and men with side-whiskers smiled out of crackled canvases. This vine-covered house was filled with a poetic, old-fashioned atmosphere like the beginning of an old English novel." (WTS 135)

[16] Massé 27.

[17] "[...] a little table in a dark passage [...] Customers were not allowed into the corridors and the only person who occasionally stole through the gloom was an assistant in a high-necked blouse [...]" (WTS 11-12)

[18] "[...] the massive silhouette of the tour Saint-Romain and the cathedral spire stand out sharply against a pearl-grey sky. Life is so quiet in this town studded with Gothic churches that it is as though I had been suddenly carried right back into the middle ages: the upthrusting lacework of stone creates a mystical atmosphere, and the slate roofs swim in so peaceful and so living a twilight that I feel rather like a fashionable young woman of former times who, touched by grace, is beginning a retreat in the peace of a nunnery." (WTS 49)

Chantal is very much aware of the omnipresence of the cathedral, describing its haunting form in such passages as this: "Sous le clair de lune, le jardin de la cathédrale avait un air fantastique, presque irréel; un chat noir miaulait parmi les pierres tourmentées" (QPS 85).[19] She compares Monique, one of her students, to a figure from a stained glass window, and relates the colours of the town to those of an old tapestry (QPS 74, 50).

All of the characters in *Quand Prime le Spirituel* associate the cathedral spire with imprisonment. Andrée, the most precocious of Chantal's students, is acutely aware of this: "La flèche de la cathédrale s'élançait au loin vers le ciel, on l'apercevait de partout; à chaque instant ces dentelles de pierre rappelaient impitoyablement à Andrée qu'elle était prisonnière à Rougemont" (QPS 72).[20] The cathedral spire, an obvious symbol of Christian spirituality, is also a phallic symbol, and of course Christian morality is one of the prime forces of patriarchal ideology in this novel.

Other images refer explicitly to the stifling constraints imposed on women, as if they were confined to a Gothic mansion. Beauvoir deliberately makes a reference to a contemporary Gothic narrative, Charlotte Perkins Gilman's *The Yellow Wallpaper,* a well-known tale of women's oppression, in the following passage where Andrée, sitting in a café, becomes transfixed by the wallpaper: "[…] ses yeux se fixèrent sur le papier qui tapissait les murs. Il était rouge et mangé par endroits de larges plaques jaunes; si on les regardait longtemps, on découvrait qu'elles avaient des formes d'animaux, de plantes" (QPS 103).[21] The image of restriction appears again in the corset shop: "[…] le ciel était toujours brouillé, pas de couleurs, rien que du gris et de temps en temps le rose fade d'un magasin de corsets" (QPS 69).[22] Here, the corsets are associated with boredom. In another passage, the corset shop is juxtaposed to the image of the church and of bourgeois conformity: "À sa place, c'est là qu'elle aurait vécu, loin des maisons blanchies à chaux, des églises dentelées, des magasins de corsets" (QPS 77).[23] This image returns

---

[19] "The cathedral garden looked fantastic, almost unreal, in the moonlight: a black cat was yowling among the tormented stones." (WTS 79)
[20] "Far away the cathedral spire thrust up into the sky: it could be seen from everywhere, and at every moment the stone lacework pitilessly reminded her that she was a prisoner in Rougemont." (WTS 68)
[21] "[…] she looked at them for a moment and then her gaze shifted to the wallpaper. It was red, and in places broad patches of yellow had eaten into it: if you looked at them for a long time you found that they had the shapes of animals, of plants." (WTS 93)
[22] "[…] the sky was always overcast; no colours, nothing but grey and from time to time the insipid pink of a corset-shop […]." (WTS 66)
[23] "Had she been Plattard, this is where she would have lived, far from the whitewashed houses, the lacework churches and the corset shops." (WTS 72)

in *Mémoires d'une jeune fille rangée* when Beauvoir explicitly connects the image of the corset to the oppression of women: "À vingt ans, engoncée dans des guimpes à baleine, habituée à réprimer ses élans et à enfouir dans le silence d'amers secrets, elle se sentait seule et incomprise; malgré sa beauté, elle manquait d'assurance et de gaieté" (MJF 53).[24] All of the heroines in *Quand Prime le Spirituel* refer to their imprisonment. Chantal says that she is suffocating in Rougemont: "J'étouffe; j'ai l'impression d'être au fond d'un tombeau" (QPS 57).[25] Monique, Chantal's favourite student, gets pregnant and will be shipped off to the country, "seule, à l'écart de la vie, enterrée en province, sans amour, sans avenir" (QPS 57).[26] Anne's home is described by Chantal as a prison where she is kept locked up (QPS 155).

These pervasive images of enclosure acutely expose the heroines' very limited possibilities in terms of transcendence. They are, as Michelle Massé writes of Gothic heroines, "trapped women".[27] The teachers and students of *l'Institut Saints-Anges* and in the Rougement *lycée* are overwhelmingly lonely and caught in a dead-end existence. Chantal pities her older colleagues: "[…] ce sont de vieilles filles desséchées, toutes fières de leur lourde et inutile culture universitaire et qui jamais n'ont regardé en face le vrai visage de la vie" (QPS 51).[28] Speaking of Mlle Bidois, the school principal, Andrée comments: "Un corps massif où le cœur bat toujours d'un rythme égal, un exact souci des conduites à tenir, et un grand vide" (QPS 89).[29] Lisa is aware that most of the girls at the *Institut* become the *femmes éteintes* later referred to in *Le Deuxième Sexe* and in "La Femme rompue":

> […] ces filles résignées qui amassent des connaissances comme d'autres filles enfilent des mailles sur des aiguilles à tricoter; jamais elles n'ont une idée, jamais elles n'ouvrent un livre qui sorte de leur programme; elles subissent un destin que le hasard leur impose; quelques-unes rêvent d'être des fermières ou des mères de famille; la plupart ne désirent jamais rien. (QPS 126)[30]

---

[24] "At the age of twenty, her neck squeezed into whalebone collars, accustomed to suppressing all her natural spontaneity, resorting to silence and brooding over bitter secrets, she felt herself alone and misunderstood; despite her great beauty, she lacked assurance and gaiety." (MDD 37)

[25] "I am stifling: I have the feeling of being buried alive." (WTS 57)

[26] "[…] alone, withdrawn from life, buried in the provinces, without love, without a future." (WTS 57)

[27] Massé 37.

[28] "[…] withered old maids, all puffed up with their heavy, useless academic culture, who have never looked real life in the face.» (WTS 52)

[29] "A massive body in which the heart always beats at a steady pace; a meticulous concern for behaviour; and a vast emptiness." (WTS 82)

[30] "[…] these resigned young women who accumulated pieces of information as others threaded loops on to knitting-needles. They never had an idea of their own; they never opened a book that was not required reading for their course; they submitted to a fate imposed on them by chance. A few of them dreamt of being farmers' wives or mothers of families; most never desired anything at all." (WTS 112-113)

The young women who either narrate their stories, or whose point of view is focalized, fear this fate and constantly express their desire for transcendence. The vocabulary used to express this yearning for fulfillment is identical to the one Beauvoir uses in her teenage diaries and in *Mémoires d'une jeune fille rangée*. Chantal describes her aspirations in terms of "faim", "ferveur" and "ivresse" (QPS 48, 49, 52),[31] words which echo those of Beauvoir's 1926 diary: "fièvre", "ardeur", "âme excessive", "brûler la vie", "vie dévorante".[32] Like her young heroines, Beauvoir says on October 16, 1926:

> Je crois que j'ai plus que lui le souci de ne rien perdre dans la vie. Rien jamais ne dort en moi, rien n'a besoin de se réveiller, tout garde une vie d'une extra-ordinaire intensité; tout me reste présent surtout, aussi bien dans l'ordre sen-timental que dans l'ordre intellectuel. Je crois que c'est là mon trait à la fois le plus essentiel et le plus distinctif. [...] Donc mes sentiments participent à ce sérieux, cette fièvre que j'apporte à toute chose.[33]

Chantal writes in a similar vein: "Il n'est rien de la vie que je veuille laisser passer auprès de moi sans le saisir" (QPS 55).[34] All of the female characters express the same wish to achieve something in life, and all of them complain about the painful emptiness in their hearts. Marcelle asks herself "si le vide de son coeur serait jamais comblé" (QPS 9).[35] Chantal, whose heart is "épris de merveilleux" (QPS 101),[36] must admit upon thinking back on her year in Rougemont that she had often felt "une impression déprimante de vide" (QPS 153).[37] Lisa claims that the force of her desire, always disappointed, leaves her soul bruised and her heart empty (QPS 117, 110). Anne, for all her passion and talent, is left with nothing but emptiness because her desire has been thwarted (QPS 183). Andrée, avidly wanting a real education, sees only empty skies (QPS 103).

---

[31] See the following pages for the complete quotations: "jamais ils n'assouvissaient ma faim" (QPS 48), "je me plongeais avec ivresse dans la solitude" (QPS 49), "jamais je ne me suis sentie si équilibrée, si forte, ni dans un tel état de ferveur" (QPS 52), "Il n'est rien dans la vie que je veuille laisser passer auprès de moi sans le saisir." (QPS 55) "[...] they never satisfied my hunger" (WTS 49); "I plunged rapturously into solitude" (WTS 50); "I have never felt so well-balanced, nor so strong, nor so enthu-siastic" (WTS 53); "I want no part of life to go by me without grasping it." (WTS 55)

[32] *Carnets de jeunesse*, Nov. 5, Nov. 13, Aug. 6, 1926.

[33] "I believe that I have the desire to take everything from life more than he does. Nothing ever sleeps within me, nothing needs to be awoken, everything has a life of extraordinary intensity; everything is present to me, both in feelings and in thoughts. That, I believe, is my most essential and distinctive characteristic [...]. So my feelings contribute to the serious attitude, the fever that I bring to every-thing." (my translation)

[34] "I want no part of life to go by without grasping it." (WTS 55)

[35] "[...] whether the emptiness in her heart would ever be filled." (WTS 16)

[36] "[...] enamoured of the wonderful [...]." (WTS 91)

[37] "[...] a depressing sensation of emptiness." (WTS 134)

Just as in Gothic novels, the heroines all seek to satisfy their desire for transcendence through love. Dominant in popular romance fiction and in Gothic novels, the quest-for-love narrative can be viewed as a perpetration of conservative values, in particular of traditional marriage and female sub-servience. However, "garbage dump" romances[38] and Gothic fiction both address society's deafness to women's most basic and urgent needs. According to Janice Radway, author of *Reading the Romance. Women, Patriarchy and Popular Culture,* romances with unhappy endings can be construed as a feminist cri-tique of women's oppression:

> [...] the romance, which is never simply a love story, is also an exploration of the meaning of patriarchy for women. As a result, it is concerned with the fact that men possess and regularly exercise power over them in all sorts of circum-stances. By picturing the heroine in relative positions of weakness, romances are not necessarily endorsing her situation, but examining an all-too-common state of affairs in order to display possible strategies for coping with it.[39]

In the same way, Gothic fiction, including novels by Emily Brontë, Jane Austen, Alice Walker, and Margaret Atwood, exposes the ideology that crushes the heroines. In her psychoanalytic study of the contemporary Gothic novel, Michelle Massé writes:

> The heroines of the Gothic, inculcated by education, religion, and bourgeois familial values, have the same expectations as those around them for what is normal. Their social contract tenders their passivity and disavowal of public power in exchange for the love that will let them reign in the interpersonal and domestic sphere. [...] The Gothic plot is thus not an "escape" from the real world but a repetition and exploration of the traumatic denial of identity found there. Both the nightmare stasis of the protagonists and the all-enveloping power of the antagonists are extensions of social ideology and real-world experience.[40]

Massé insists on this point: "Girls who, seeking recognition and love, learn to forget or deny that they also wanted independence and agency, grow up to become women who are Gothic heroines."[41]

Beauvoir stated that her goal in *Quand Prime le Spirituel* was to expose the spiritualism that had so oppressed her in her youth. Elizabeth Fallaize offers this definition of spiritualism: "a mystical belief in a religion, intellectual or

---

[38] This is the term used by Janice Radway in *Reading the Romance. Women, Patriarchy and Popular Culture* (Chapel Hill & London: University of North Carolina Press, 1991) 178.
[39] Radway 75.
[40] Massé 18.
[41] Massé 3.

aesthetic absolute held to be superior to the material world."[42] Beauvoir also said that her aim was to use language "[pour] faire entendre les voix – et les silences – du mensonge. Comme beaucoup plus tard dans *La Femme rompue,* j'ai usé du langage pour dissimuler la vérité" (QPS vii).[43] Although Beauvoir and most of her commentators have stressed the heroines' bad faith,[44] the lies that are exposed in this novel are those of the heroines' conditioning. Beauvoir developed this point at great length in *Le Deuxième Sexe,* for example in the following passages:

> Ainsi, la passivité qui caractérisera essentiellement la femme "féminine" est un trait qui se développe en elle dès ses premières années. Mais il est faux de prétendre que c'est là une donnée biologique: en vérité, c'est un destin qui lui est imposé par ses éducateurs et par la société. (DS II 29)[45]

> Fantasmes, comédies, puériles tragédies, faux enthousiasmes, bizarreries, il en faut chercher la raison non dans une mystérieuse âme féminine mais dans la situation de l'enfant. (DS II, 52)[46]

> [...] la femme est invitée à la complicité. J'ai rappelé déjà qu'à côté de l'authentique revendication du sujet qui se veut souveraine liberté, il y a chez l'existant un désir inauthentique de démission et de fuite; ce sont les délices de la passivité que parents et éducateurs, livres et mythes, femmes et hommes font miroiter aux yeux de la petite fille; dans sa toute petite enfance, on lui apprend déjà à les goûter; la tentation se fait de plus en plus insidieuse; et elle y cède d'autant plus fatalement que l'élan de sa transcendance se heurte à de plus sévères résistances. [...] Elle a douze ans et déjà son histoire est inscrite dans le ciel. (DS II 53)[47]

---

42 Fallaize, *Novels,* 145.
43 "[...] to have people hear the voices – and the silences – of lies. As I did much later in *La Femme rompue,* I used language to hide the truth." (my translation)
44 See for example Terry Keefe's *Beauvoir,* page 15, where he says that Marcelle is not a victim because "she is so willing to go along with any spiritualism offered to her", and also page 17: "We are bound to see the dominant feature of her personality as her boundless mauvaise foi or self-deception." Elizabeth Fallaize also comments on Marcelle's bad faith in *Novels,* page 145: "Marcelle's self-delusions are insisted upon in the story. [...] Marcelle is thus poised as a case in which complicity is strong; her sexual masochism underlies this point heavily."
45 "Thus the passivity that is the essential characteristic of the 'feminine' woman is a trait that develops in her from the earliest years. But it is wrong to assert that a biological datum is concerned; it is in fact a destiny imposed upon her by her teachers and by society." (SS 280)
46 "Fantasies, histrionics, childish tragedies, false enthusiasms, odd behavior – the reason for all these must be sought not in a mysterious feminine soul but in the child's environment, her situation." (SS 297)
47 "[...] woman is offered inducements to complicity. I have previously called to mind the fact that along with the authentic demand of the subject who wants sovereign freedom, there is in the existent an inauthentic longing for resignation and escape; the delights of passivity are made to seem desirable to the young girl by parents and educators, books and myths, women and men; she is taught to enjoy them from earliest childhood; the temptation becomes more and more insidious; and she is the more fatally bound to yield to those delights as the flight of her transcendence is dashed against harsher obstacles. [...] She is twelve years old and already her story is written in the heavens. (SS 298)

Beauvoir puts woman's bad faith squarely on the shoulders of patriarchal ideology, which imbibes every facet of her life. Therefore when Beauvoir seemingly criticizes her heroines' bad faith, she is exposing the educational system and ideological framework which are responsible for this "mauvaise foi". Recent studies of *Quand Prime le Spirituel* have stressed the importance of the social context which is largely responsible for the female characters' shortcomings. In a book published in 2002, Sarah Fishwick emphasizes "the cultural pressure surrounding feminine bodily stylization", pointing out the role played by popular literature rather than religious oppression.[48] In her 2004 psychoanalytic reading of Beauvoir's fiction, Genevieve Shepherd begins with Beauvoir's stated intention of exposing the bad faith of spiritualism in which all five protagonists are trapped,[49] but she also studies the cultural construction of masochism, a motif which this chapter will further develop. Beauvoir's strategy in *Quand Prime le Spirituel,* which totally escaped Gallimard and Grasset in 1938, was to deconstruct the discourse of romance fiction, which is what Gothic fiction does, seen from a feminist perspective.

Beauvoir carefully builds the foundation of romance's mythologizing discourse. She focuses on young women's upbringing and education, stressing the books that they are allowed to read, those that are banned, and especially the values transmitted by the parents' or educators' language. In *Le Deuxième Sexe,* she says that women interiorise the negative images about women that are transmitted through books and myths (DS II, 471). Andrée Lacombe's father plasters his daughter's walls with quotations taken from the best French authors (QPS 68). In *Quand Prime le Spirituel,* young women are not permitted to read any "immoral" novels, and if they do, they are briskly chastised. Having found such literature in Anne's room, Mme Vignon reprimands her daughter: "J'ai inspecté ta bibliothèque hier soir, je suis tombée sur des pages qui m'ont fait rougir. [...] Si tu veux t'enrichir, lis les Pères de l'Église ou sainte Thérèse" (QPS 143).[50] But the representation of femininity in Christian literature unfortunately corresponds exactly to what the young women find in fairy tales and children's books: the image of the suffering woman, the martyr. Growing up

---

[48] Sarah Fishwick, *The Body in the Work of Simone de Beauvoir* (New York: Peter Lang, 2002) 236.
[49] Genevieve Shepherd, *Simone de Beauvoir's Fiction. A Psychoanalytic Reading* (New York: Peter Lang, 2004) 51.
[50] "I inspected your books yesterday evening, and I chanced across some pages that made me blush. [...] If you want to enrich your mind, read the Fathers of the Church or Saint Theresa." (WTS 127)

in a Catholic environment, Marcelle is fascinated by the legends that she comes across in approved books: Blue-Beard, Greselda, Genevieve of Brabant (QPS 6).[51] In the much broader context of the socialization of girls, these texts become the site for masochistic fantasies:

> La cruauté de Barbe-Bleue, les épreuves infligées à la douce Grisélidis par un époux au cœur inquiet, la rencontre du duc de Brabant avec l'infortunée Geneviève, toute nue sous ses longs cheveux, remplissaient Marcelle d'un trouble extraordinaire; elle s'enchantait inlassablement de cette histoire: une femme maltraitée par un maître superbe finit par conquérir son cœur à force de soumission et d'amour. Marcelle s'identifiait à cette héroïne qu'elle imaginait parfois innocente et méconnue, mais le plus souvent coupable d'une lourde faute, car elle aimait frissonner de repentir aux pieds d'un homme beau, pur et terrible. Il avait droit de vie et de mort sur elle et elle lui disait "Seigneur"; il la faisait mettre nue devant lui et, pour monter sur son cheval richement caparaçonné, il se servait de son corps comme d'un marchepied. Elle prolongeait avec volupté ce moment où la tête courbée, le cœur empli d'adoration, d'une humilité passionnée, elle sentait un dur éperon écorcher son dos d'esclave. Quand, vaincu par la pitié et par l'amour, le justicier aux yeux sévères posait la main sur sa tête en signe de pardon, elle embrassait ses genoux en défaillant délicieusement. (QPS 6)[52]

In another passage, Marcelle briefly lives out this masochistic fantasy:

> Elle souleva les paupières; le visage de Denis lui apparut, changé par le désir, avide, presque méconnaissable; il semblait capable de la battre, de la torturer; cette vue remplit Marcelle d'une jouissance si aiguë qu'elle se mit à gémir. 'Je suis à sa merci', se dit-elle et elle sombra dans une extase où se mêlait la honte, la crainte et la joie. [...] Elle aurait voulu crier qu'elle était sa chose, son esclave, et des larmes coulèrent sur ses joues. [...] Elle acceptait avec une soumission passionnée chacun des coups que Denis lui portait [...]." (QPS 29)[53]

---

[51] See also Fishwick, p. 179: "Marcelle's exposure to a model of erotic femininity – one that is transmitted through literature and is culturally validated – is shown to shape her fantasies."

[52] "Bluebeard's cruelty, the trials imposed upon the gentle Griselda by her suspicious husband, the Duke of Brabant's meeting with the unfortunate Geneviève, stark naked under her long hair – all these perturbed and excited Marcelle to a remarkable degree. The story of a woman, cruelly and harshly treated by an arrogant master, who eventually wins his heart by her submissiveness and her love was one that never failed to delight her. She identified herself with this heroine, sometimes imagining her innocent and misunderstood, but more often guilty of some grave offence, for she was fond of quivering with repentance at the feet of a sinless, beautiful and terrible man. He had the right of life and death over her, and she called him 'Lord': he made her strip herself naked before him, and he used her body as a step when he mounted his splendidly decked charger. With a sensuous delight she drew out this moment of feeling the harsh spur flay her servile back as she knelt there, her head bowed, her heart full of adoration and passionate humility. And when the stern-eyed avenger, vanquished by pity and love, laid his hand on her head as a sign of forgiveness, she clasped his knees in an exquisite swoon." (WTS 13) The same stories are told in *Le Deuxième Sexe* II 45. (SS 291-2)

[53] "She opened her eyes: Denis' face appeared before her, changed with desire, intensely eager, almost unrecognizable: he looked capable of beating her, torturing her, and the sight filled Marcelle with so

"Une femme maltraitée par un maître superbe finit par conquérir son cœur à force de soumission et d'amour": this is the formulaic plot of all Harlequin romances. In *Romance and the Erotics of Property. Mass-market Fiction for Women,* Jan Cohn explains that the basic plot is always the same: at first the hero is ill-mannered, indifferent or even cruel, but he finally recognizes the heroine's purity and heart of gold and falls in love with her.[54] In *Reading the Romance. Women, Patriarchy and Popular Literature,* Janice Radway arrives at the same conclusion: the dark hero is transformed by love.[55] In Gothic novels, the hero does not go through such a metamorphosis, and the hero-ine idealizes her suffering, viewing it as a proof of love. This leads to masochism, as Michelle Massé writes:

> Masochism is the end result of a long and varyingly successful cultural train-ing. The training leaves its traces upon individual characters and upon the Gothic itself, which broods upon its originating trauma, the denial of auton-omy or separation for women, throughout the centuries. Women's schooling in masochism, the turning inward of active drives, seems to naturalize that denial and makes it appear to spring from within rather than without. Insofar as a Gothic protagonist internalizes these lessons, she sees her trials as unique to herself and avoids systemic inquiry about the source of her suffering. She carefully monitors herself, finds her virtue in her renunciation, and teaches other women to do so as well.[56]

In other words, there is a societal expectation that "they *should* be masochis-tic if they are 'normal' women".[57] In her work as a youth leader, Marcelle explains women's social mission, which she links to the notion of suffering (QPS 18).[58] This is not because she is particularly weak or passive, but because of the Gothic's "ubiquitous strength" in its linking of love and domination.[59] Feminist psychoanalysts such as Karen Horney, Clara Thompson, Paula Caplan, Jessica Benjamin, and Louise Kaplan deny that

---

piercing a pleasure that she began to groan. 'I'm at his mercy,' she said to herself and she was engulfed by an ecstasy in which shame and fear and joy were all intermingled. [...] She would have liked to call out to Denis that she was his thing, his slave: and tears ran down her cheeks. [...] She took every one of Denis's piercing thrusts with passionate submission [...]." (WTS 32-3)

[54] Jan Cohn, *Romance and the Erotics of Property* (Durham and London: Duke University Press, 1988) 8.

[55] Radway143.

[56] Massé 3.

[57] Massé 2.

[58] See also page 21: "[...] elles ne comprenaient pas que la femme mariée dût renoncer à travailler en-dehors pour se consacrer aux soins du foyer; sur la résignation et le dévouement, Marcelle leur fit de belles conférences qui les laissèrent insensibles." "They could not understand why a married woman should give up her job to look after the house. And Marcelle's fine lectures on resignation and self-sacrifice did not move them at all." (WTS 26)

[59] Massé 231.

women are "naturally" masochistic; rather, they are trained to associate love and pain.[60] In *Le Deuxième Sexe* Beauvoir had already dissected the myth of women and pain:

> Ainsi le narcissisme conduit au masochisme: cette liaison se rencontrait déjà chez l'enfant rêvant à Barbe-Bleue, à Grisélidis, aux saintes martyres. Le moi est constitué comme pour autrui, par autrui: plus autrui est puissant, plus le moi a de richesses et de pouvoirs; captivant son maître, il enveloppe en soi toutes les vertus que celui-ci détient [...]. (DS II, 116)[61]

Gothic fiction therefore focuses less on women's weakness and more on the ideology of oppression. Massé writes: "The Gothic's repeated, excruciatingly detailed representation of how women come to interweave love and pain helps us to understand how we too might awaken some day from the Gothic nightmare that is our own as well as our culture's."[62]

Marcelle's masochistic fantasies quickly dissipate during the honeymoon vacation with Denis, for as Beauvoir says in *Le Deuxième Sexe,* most women do not wish to carry out such fantasies in real life: "[...] la plupart du temps la jeune fille accepte dans *l'imaginaire* la domination d'un demi-dieu, d'un héros, d'un mâle; mais ce n'est encore qu'un jeu narcissiste. Elle n'est aucunement disposée par là à subir dans la réalité l'expression charnelle de cette autorité [...]" (DS II 185).[63] However, Marcelle does turn into a martyr, taking to her bed after Denis abandons her, wasting away until her health becomes compromised. Her sister Marguerite also had masochistic fantasies when she was a girl: "J'adorais m'imposer des mortifications [...]; je me fouettais avec une petite chaîne d'or; je me frottais aussi les cuisses à la pierre ponce [...]." (QPS 196-7).[64] She later becomes

---

[60] Massé 6.
[61] "Thus narcissism leads to masochism, as we see in the child already dreaming of Bluebeard and the holy martyrs. The ego is formed as it were for others, by others: the more powerful the others are, the richer and more powerful the ego is." (SS 348)
[62] Massé 9.
[63] "[...] usually the young girl accepts *in imagination* the domination of a demigod, a hero, a male; but this is no more than a narcissistic game." (SS 398) See also pages 582-3: "Qu'il s'agisse d'un médecin, d'un prêtre ou de Dieu, elle connaîtra les mêmes incontestables évidences, elle accueillera en esclave dans son cœur les flots d'un amour qui tombe d'en haut. Amour humain, amour divin se confondent, non parce que celui-ci serait une sublimation de celui-là, mais parce que le premier est aussi un mouvement vers un transcendant, vers l'absolu." "Be it a doctor, priest, or God, woman will feel the same unquestionable certainties, as hand-maiden she will receive in her heart the love that comes flooding from on high. Human love and love divine commingle, not because the latter is a substitute of the former, but because the first is a reaching out toward a transcendent, an absolute." (SS 670)
[64] "I loved imposing mortifications on myself [...]; I would often lock the lavatory door and whip myself with a little gold chain; I also rubbed my thighs with pumice-stone [...]". (WTS 170)

so devoted to Denis that she is ready to sell contraband drugs with him in Saigon. It takes her a full two years to achieve a relative autonomy after Denis drops her and returns to Marcelle. In Anne's case, masochism turns deadly. Chantal had already remarked Anne's propensity to accept suffering as her lot: "Chantal se ressaisit: elle savait bien qu'Anne était capable de gaspiller ridiculement des trésors d'héroïsme; elle ne les employait qu'à souffrir, à se nier [...]" (QPS 160).[65] Already prone to suffering because of love, Anne cuts her foot with an axe in order to be left alone. Convinced that the price of love is suffering, she does not confront Pascal with his indifference and at the end, dies of a broken heart. These examples demonstrate that the masochism typical of Gothic heroines is the direct result of traditional romantic discourse. Women associate love and pain, and since love is their supreme value, love turns into a perverse kind of mysticism. As Beauvoir explains in *Le Deuxième Sexe:* "L'amour a été assigné à la femme comme sa suprême vocation et, quand elle l'adresse à un homme, en lui elle recherche Dieu" (DS II 582).[66] Only through humiliation and suffering will she achieve some form of apotheosis.

Masochism may be a way to sublimate unacceptable sexual fantasies. Anne Vignon sublimates her sexual drive because she is crushed by a very restrictive morality: "[...] pour chacun des livres que j'ai lus, chaque sortie, chaque pensée, j'ai lutté [...]" (QPS 160).[67] Lisa's libido is expressed rather humourously through her obsession with hands, either caressing or masturbating hands, or hands representing male genitals: "[...] le docteur Desvignes lave ses mains. Lisa suit, comme fascinée, les mouvements de ces mains couvertes de mousse qui se pétrissent l'une contre l'autre, s'étreignent, se quittent, se reprennent [...] Lisa est entièrement abandonnée entre ses mains. [...] Rien n'existe que ses mains, ses mains habiles, ce sont des mains potelées et diaphanes, aux ongles soigneusement taillés. [...] De nouveau la main souple et grasse frôle les lèvres et le menton; sous cette caresse [...] Lisa sent son corps s'alanguir. [...] Il lui semble soudain que sa chair est devenue douce au toucher, tendre et riche" (QPS 122-4).[68]

---

[65] "She knew very well that Anne was capable of wasting treasures of heroism in the most ridiculous way – using them up in suffering, in self-denial." (WTS 140)

[66] "Love has been assigned to woman as her supreme vocation, and when she directs it toward a man, she is seeking God [...]" (SS 670)

[67] "[...] I've struggled for every book, for every thought, for every time I wanted to go out." (WTS 140)

[68] "[...] Dr Desvignes washed his hands. As though she were fascinated Lisa watched the motion of these froth-covered hands, the one kneading the other, their ritual grasping, separating, coming

Just before being treated by the dentist, she contemplates the waiting room, heavily charged with the image of female genitalia: "Des rideaux de damas rose aux franges d'or s'entrouvrent sur deux larges baies voiles d'un réseau de gros tulle; un radiateur répand dans la pièce une chaleur égale et un peu entêtante" (QPS 121).[69] Later, when she goes to bed, she fantasizes about the dentist's hands, which become Pascal's; hers then take over:

> Mains tièdes, mains de guimauve encore humides de mousse. Vous êtes la pluie des caresses légères. [...] Les mains de Pascal effleurent les cheveux, le cou; [...] des mains répandues sur la chair secrète, mains d'archange descendant lentement le long d'une tendre victime, ta main chair frissonnante, ta chère main d'archange bien-aimé; bien-aimé, bien-aimé.
>
> La main de Lisa a laissé tombé dans le cendrier la cigarette et s'est glissée sous la soie du pyjama; elle ne sent plus son bras, sa main n'est plus la sienne et les douces muqueuses humides tressaillent sous la caresse de ces doigts étrangers.
>
> Ta chère main d'archange bien-aimé, bien-aimé. (QPS 129)[70]

Passages such as this one may have simply been too much for Gallimard and Grasset! Here, Beauvoir imitates the heavy breathing of the aroused woman by repeating "bien-aimé" and by truncating the syntax, a technique she uses much later in "Monologue," one of the three short stories in *La Femme rompue*. Likewise, the passages on lesbian desire may have been too strong for the publishing industry at the time. In two separate stories, the young women approached by another woman find their advances disgusting, as Marcelle says about the forty-year old Germaine Masson who is in love with her: "[...] cette femme presque vieille se nourrissait comme un vampire de la jeunesse et de l'entrain de son amie" (QPS 13).[71]

---

together. [...] Lisa, half-lying in the chair, was wholly in his power; [..] nothing existed apart from his hands, his skilful hands. She half opened her eyes: they were plump, translucent hands with carefully cut nails [...]. Once again the plump, supple hands brushed her lips and her chin: under this caress [...] Lisa felt her body relax [...]. It seemed to her that her flesh had become soft to the touch, yielding and rich." (WTS 109-111)

69 "The half-opened pink damask curtains with gold fringes showed two broad windows veiled with wide-meshed tulle: a radiator emitted an even, slightly heady warmth." (WT 109)

70 "Warm hands, lily-soft hands still damp with moss. You are the light rain of caresses. [...] Pascal's hands stroking hair and neck, [...] hands moving over the secret flesh, archangel's hands gliding slowly down a tender victim, your hand quivering flesh, your dear archangel's hand beloved: beloved, beloved. Lisa's hands dropped the cigarette into the ashtray and slipped under the pyjama's silk: she no longer felt her arm – her hand was no longer hers and it was under the caress of these stranger's fingers that the soft moist inner tissues thrilled and quivered. Your dear archangel's hands beloved, well-beloved." (WTS 115)

71 "[...] she was almost an old woman and she fed on her friend's youth and zest for life like a vampire." (WTS 19)

Marcelle's sister Marguerite recoils in horror when the older Marie-Ange tries to seduce her: "Mon cœur s'est mis à battre; je n'osais pas la repousser mais tout mon corps s'est crispé; [...] sa main se promenait par tout mon corps, elle se glissait sous ma veste, descendait le long du ventre; je serrais fortement les jambes l'une contre l'autre, je ne faisais pas un geste" (QPS 240).[72] All of their upbringing has conditioned them to think that they are destined to men, as Beauvoir says in *Le Deuxième Sexe:* "Elle est vouée à l'homme, elle le sait; et elle veut une destinée de femme normale et complète" (DS II 113).[73]

The young women are educated to believe that sexual desire, even for a man, is unacceptable and shameful. Genevieve Shepherd explains Marcelle's masochism as the product of a severely repressed sexuality which is bound up in Catholic doctrine: "What Marcelle is both projecting and hiding behind these saintly fantasies is nothing other than her own strong sexuality."[74] This may be why Chantal explicitly transforms romantic discourse into a form of mysticism. She idealizes Monique and Serge, a young couple, projecting her own romantic ideal onto them, like the protagonists of *Le Grand Meaulnes:* "[...] sur un invisible autel se célèbrent les mystères de la jeunesse et de l'amour et j'incline mon front avec ferveur" (QPS 84).[75] Like Laurence's father in *Les Belles Images,* she transforms human suffering into beauty: "Tenez: le vieux mendiant qui est toujours là, à vendre des lacets et du papier d'Arménie, si je le regarde comme l'incarnation d'un de ces avortons prodigieux qu'a dessinés Goya, il ne me semble plus répugnant, mais beau" (QPS 75).[76] Chantal literally lives her life as if she were the heroine of a novel: "Lorsque je regarde ma vie comme un roman dont je suis l'héroïne, les heures de tristesse se transforment en des pages émouvantes dont il m'est possible de tirer de la joie" (QPS 82).[77] But the romantic discourse gleaned from fiction makes her unfit for tough ethical decisions such as helping her preg-

---

[72] "My heart began to thump; I did not like to push her away, but my whole body grew rigid. [...] Her hand moved all over my body, sliding under my jacket and down my belly: I clamped my legs together, making no movement at all." (WTS 205)
[73] "She is destined for man, and knows it; and she wants the normal and complete lot of woman." (SS 347)
[74] Shepherd 56, 60.
[75] "[...] the mysteries of youth and love are being celebrated on an unseen altar and earnestly, fervently I bow my head." (WTS 78)
[76] "Take the old beggar by the lycée, for example, the one who is always there selling shoe laces and fumigating paper: if I look upon him as the incarnation of one of Goya's prodigious freaks he no longer seems to me repulsive but beautiful." (WTS 71)
[77] "When I see my life as a novel of which I am the heroine, the hours of sadness are transformed into touching passages – pages from which I can draw pleasure." (WTS 76)

nant student get an abortion. Instead, she focuses on her appearance, getting makeovers, new clothes and taking in the important lessons learned from *Vogue, Femina* and *Votre Beauté:* "[Chantal et Jeannine] avaient retenu ces principes essentiels: que le noir est toujours élégant, que la classe d'une toilette dépend en grande partie des souliers qui l'accompagnent" (QPS 61).[78] As emancipated as she thinks she is, Chantal conforms to the image of the self-sacrificing woman when she is bent on seducing Paul Baron: "[…] elle apprit les sports qu'il aimait, elle suivit des cours de danse pour danser avec lui; elle lu avidemment les journaux pour qu'il la consultât sur les questions de politique; c'était un énorme travail" (QPS 164).[79] Later, she ends up marrying a doctor and more than likely becoming a traditional housewife.

Young women are not taught to read fiction with a critical eye and to become aware of the destructive messages transmitted by the language of fiction or of popular culture. One product of this education is Marguerite who reads novels without the faintest notion of the misogyny inscribed in their pages: "J'avais l'esprit décidément tourné vers le sublime; pour moi, les romans les plus obscènes racontaient tous, symboliquement, l'éternel drame de l'homme à la poursuite de l'absolu; si le héros accomplissait un viol atroce, un acte de sadisme, c'est qu'il cherchait à combler le vide de son âme […]" (QPS 206).[80] This is no surprise, given the training that she received at *l'Institut Saints-Anges.* Mlle Lacombe, one of the institute's finest teachers, teaches the girls to take down notes passively and to regurgitate them in the final exam:

> Mlle Lacombe avait posé à côté d'elle une liasse de papiers couverts d'écriture et découpés en rectangles; sur chaque auteur au programme, elle avait constitué un dossier portatif comprenant un récit de sa vie et une appréciation de son œuvre d'après les critiques les plus autorisés; chaque année, sans en changer une ligne, elle lisait ces notes à ses élèves qui les copiaient docilement sur leurs cahiers. Cette méthode donnait aux examens d'excellents résultats et Mlle Lacombe était un professeur estimé. (QPS 88)[81]

---

[78] "[…] they had retained these basic principles – that black is always elegant, and that being well dressed depends in a large degree upon the shoes one wears." (WTS 60)

[79] "[…] she learnt the games he liked, she took dancing lessons in order to be able to dance with him, and she avidly read the newspapers so that he should consult her on political matters; it was a prodigious task." (WTS 143-4)

[80] "My mind had a most decided turn for the sublime: as far as I was concerned all these novels, even the most obscene, were symbolic accounts of the eternal drama of man in pursuit of the absolute, and if the hero carried out an appalling rape or a sadistic act it was because he was trying to fill the emptiness of his soul." (WTS 178)

[81] "Mlle Lacombe had a pile of square-cut, closely-written papers beside her: she had compiled a portable dossier on each of the authors of the set books, a file that contained an account of the author's

Marguerite has absorbed the male point of view from the texts that she has passively studied in school. As Patrocinio Schweickart writes: "As readers and teachers and scholars, women are taught to identify with a male point of view, and to accept as normal and legitimate a male system of values, one of whose central principles is misogyny."[82] Mlle Bidois, the school principal, concentrates only on infractions to the dress code: "Vous savez que vous ne devez pas vous rendre au lycée en manches courtes, reprit-elle, et nous ne devez pas vous contenter de jeter vos manteaux sur vos épaules" (QPS 89).[83] These "lessons" are immediately juxtaposed to real-life stories of women and their predicaments: painful periods, miscarriages, unwanted pregnancies, poverty, solitude (QPS 91-92). Clearly, the girls are not being prepared to improve their lot but rather to accept suffering as part of their destiny, as Mme Vignon tells her daughter Lucette: "[…] tes devoirs d'État à présent sont ceux d'une épouse et d'une mère, c'est immoral ce refus de remplir ta mission de femme […]. Si tu comprenais un peu mieux ce que doit être le mariage pour une chrétienne, tu ne ferais pas intervenir tant de vanité […]. Crois bien que si je n'avais pensé qu'à mon plaisir, tu ne serais pas de ce monde" (QPS 137, 139).[84] Women must learn self-abdication and accept suffering as their lot, as she tells her other daughter Anne: "Il faut faire ce que nous avons à faire sans tenir compte de nos humeurs, Anne. […] J'ai été comme toi; mais on apprend à ne pas s'écouter" (QPS 146).[85] Later in *Mémoires d'une jeune fille rangée,* Beauvoir says that her mother taught her to silence her needs: "J'appris de maman à m'effacer, à contrôler mon langage, à censurer mes désirs, à dire et à faire exactement ce qui devait être dit et fait" (MJF 58).[86] Both Anne and her mother subcon-

---

life and an appreciation of his works based on the most approved critics; and every year, without changing a line, she read these notes out to her pupils, who submissively copied them into their exercisebooks. This method produced excellent results in the examinations and Mlle Lacombe was a respected teacher." (WTS 81)

[82] Patrocinio P. Schweickart, "Reading Ourselves: Toward as Feminist Theory of Reading", Ed. E. Flynn and P. Schweickart, *Gender and Reading* (Baltimore and London: Johns Hopkins University Press, 1968) 41.

[83] "'You know that you are not to come to school in short sleeves, she went on, 'and that you are not merely to throw your coats over your shoulders […]'". (WTS 81)

[84] "[…] *her civic duties are those of a wife and mother and this refusal to fulfil her mission as a woman is immoral.* […] 'If you had a slightly better understanding of what marriage ought to be for a Christian woman, you would not let questions of vain pride enter into it. […] 'Believe me, […] if I had only thought about *my* pleasure, you would never have come into the world'." (WTS 122-3)

[85] "'We must do what we have to do without taking our feelings into consideration, Anne. […] I used to be like you: but one learns not to pay attention to oneself.'" (WTS 129)

[86] "[…] I learnt from Mama to keep in the background, to control my tongue, to moderate my desires, to say and do exactly what ought to be said and done." (MDD 41)

sciously sense their entrapment in this ideology, as they both feel the collars around their necks: "Mme Vignon toucha le lourd fermoir d'or que retenait autour de son cou un ruban de velours noir" (QPS 139); "son visage demeurait sérieux et fermé et elle ne faisait pas un geste; de temps en temps, elle caressait son collier de corail" (QPS 156).[87] Beauvoir was no doubt thinking of Colette's *La Vagabonde,* a novel which she quotes often in *Le Deuxième Sexe,* in particular of this passage: "[…] mon regard de chienne soumise, un peu penaude, un peu battue, très choyée, et qui accepte tout, la laisse, le collier, la place aux pieds de mon maître".[88]

The education that the young women receive prepares them for the subservience awaiting them in marriage. This is part of the ideology that Beauvoir denounces in this novel. The young women must be trained to become Gothic heroines. They must learn the lessons of romantic discourse through religion, high and popular culture, education, and bourgeois values. Beauvoir cleverly mocks these serious institutions by humorously juxtaposing them with spiritualist and occult beliefs. Lisa's dentist is a theosophist who talks at length about out-of-body experiences and reincarnation. Marie-Ange Lamblin, an older woman who tries to seduce Marguerite, reads palms, has premonitory dreams and can see germs in dishes. Spiritualism and spirituality are conflated into one big myth, so that the "spirituel" in the title of the novel ends up meaning "false and harmful discourses."

The male protagonists have also learned their lessons well. Like the dark heroes of Gothic fiction, their primary function is to make the heroines suffer. The most selfish and arrogant of the men in *Quand Prime le Spirituel* is Denis Charval, a spoiled, lazy and misogynist man whose mission in life is to exploit women. Denis marries Marcelle for the financial support she can provide. In bed, he becomes authoritative and domineering, and Marcelle thinks that he would be capable of beating and torturing her. He does indeed end up torturing her emotionally, cheating on her, squandering her money, and treating her with utter contempt. Marcelle's sister Marguerite also falls in love with him, and is ready to sacrifice her life for him. He repays her devotion with indifference and neglect. His egotism is never questioned or chastised by the two sisters, or by Denis himself. According

---

[87] "Mme Vignon put her hand to the heavy gold clasp of the black velvet ribbon around her neck" (WTS 123); "[…] her face remained closed and grave and she hardly moved at all, though from time to time she touched her coral necklace." (WTS 136-7)

[88] Colette, *La Vagabonde* (Paris: Livre de Poche, 1990) 164.

to Michelle Massé, Gothic husbands believe in their own entitlement: "In each of these stories, the husbands' actions are wholly explicable in his own mind, and often those of others, because he believes that his wife should be a narcissistic extension of himself rather than a discrete personality."[89]

The other male characters all treat the female protagonists with contempt or indifference. Pascal has inspired a passionate infatuation in Lisa, who tries to get his attention by waiting for him at a bus stop near Musset's statue with a pathetic bouquet of violets. His emotional withdrawal from Anne is just as harmful as any Gothic hero's violence, leading directly to her death. The novel that Anne was reading during one of her last encounters with Pascal was titled *L'Égoïste*. Serge, the student who gets Monique pregnant, treats her with condescension, even going so far as to hit her. "Il ne m'aime pas", says Monique, "il n'est pas capable d'aimer personne, il est tout juste bon à jouer au billard ou à la manille du matin au soir; c'est un égoïste stupide" (QPS 94).[90] This man is a clone of Denis Charval.

Gothic heroes abuse, control, and silence their women. During their honeymoon, Marcelle would have liked to tell Denis about her childhood, "mais il ne s'y intéressait pas beaucoup" (QPS 31).[91] He refuses to listen to Marcelle when she has serious issues to discuss: "Il ne semblait pas du tout prendre Marcelle au sérieux [...]. Il était instable, nerveux et il affectait d'éviter les conversations sérieuses" (QPS 35-6).[92] He is bored by Marguerite and refuses to let her speak: "[...] il lui arrivait souvent de m'accueillir d'un air ennuyé, lointain ou ironique; il écartait avec impatience toute allusion à nos conversations passées, il ne répondait pas à mes questions [...]" (QPS 228).[93] In another passage, Denis cuts off all of her attempts to communicate with him: "[...] il était toujours de mauvaise humeur; quand je l'interrogeais sur l'emploi de sa journée, il ne me répondait que par monosyllables, il n'écoutait pas mes récits. Alors je buvais mon café et je me taisais" (QPS 242).[94] Michelle Massé writes that

---

[89] Massé 26.

[90] "'He doesn't love me; he's not capable of loving anyone. All he's good for is playing billiards or cards from morning till night: he's a stupid egoist.'" (WTS 86)

[91] "[...] but it was not a subject that he found very interesting." (WTS 35)

[92] "He did not seem to be taking Marcelle at all seriously. [...] He was irritable and on edge and he made a point of avoiding serious conversations." (WTS 38)

[93] "Often he would receive me with a bored, distant or ironic look: impatiently he repelled any allusion to our earlier conversations, he did not answer my questions [...]." (WTS 197)

[94] "[...] he was always ill-tempered. When I asked him how he had spent his day he only answered with monosyllables; he did not listen to my accounts. So I drank my café crème too and held my tongue." (WTS 207)

Gothic heroines have difficulty getting their stories told, and their difficulties in speaking to others are accompanied by "a kind of despair about any direct use of language".[95] "The plea of the heroine in marital Gothic," she writes, "[is] to have her voice heard and her existence acknowledged."[96] The silencing of women in this novel is akin to violence.

Marguerite encounters a different form of male violence in the strangers she meets in bars. Marguerite has been brainwashed by the new novelists she has been reading: André Gide, Jacques Rivière, André Breton, whose message is to be always "disponible", to refuse nothing (QPS 215). This may be fine for men, but it is downright suicidal for women, as Marguerite finds out the hard way. On many occasions, men threaten her, and she barely escapes being beaten and raped: "[…] l'homme m'a saisie aux épaules: 'Maintenant je sais que tu te moques de moi, m'a-t-il dit, […] tu mérites une bonne leçon, ma petite: je deviens méchant quand on me contrarie; tu as eu tort de vouloir me faire marcher'" (QPS 217).[97] All of the male characters use the discourse of domination and intimidation. In *Quand Prime le Spirituel,* Beauvoir criticizes male behavior and holds them responsible for the suffering they inflict on women. "The very meaning of masculinity must change," writes Denise Thompson. "It must be divested of its contempt for and dread of the female, its competitiveness, aggression, violence and addiction to hierarchy […]".[98]

Beauvoir was clearly trying to demystify the discourse of masculinity. By depicting female suffering, Gothic fiction implicitly advocates the opposite: a love not founded on domination but on reciprocity. Although *Quand Prime le Spirituel* is largely based on Beauvoir's own experience, she was able to detect the lies embedded in romantic discourse because she had a firm idea of what she wanted in a love relationship at a very early age. In her teenage diaries, she says that what she hates in love is the abdication of one's identity: "Je n'en fais pas une question de dignité mais de morale; je consentirais volontiers tous les sacrifices pour un être que j'aimerais, mais je ne voudrais pas n'exister qu'à travers lui – le chantage sentimental pousse les femmes surtout à voir dans celui qu'elles aiment un être chargé de

---

[95] Massé 20.
[96] Massé 28.
[97] "[…] the man took me by the shoulders again. 'Now I know you're making a fool of me,' he said. […] You deserve a good lesson, my chick; I grow nasty when I'm crossed. You got it all wrong, trying to string me along.'" (WTS 187)
[98] Thompson 88.

partager le fardeau de leur âme qu'elles sont trop faibles pour porter."[99] The expression that returns throughout her diary is "se donner tout en se réservant", the idea that a woman must not sacrifice her life for love.[100]

Gothic heroines like the ones in *Quand Prime le Spirituel* do sacrifice themselves for love. Marguerite achieves a shallow kind of victory in that she realizes – after a two year struggle – that she can live without Denis, but she pays the same price for her autonomy as Renée Néré in *La Vagabonde:* solitude. Monique, the pregnant student, expresses her hatred for Serge, but she is forced to accept her destiny as a wife and mother. The language of romance that she has learned translates into a feminist consciousness of authentic and legitimate female desire, but her revolt is ineffectual. In a book dedicated to Simone de Beauvoir, *The Dialectic of Sex. The Case for Feminist Revolution,* Shulamith Firesone writes: "Women and love are underpinnings. Examine them and you threaten the very structure of culture."[101]

As I mentioned at the beginning of this chapter, Beauvoir said that in *Quand Prime le Spirituel,* she wished to expose the spiritualism that had so oppressed her in her youth (QPS vii). Marguerite uses the term as defined by Fallaize ("a mystical belief in a religion, intellectual or aesthetic absolute held to be superior to the material world")[102] when she says that her whole family is devoted to some form of spiritualism – her father to literature, her mother to Christian virtues, her brother and sister to poetry and inner life (QPS 195). In a chapter devoted to *Quand Prime le Spirituel,* Eleanor Holveck points out how each character represents a form of spirituality that Beauvoir ended up rejecting – Rimbaud, Rilke, Baruzi, Leibniz, Kant, Brunschwicg, Maritain; she argues that Beauvoir "is doing a phenomenological description of the idealistic beliefs that formed the life-world of her philosophical childhood."[103] In other words, Beauvoir used language to deconstruct the fictions proposed by bourgeois patriarchal ideology.

---

[99] *Carnets de jeunesse,* Aug. 27, 1926.

[100] See for example Aug. 13 and 27, 1926, and Nov. 5, 1926: "[…] l'amour ne saurait être un simple incident; il tend à absorber tout, à apporter toute la vie à l'amour; à enrichir la vie par l'amour. Mais il ne faut pas sacrifier l'un à l'autre; il ne faut pas surtout prétendre les confondre." "[…] love is certainly no trifling incident; it tends to absorb everything, to bring everything to love, to enrich life by love. But you musn't sacrifice one for the other; above all one musn't claim they are the same." (my translation)

[101] Shulamith Firestone, *The Dialectic of Sex. The Case for Feminist Revolution* (New York: William Morrow & Co., 1970) 142.

[102] Fallaize 145.

[103] Eleanor Holveck, *Simone de Beauvoir's Philosophy of Lived Experience. Literature and Metaphysics* (Oxford: Rowman & Littlefield Publishers, 2002) 45–46.

In her teenage diaries, Beauvoir says that, as a writer, one should not strive to be understood right away: "[...] ce qui est intéressant, c'est ce qu'on lit entre les lignes."[104] For a long time, for example, readers did not understand her use of irony in *The Second Sex,* and misread the message that she considered quite obvious, and which she stated clearly in different parts of the text: that myths are discourses that hurt women and therefore must be denounced as false and harmful. Sooner or later, she writes, the reader will figure out the ideas that are suggested by the text.[105] Beauvoir uses language subversively, undermining patriarchal discourse from within, and this subversion, according to Michelle Massé, involves a "secret knowingness."[106] What Beauvoir meant by *spirituel* was the discourse of patriarchal ideology that brainwashes young women. *Quand Prime le Spirituel* attempts to dismantle these discourses so that women can reject the Gothic script that is still ours to a great extent today.

---

104 "It's what's between the lines that's interesting." (my translation)
105 *Carnets de jeunesse,* 10 Sept. 1927.
106 Massé 250.

Works Cited

Bair, Deirdre. *Simone de Beauvoir. A Biography.* New York: Summit Books, 1990.

Beauvoir, Simone de. *Carnets de jeunesse,* Holograph manuscript, Paris: Bibliothèque Nationale, Site Richelieu, 1926-1930.

_____. *Quand Prime le Spirituel.* Paris: Gallimard, 1979.

_____. *When Things of the Spirit Come First.* Trans. Patrick O'Brian, London: HarperCollins, Flamingo, 1983.

_____. *Le Deuxième Sexe.* Paris: Gallimard, 1949.

_____. *The Second Sex.* Trans. H. M. Parshley, Harmondsworth: Penguin, 1972.

_____. *Mémoires d'une jeune fille rangée.* Paris: Gallimard, 1957.

_____. *Memoirs of a Dutiful Daughter.* Trans. James Kirkup, Harmondsworth: Penguin, 1987.

_____. *La Force de l'âge.* Paris: Gallimard, 1960.

_____. *The Prime of Life.* Trans. Peter Green, Harmondsworth: Penguin, 1965.

_____. *Les Belles Images.* Paris: Gallimard, 1966.

_____. *Les Belles Images.* Trans. Patrick O'Brian, London: Fontana, 1969.

_____. *La Femme rompue.* Paris: Gallimard, 1967.

_____. *The Woman Destroyed.* Trans. Patrick O'Brian, London: HarperCollins, Flamingo Modern Classics, 1994.

Cohn, Jan. *Romance and the Erotics of Property.* Durham & London: Duke University Press, 1988.

Colette, *La Vagabonde.* Paris: Livre de Poche, 1990.

Firestone, Shulamith. *The Dialectic of Sex. The Case for Feminist Revolution.* New York: William Morrow & Co., 1970.

Fishwick, Sarah. *The Body in the Work of Simone de Beauvoir.* New York: Peter Lang Publishers, 2002.

Fallaize, Elizabeth. *The Novels of Simone de Beauvoir.* London: Routledge, 1988.

Fetterley, Judith. "Reading about Reading. *A Jury of Her Peers, The Murder in the Rue Morgue* and *The Yellow Wallpaper,*" in Elizabeth A. Flynn and Patrocinio P. Schweickhart. *Gender and Reading. Essays on Readers, Texts and Contexts.* Baltimore: Johns Hopkins University Press, 1968. 147-164.

Gilman, Charlotte Perkins. *The Yellow Wallpaper,* Boston: Bedford Books, 1998.

Holveck, Eleanor. *Simone de Beauvoir's Philosophy of Lived Experience. Literature and Metaphysics.* Oxford: Rowman & Littlefield, 1995.

Keefe, Terry. *Simone de Beauvoir.* New York: St. Martin's Press, 1998.

Massé, Michelle A. *In the Name of Love. Women, Masochism and the Gothic.* Ithaca and London: Cornell University Press, 1992.

Radway, Janice A. *Reading the Romance. Women, Patriarchy and Popular Literature.* Chapel Hill & London: University of North Carolina Press, 1991.

Sage, Lorna. "Simone de Beauvoir: Transcending Fictions." Ed. Ruth Evans, ed. *Simone de Beauvoir's The Second Sex. New Interdisciplinary Essays.* Manchester: Manchester University Press, 1998. 97-121.

Shepherd, Genevieve. *Simone de Beauvoir's Fiction. A Psychoanalytic Reading.* New York: Peter Lang Publishers, 2004.

Thompson, Denise. *Radical Feminism Today.* London: Sage, 2001.

2 Intimacy and Revenge: Language and Power in *L'Invitée*

Alison T. Holland

This chapter offers a close reading of *L'Invitée*, Beauvoir's first published novel. It focuses on a number of the key relationships of Françoise, the central protagonist. Firstly it explores Françoise's intense relationships, with Élisabeth and Xavière. As we shall see, to use the term "intimate friendships" would be to oversimplify. In many ways, Françoise's relationship with Xavière is the central relationship in *L'Invitée*; as Beauvoir tells us, the story begins when Xavière, a stranger, enters her life (FA 385). The echoes and parallels in Françoise's relationship with Élisabeth are striking. This chapter also explores the complex relationship of Françoise with language. Firstly in terms of language and representation, Françoise fears the power of others to narrate her story and (ab)uses narrative power to exact revenge on Élisabeth and Xavière. This narrative violence culminates in murder on the level of story. Françoise kills Xavière explicitly for narrative control. Secondly in terms of language and signification; Françoise experiences language as problematical. The explorations of Françoise's intense relationships and of her relationship with language are inextricably bound together. The third dimension of my reading is Beauvoir's writing practice. It reveals that the how of the telling of the story is to a great extent the meaning of the story.

The drama of Françoise's relationships with Élisabeth and Xavière is played out against the backdrop of Françoise's relationship with Pierre. A similar pattern recurs in all three relationships, a pattern involving desire for confluence, loss of self and the pain of abandonment.[1] The fact that Françoise's relationship with Pierre is based on complete unity is repeatedly foregrounded in the first part of the narrative. Pierre and Françoise believe they are one: "Toi et moi, on ne fait qu'un", Pierre tells her (I 29). "On ne fait qu'un", she repeats to herself (I 30). Watching Pierre on stage during a dress-rehearsal, she sees him as an extension of herself (I 61). Paradoxically, to begin with, this symbiosis does not threaten Françoise's sense of

---

[1] Confluence is a form of symbiosis in which two individuals merge with one another and behave as if they are one person. See Petrūska Clarkson, *Gestalt Counselling in Action* (London: Sage, 1989) 55.

identity. She willingly invests her identity in Pierre. Yet the warning signs
are there; this symbiosis is already a source of mild anguish as Françoise
realises that it brings responsibility for Pierre's performance without the
power to do anything about it. *L'Invitée* is the story of Françoise's painful
separation from him, her realisation that she has lost herself in the unity
with Pierre – she comes to realise, as Toril Moi puts it, that they are one
but that Pierre "is the one they are".[2] When Pierre withdraws from the
confluence on which her identity depends, Françoise experiences unbear-
ably painful feelings of abandonment. Exiled from Pierre one afternoon
when he is with Xavière, Françoise understands that her happiness
depends on Pierre's desiring for himself what Françoise desires for him and
that she has no control whatsoever over what Pierre desires (I 213). On the
verge of physical and emotional collapse, Françoise is utterly alienated: "Il
aurait fallu que quelqu'un fût là pour dire; 'je suis fatiguée, je suis mal-
heureuse' [...]. Mais il n'y avait personne" (I 216). She blames herself for
no longer being someone, for not even having a face, for never saying "I"
whilst Pierre is able to decide his own future, follow his own heart and to
live his own life.

Françoise's relationship with Pierre forms the context for her intense
relationships with Élisabeth and Xavière and it is to these relationships and
the parallels between them that I now turn. The early years of Françoise's
relationship with Élisabeth are related in the second of the two chapters discarded from the novel on the advice of Brice Parrain at Gallimard, her
publisher.[3] This chapter adds a great deal to our understanding of the relationship between the two women in the published novel. From the beginning,
Françoise is bowled over by the new, self-possessed, flamboyant, daring
young woman at the *lycée* who wants to be her friend. She is fascinated by
Élisabeth's difference. It soon emerges that Françoise's sense of self is
threatened by her relationship with Élisabeth. *In La Force de l'âge* Beauvoir
explains that Françoise lacks solid boundaries and a clear sense of self; for
Beauvoir this arises out of Françoise's view of herself as pure consciousness, a sovereign subject whose role it is to reveal the world: "La rançon de
ce privilège c'est que, se confondant avec tout, elle ne possédait pas, à ses

---

[2] Toril Moi, *Simone de Beauvoir: The Making of an Intellectual Woman* (Oxford: Blackwell, 1994) 108.
[3] See FA, pp. 384-85. "Deux chapitres inédits de *L'Invitée*", Ed. Claude Francis and Fernande Gontier
(Paris: Gallimard, 1979) 275-316. Further references to these chapters are given in abbreviated form
(DCI) in the main body of the text.

propres yeux, de figure définie" (FA 385).[4] Élisabeth, on the other hand, knows who she is, what she thinks and what she wants. And she likes herself. In her encounter with Élisabeth, Françoise is struck by the painful realisation that the world exists independently of her. Élisabeth also has the power to make the world exist: "Les choses se sentaient exister sans elle; un autre regard, une autre pensée que la sienne jetait sur la surface du ciel une ombre mélancolique. C'était presque intolérable" (DCI 296).[5] The adolescent Françoise's dismay is captured by the unexpected image of a shadow cast on the sky. Élisabeth directly challenges Françoise's sovereign status in the world: "Élisabeth était réelle" (DCI 296).[6] Extremely disconcerted by Élisabeth's assumption that the world revolves around her, Françoise makes a deliberate decision to get close to Élisabeth ("devenir intime avec elle" [DCI 298]) to set the record straight and impose her own existence. When Élisabeth tells her she is pleased to have found a friend, Françoise does not reply; for her it is not a question of friendship at all (DCI 302). Élisabeth's self-assurance (her "dures résistances") makes Françoise acutely aware of the emptiness in herself: "Qu'est-ce que je suis, moi? [...] Elle ferma les yeux. Plus rien n'existait ni autour d'elle, ni en elle; rien que la conscience aiguë de ce néant" (DCI 302).[7]

Françoise desires symbiosis with Élisabeth. Symbiosis brings relief as when Françoise merges with Élisabeth, she is no longer an alien consciousness, a stranger:

> La voix d'Élisabeth, une odeur de charbon dissipaient l'envie, la rancune; assise dans le fauteuil de tapisserie, à côté de la salamandre, Françoise renonçait d'un seul coup à son orgueil, à son passé, à tout désir. Elle regardait les cheveux roux d'Élisabeth, elle écoutait, et elle oubliait sa propre existence. Alors tout devenait facile; aucun obstacle ne se dressait plus entre Élisabeth et elle; elle n'avait plus d'autre histoire que l'histoire d'Élisabeth; et Élisabeth n'était rien d'autre que cette histoire qu'elle racontait. (DCI 305)[8]

---

4 "But there was a price to pay for this privilege: by merging her identity with everything she saw she lost all sharply defined individualism in her own eyes." (PL 338)

5 As no English translation of these chapters has been published, all translations are my own. "Things were aware of their existence without her; someone else's look, someone else's thought cast a melancholy shadow on the surface of the sky. It was almost intolerable."

6 "Élisabeth was real."

7 "What am I? [...] She closed her eyes. Nothing at all existed either around her or within her; nothing but the acute awareness of this nothingness."

8 "The voice of Élisabeth, the smell of the coal fire made envy, bitterness disappear; sitting in the tapestry arm chair next to the stove, Françoise all at once gave up her pride, her past, everything she desired. She looked at Élisabeth's red hair, she listened, and she forgot her own existence. Then everything became easy; there was no longer any obstacle between Élisabeth and herself; the only story she had was Élisabeth's story; and Élisabeth was nothing but the story she was telling."

Françoise wants to know Élisabeth absolutely, her quest is for absolute knowledge. From the first, Françoise wants to understand Élisabeth, to know what she is thinking (DCI 294). This is more than simple curiosity. She invests Élisabeth with an air of mystery. The knowledge she craves will allow her to overcome her obsession. Invited to Élisabeth's for the first time, Françoise stands on the landing, aware of her friend behind the door, living a separate existence that Françoise can never truly know (DCI 298). Françoise wants to know everything that Élisabeth knows (DCI 305). She has the sense of being shut out of a secret: "Il semblait à Françoise que le jour où elle connaîtrait parfaitement Élisabeth, elle finirait par la mépriser ou par l'aimer; de toute façon, ce serait une délivrance; avec obstination elle essayait de glisser au coeur de cette vie interdite" (DCI 306).[9] As Françoise waits for Élisabeth in her bedroom, she is moved by the sense that the absent Élisabeth is somehow in the objects around her, tries to see the room through Élisabeth's eyes, to "be" Élisabeth. She is bitterly disappointed that she can never truly know who Élisabeth is. On another occasion, Françoise secretly follows Élisabeth to the theatre where she has gone to join her brother Pierre at a dress-rehearsal. Françoise is filled with self-pity, realising that "de la vie d'Élisabeth elle ne connaîtrait jamais que des dehors, que des envers" (DCI 308-09).[10]

Françoise is at once attracted and repelled by Élisabeth. One of the first things she notices is Élisabeth's "mains de paysanne" (country-woman's hands) with their bright red nails (DCI 293). Françoise experiences an immediate powerful physical, sexual attraction to her. After Élisabeth's first day at school, Françoise walks her home and watches her comb her hair in front of the mirror in the hallway:

> Le peigne descendait le long des mèches rousses, la lourde toison se gonflait et frissonnait contre la nuque. Une fois, deux fois, dix fois: d'un geste régulier, la main aux ongles rouges guidait le peigne à travers la masse cuivrée; le peigne passait et repassait le long des mèches houleuses; une fois encore; encore une fois. C'était fascinant. Françoise ne sentait plus son corps; des cheveux caressaient une nuque, une joue; elle ne sentait que cette caresse soyeuse effleurant une chair qui n'était pas la sienne. Le peigne glissait lentement; les cheveux de soie frôlaient la peau blanche et la caressaient, délicieuse et cruelle. Élisabeth poussa la seconde porte et commença de monter

---

[9] "It seemed to Françoise that the day she knew Élisabeth absolutely, she would end up either despising her or loving her; in either case, it would be a release; she obstinately tried to slip into the heart of this life that was closed to her."

[10] "She would never know anything but the outside, the wrong side of Élisabeth's life."

l'escalier. L'escalier existait et le tapis, la rampe où se posaient les doigts aux ongles peints. Françoise avait cessé d'exister. (DCI 295)[11]

The text conveys Françoise's heightened sense of physical awareness at the same time as she loses herself and merges with Élisabeth. The use of repetition gives the text an hypnotic quality. At times, the insistant rhythm suggests sexual arousal: "une fois, deux fois, dix fois"; "une fois encore; encore une fois". Once home, Françoise sits in the darkened library, imagining Élisabeth who continues to exist without her. The picture she invents is very sensual, evocative of sexual fantasy: "Un souple corps en robe de soie collante s'allongeait sur les coussins d'un divan et la bouche épaisse rejetait des volutes de fumée bleue" (DCI 296).[12]

In the published novel, the relationship between Françoise and Élisabeth has changed. The rosy picture of their shared adolescence, evoked by Françoise, is unrecognisable: "Elle eut un élan de sympathie vers [Élisabeth]; elle éprouvait la même impression de camaraderie et de détente qu'autrefois, lorsqu'au sortir d'un cours intéressant et difficile, elles se promenaient bras dessus bras dessous dans la cour du lycée" (I 56).[13] Of course, it can be argued that Beauvoir's conception of the character of Élisabeth has completely changed, that the Élisabeth in the published novel is not at all the Élisabeth of the omitted chapters but this change too is interesting. In the published novel Françoise sums up Élisabeth for Xavière; she describes her as an eternal adolescent who still looks to others for approval and models of behaviour. What Françoise and Pierre find so annoying about Élisabeth is the way she listens to them so slavishly and constantly re-invents herself in a clumsy attempt to bolster her self-esteem (I 170).

There has clearly been a reversal of roles; the message intended is that Françoise is now capable, strong and confident; Élisabeth is the one whose

---

11 "The comb ran down the length of the red locks, the thick mane expanded and rippled against her neck. Once, twice, ten times: with a regular movement, the hand with the red nails guided the comb through the copper mass; the comb ran again and again through the long messy locks; once again; one more time. It was spellbinding. Françoise could no longer feel her body; hair was caressing a neck, a cheek; she only felt this silky caress brushing against a flesh that wasn't her own. The comb slid gently; the silky hair brushed the white skin and caressed it, delicious and cruel. Élisabeth went through the inner door and began to climb the stairs. the staircase existed and the carpet, the banister touched by the fingers with the varnished nails. Françoise had ceased to exist."

12 "A supple body in a clingy silk robe was lying stretched out on the cushions of a sofa and the generous mouth was blowing out curls of blue smoke."

13 "She felt a burst of affection for Elizabeth. She had the same feeling of camaraderie and ease as when, in the past, they had come out of a difficult and interesting class and strolled arm in arm in the *lycée* yard. (SCS 39)

faltering sense of self leads her to depend on Françoise for a sense of who she is. Now it is Élisabeth who is driven to know Françoise absolutely. In a scene which is the mirror image of the scene in the omitted chapters where the adolescent Françoise waits for Élisabeth in her bedroom, Élisabeth goes alone to Françoise's hotel room to borrow some nail varnish remover. She closes her eyes and wills herself to be Françoise. She senses the absent Françoise in the objects around her:

> Ces objets abandonnés offraient de Françoise une image plus intolérable que sa présence réelle. Quand Françoise était auprès d'elle, Élisabeth éprouvait une espèce de paix: Françoise ne livrait pas son vrai visage, mais du moins pendant qu'elle souriait avec amabilité, ce vrai visage n'existait plus nulle part. Ici, c'était la vraie figure de Françoise qui avait laissé sa trace, et cette trace était indéchiffrable. (I 87)[14]

A telling detail is that, for Élisabeth, Françoise's actual writing, the ink on the page, asserts her indestructable existence ("existence indestructible") (I 87). The depth of Élisabeth's anger and frustration − frustration of her desire to become Françoise, for symbiosis with her − is palpable. It is reinforced by the jerky rhythm of the fragmented syntax: "Élisabeth repoussa les papiers avec violence; c'était idiot; elle ne pouvait ni devenir Françoise, ni la détruire" (I 87).[15] The unspoken levels of anger and hostility between the two women are striking. Élisabeth deliberately sets out to harm the Françoise-Xavière-Pierre trio.[16] Françoise is aware of her hatred (I 177). Somewhat disingenuously she appears to accept no responsibilty for the fact that Élisabeth no longer confides in her. That Élisabeth would not do so seems hardly surprising given the noticable lack of honesty and sincerity in almost all their exchanges. In summary, Françoise's relationship with Élisabeth is characterised by a threat to Françoise's sense of self, a powerful desire for symbiosis, an ambivalent sexual attraction and intense hostility. I will now turn to Françoise's relationship with Xavière where the parallels are unmistakable.

When Françoise befriends Xavière she anticipates that she will annexe her existence to her own and at first Xavière appears to be entirely submissive ("elle lui était tout entière livrée" [I 45]). This does not last. There is

---

[14] "These discarded objects gave a more unbearable picture of Françoise than would her real presence. When Françoise was near her, Elizabeth felt a kind of peace: Françoise never gave away her real, true face but at least, when her smile was friendly, her true face did not exist at all. Here, in this room, Françoise's true face had left its mark and this mark was inscrutable." (SCS 65)
[15] "Elizabeth pushed away the papers in sudden fury. This was ridiculous. She could neither become Françoise, nor could she destroy her." (SCS 65)
[16] See *L'Invitée* 104, 283.

a clear shift in the balance of power. Xavière's importance grows and Françoise is forced to admit there is no turning back: "Xavière existait" (I 83).[17] Once she has committed herself to the trio, Françoise becomes as dependent on Xavière as she has been on Pierre. This is epitomised by what happens early one morning after a night spent walking in Paris, when the trio are having breakfast at the café, *Le Pôle Nord.* Françoise has resigned herself to giving up on her own needs and ambitions (I 288). She is filled with a sense of well-being: "Elle regarda Xavière, puis Pierre; elle les aimait, ils s'aimaient, ils l'aimaient; depuis des semaines ils vivaient tous les trois dans un enchantement joyeux". (I 289).[18] The use of repetition and the rhythm of the text suggest Françoise's light-heartedness. However this is short-lived. Xavière gets angry and directs her anger at Françoise in particular. Françoise is defenceless against her poisonous thoughts: "elle aimait Xavière; elle ne pouvait plus supporter sa haine" (I 293).[19] Françoise is at the mercy of Xavière to the extent that "elle n'existait plus qu'à travers les sentiments capricieux que Xavière lui portait; cette sorcière s'était emparé de son image et lui faisait subir à son gré les pires envoûtements" (I 298).[20] Françoise's happiness and her very being depend on Xavière, an alien and rebellious consciousness (I 299). Françoise loaths her dependance but is powerless. Xavière's hatred is toxic: "Le brouillard maléfique restait suspendu à travers le monde, il empoisonnait les bruits et les lumières, il pénétrait Françoise jusqu'aux moelles. Il fallait attendre qu'il se dissipât de lui-même; attendre et guetter et souffrir, sordidement" (I 302).[21] The sense of inevitability is reinforced by the rhythm of the final clause.[22]

---

[17] This echos the language used about Élisabeth: "Élisabeth était réelle" (DCI 296). "Élisabeth was real."

[18] "She looked at Xavière, then at Pierre. She loved them; they loved each other; they loved her. For weeks all three of them had been living in happy enchantment." (SCS 229) This is reminiscent of the young Françoise's renunciation of self and feelings of well-being as she listened to Élisabeth telling stories by the fire. (DCI 305)

[19] "She loved Xavière. She could no longer stand her hatred." (SCS 233)

[20] "She now existed only through Xavière's capricious feelings for her. This sorceress had taken possession of her wax image and was sticking pins into it to her heart's content." (SCS 237)

[21] "The maleficent mist still remained suspended across the world, poisoning sounds and lights, and penetrating to the very marrow of her bones. She would have to wait until it dissipated of itself: wait and watch, and suffer, squalidly." (SCS 240)

[22] See also at the Spanish nightclub: "Ça reprenait; à nouveau corrosive comme un acide, la haine s'échappait de Xavière en lourdes volutes; c'était inutile de se défendre contre cette morsure déchirante, il n'y avait qu'à subir et attendre, mais Françoise se sentait à bout de forces." (I 361) "It was beginning over again. Dense vapours of hatred, as corrosive as an acid, were once more emanating from Xavière, and there was no defence against its excruciating bite. There was nothing to do but endure it and wait. But Françoise felt completely exhausted." (SCS 290)

Like the adolescent Élisabeth, Xavière threatens Françoise's sense of self. The threat that Xavière represents to Françoise culminates in an incident in the Spanish night-club when Xavière deliberately burns herself with a cigarette.[23] Françoise realises that she has not had the courage to be herself and as a result of her cowardice she has been reduced to nothing (I 359). Afterwards as they listen to a poem, Françoise is overwhelmed by fear:

> Cette présence ennemie qui s'était révélée tout à l'heure dans un sourire de folle devenait de plus en plus proche, il n'y avait plus moyen d'en éviter le dévoilement terrifiant; jour après jour, minute après minute, Françoise avait fui le danger, mais c'en était fait, elle l'avait enfin rencontré cet infranchissable obstacle qu'elle avait pressenti sous des formes incertaines depuis sa plus petite enfance; à travers la jouissance maniaque de Xavière, à travers sa haine et sa jalousie, le scandale éclatait, aussi monstrueux, aussi définitif que la mort; en face de Françoise, et cependant sans elle, quelque chose existait comme une condamnation sans recours: libre, absolu, irréductible, une conscience étrangère se dressait. C'était comme la mort, une totale négation, une éternelle absence, et cependant par une contradiction bouleversante, ce gouffre de néant pouvait se rendre présent à soi-même et se faire exister pour soi avec plénitude; l'univers tout entier s'engloutissait en lui, et Françoise, à jamais dépossédée du monde, se dissolvait elle-même dans ce vide dont aucun mot, aucune image ne pouvait cerner le contour infini. (I 363-64)[24]

Syntax in *L'Invitée* replicates Françoise's emotional and metaphysical crisis on a textual level. These two sentences are Gothic in their complexity, their convolutions. The accumulation here of clause upon clause, combined with enumeration and repetition, conveys a sense of relentlessness and inevitability as well as infinity. These long uncoordinated sentences that are characteristic of the text harmonize with and contribute to the sense of suffocation and enclosure evoked.[25] Moreover, such sentences

---

[23] It is worthy of note that Xavière is driven to self-harm by a combination of self-loathing and Pierre's unspoken jealousy and anger because she has spent an evening with Gerbert. This is made explicit. (I 357)
[24] "This hostile presence, which earlier had betrayed itself in a lunatic's smile, was approaching closer and closer: there was now no way of avoiding its terrifying disclosure. Day after day, minute after minute, Françoise had fled the danger; but the worst had happened, and she had at last come face to face with this insurmountable obstacle which she had sensed, behind a shadowy outline, since her earliest childhood. At the back of Xavière's maniacal pleasure, at the back of her hatred and jealousy, the abomination loomed, as monstrous and definite as death. Before Françoise's very eyes, and yet apart from her, something existed like a sentence without an appeal: detached, absolute, unalterable, an alien conscience was taking up its position." (SCS 292)
[25] Beauvoir's writing in *L'Invitée* is characterised by parataxis which is the placing of sentences, clauses, or propositions together without connectives. She tends to write simple sentences or sentences made up of series of clauses, sometimes including subordinate or coordinate clauses, separated or linked by semi-colons and colons and commas. There is a sense in which such sentences could go on and on, clauses

resist any imposition of closure or conclusiveness. This syntax is in keeping with Françoise's sense of being overwhelmed and the illimitable peril that Xavière personifies.

Françoise is incapable of choosing herself, of saying "me". She has become Xavière's prey. Xavière on the other hand is nothing more than a living affirmation of herself, "une vivante affirmation de soi" (I 364). Françoise has allowed herself to put Xavière before herself and has destroyed herself in the process; she has seen things through Xavière's eyes; she has come to know herself only through Xavière's feelings for her and now wants to merge with her and her vain attempts to do so have meant her destruction: "Déjà il lui était arrivé de sentir comme ce soir son être se dissoudre au profit d'êtres inaccessibles, mais jamais elle n'avait réalisé avec une lucidité si parfaite son propre anéantissement" (I 365).[26] In a repetition of the experience she had with Élisabeth, Françoise has been brought face to face with the fact that Xavière has a consciousness just like her own (I 369): "Voilà que maintenant le monde se dressait en face d'elle comme un immense interdit: c'était la faillite de son existence même qui venait de se consommer" (I 370).[27]

Françoise desires symbiosis with Xavière just as she had with Élisabeth and Pierre. Françoise recognises that confluence with Xavière is impossible. This is of crucial importance. She can no longer say "my future" because she cannot separate from Pierre and Xavière but nor can she now say "our future"; with Pierre it had made sense because they shared "une vie, une oeuvre, un amour" (one life, one life's work, one love); this is not the case with Xavière: "On ne pouvait pas vivre avec elle, mais seulement à côté d'elle" (I 291).[28] After an evening spent dancing together, Françoise

---

added to infinity. Such sentences follow the principles of attributive structure as it is presented by Liisa Dahl. This sentence structure is characteristic of interior monologue and conveys the flux of consciousness. Dahl argues that "different additions can be made, because there is no definite subordination to which a new word should conform. The connection between the parts is 'half open', for the starting point is the subject but it has no fixed termination". See Liisa Dahl, "The Attributive Sentence Structure in the Stream of Consciousness Technique with Special Reference to the Interior Monologue used by Virginia Woolf, Joyce and O'Neill", *Neuphilogische Mitteilungen*, 68 (1967) 443.

[26] "It had happened to her before, as now it was happening tonight, that she had felt her being dissolve to the advantage of inaccessible other beings; but never had she been aware of her own annihilation with such perfect lucidity." (SCS 293)

[27] "The world now stood before her like a gigantic interdict. The failure of her very existence was now brought to completion." (SCS 297) Although this is not clear from the published translation, there is a direct echo here of the language used to relate her earlier experience: "Comment avait-elle pu imaginer que le monde se confondait avec ce qu'elle en saisissait? Il était là devant elle comme un immense interdit." (DCI 296) "How could she have imagined that the world coincided with what she experienced of it? It was there in front of her like a vast forbidden place."

[28] "It was not possible to live with her, but only beside her." (SCS 231)

has the illusion of symbiosis. She imagines that she forms the very substance of Xavière's existence, that Xavière experiences everything through her and that even in spite of herself she belongs to Françoise. However, the illusion is short-lived; Xavière is out of reach, "hors d'atteinte" and Françoise is forced to acknowledge that the only ties for Xavière are the ties she chooses for herself (I 315). When Xavière is distraught after making love with Gerbert, Françoise shares her pain: "Françoise se sentit d'un coup arrachée à elle-même et dévorée par cette intolérable douleur" (I 395).[29] More than anything, Françoise wants Xavière to confide in her. This would be the symbiosis she so desires: "D'une seule phrase, Xavière allait créer ce que Françoise désirait depuis si longtemps; une union totale qui confondrait leurs joies, leurs inquiétudes, leurs tourments" (I 398-99).[30] But Xavière refuses to confide in Françoise and rejects her: "[Françoise] s'était sentie prête à se donner à Xavière sans réserve et si ce don avait été accepté, elle aurait été délivrée à la fois d'elle-même et de cette douloureuse présence étrangère qui sans cesse lui barrait la route; mais Xavière l'avait repoussée" (I 399).[31] In the month that follows, Françoise continues to try to get close to Xavière but Xavière remains separate from her, "une étrangère" (I 420). The only way of overcoming the terrifying duality Françoise experienced for the first time in the Spanish nightclub would be for Françoise to merge with Xavière in a unique friendship, but Xavière will never forget herself (I 420). Françoise is forced to admit defeat; the friendship which alone could have saved her is impossible (I 429).

With Xavière, Françoise experiences the same desire for absolute knowledge and has the same sense of being shut out of a secret as she had with Élisabeth. Xavière like the adolescent Élisabeth is endowed with mystery. Françoise stands outside Xavière's door in a scene reminiscent of the scene where she waits on the landing for Élisabeth to open the door in the unpublished chapter: "Derrière la porte, il y eut un vague bruissement; on aurait cru entendre palpiter les secrètes pensées que Xavière caressait dans sa solitude" (I 341).

In a direct echo of her adolescent relationship with Élisabeth, Françoise

---

[29] "Françoise suddenly felt torn asunder, and overcome herself by this unbearable pain." (SCS 319)
[30] "In one sentence, Xavière was on the verge of bringing about what Françoise had so long desired: the complete union, which would encompass their joys, their worries, and their torments." (SCS 321)
[31] "She had felt ready to give herself to Xavière unreservedly, and had this gift been accepted, she would have been freed both from herself and from this woeful alien presence which constantly barred her path. But Xavière had repelled her." (SCS 322)

is destabilised by a powerful sexual attraction for Xavière that she struggles to understand and is unable to act on.[32] Her maternal feelings are blended with unmistakable lesbian desire which comes to a head one evening as the couple are dancing together:

> Elle sentait contre sa poitrine les beaux seins tièdes de Xavière, elle respirait son haleine charmante; était-ce du désir? Mais que désirait-elle? Ses lèvres contre ses lèvres? Ce corps abandonné entre ses bras? Elle ne pouvait rien imaginer, ce n'était qu'un besoin confus de garder tourné vers elle à jamais ce visage d'amoureuse et de pouvoir dire passionnément: elle est à moi. (I 310)[33]

Later, back in Xavière's hotel room, Françoise is still unsettled by the physical closeness of Xavière and intimidated by the beautiful grace of Xavière's body "qu'elle ne savait pas desirer" (I 316). When, on impulse, she takes Xavière in her arms as she is leaving, Françoise's uncertainty about what Xavière wants from her is agonising. She leaves Xavière and goes back to her own room, ashamed of her feelings, her "tendresse inutile" (I 316). This is one of many allusions to Françoise's sexual response to Xavière, allusions which gather momentum in the text from Xavière's first appearance in Françoise life. The end of Chapter 2 (part I) is the first of a number of scenes suggestive of romantic, physical love:

> [Xavière] se laissa aller de tout son poids contre l'épaule de Françoise; un long moment elles demeurèrent immobiles, appuyées l'une contre l'autre; les cheveux de Xavière frôlaient la joue de Françoise; leurs doigts restaient emmêlés.
> "Je suis triste de vous quitter", dit Françoise.
> "Moi aussi", dit Xavière tout bas.
> "Ma petite Xavière", murmura Françoise; Xavière la regardait, les yeux brillants, les lèvres entrouvertes; fondante, abandonnée, elle lui était tout entière livrée. C'était Françoise désormais qui l'emporterait à travers la vie.
> "Je la rendrai heureuse", décida-t-elle avec conviction. (I 45)[34]

---

[32] This aspect of Françoise's relationship with Xavière has attracted more critical attention recently, notably in Sarah Fishwick's book, *The Body in the Work of Simone de Beauvoir* (Oxford: Peter Lang, 2002) 193-211. See also Alison Holland, "Identity in Crisis: The Gothic Textual Space in *L'Invitée*", *Modern Language Review* 98 (April 2003) 327-34.

[33] "She felt Xavière's beautiful warm breasts against her, she inhaled her sweet breath. Was this desire? But what did she desire? Her lips against hers? Her body surrendered in her arms? She could think of nothing. It was only a confused need to keep forever this lover's face turned towards hers, and to be able to say with passion: 'She is mine.'" (SCS 246)

[34] "She sank with all her weight against Françoise's shoulder; for some time they remained motionless, leaning against each other. Xavière's hair brushed against Françoise's cheek. Their fingers remained intertwined.
'It makes me sad to leave you,' said Françoise.
'So it does me,' said Xavière softly.

It is interesting to note that in a direct parallel to Françoise's response to the adolescent Élisabeth, her physical response to Xavière is condensed in her acute awareness of Xavière's hands, which are sometimes even described in the same terms, "a country woman's hands".[35]

Hatred is a key motif in the relationship between Françoise and Xavière, as it is in Françoise's relationship with Élisabeth. Françoise's feelings for Xavière transmute into hatred when, reunited with Pierre, she is disloyal to Françoise and half succeeds in getting Pierre to be disloyal to her too. Françoise welcomes the wave of hate she feels: "En face de Xavière, elle sentait avec une espèce de joie se lever en elle quelque chose de noir et d'amer qu'elle ne connaissait pas encore et qui était presque une délivrance: puissante, libre, s'épanouissant enfin sans contrainte, c'était la haine" (I 445).[36] The women's hatred is mutual. By the time they are sharing a flat after the outbreak of the Second World War, Xavière's childish hostility has become a "une vraie haine de femme", the real hatred of a woman (I 483). In the meantime, Françoise's behaviour towards Xavière has been, to use the diction of the novel, extremely treacherous. Not only has she begun a secret love affair with Gerbert, but she has exacerbated his disloyalty to Xavière by encouraging him to love her, Françoise, exclusively (I 463). This is not all. She also colludes with Pierre in deceiving Xavière about his true feelings for her, providing her with a daily ration of reassuring lies. Françoise is triumphant: "Méprisée, dupée, ce n'était plus [Xavière] qui disputerait à Françoise sa place dans le monde. [...] De nouveau, elle existait seule, sans obstacle au coeur de sa propre destinée" (I 467).[37]

Before addressing the issue of power, I want briefly to draw attention to the formal pattern of triangles in *L'Invitée*. The two intense relationships on which this chapter focuses each forms part of a triangular relationship. Indeed, there are a conspicuous number of triangular relationships in *L'Invitée*. The Françoise-Élisabeth-Pierre triangle is one. The most complex

---

'My dear little Xavière, murmured Françoise. Xavière looked at her, with eyes shining, parted lips; mollified, yielding, she had abandoned herself completely. Henceforth Françoise would lead her through life. 'I shall make her happy,' she decided with conviction." (SCS 30) See also SCS 219, 263, 398.

[35] See, for example, "ses douces mains de femme, rouges comme des mains de paysanne" (I 265); "'with gentle feminine hands, as red as those of a peasant woman" (SCS 212); "ses mains caressantes d'homme" (I 260); "caressing masculine hands." (SCS 208) The published translation mistakenly attributes this description to Pierre.

[36] "With respect to Xavière, she felt rising within her, with a kind of joy, something black and bitter that she did not yet know and which was almost deliverance: powerful, free, finally bursting unhindered into bloom. It was hate." (SCS 360)

[37] "Scorned, duped, she would no longer dispute Françoise's place in the world. [...] Once again she existed alone, with no obstacle at the heart of her own destiny." (SCS 378-79)

is the Françoise-Xavière-Pierre triangle, based on the real life trio Beauvoir-Sartre-Olga Kosakievicz. This triangle overlaps with both the Françoise-Xavière-Gerbert triangle and the Xavière-Pierre-Gerbert triangle. The minor Françoise-Pierre-Gerbert triangle is portrayed as unproblematical, causing neither conflict or jealousy unlike the Élisabeth-Claude-Suzanne triangle which is, however, given little space.[38]

Considerable critical attention has been given to the Françoise-Xavière-Pierre triangle which has been read as a mother-daughter-father triangle with Françoise and Pierre as parent figures and Xavière as their recalcitrant adolescent daughter.[39] Toril Moi has offered a fascinating psychoanalytical reading of this triangle with Xavière as the mother-monster figure.[40] It is beyond the scope of this chapter to analyse these triangular relationships in any detail, but it is interesting to pause and consider what mechanism might be at work. One possible explanation is that Françoise triangulates her intense, threatening relationships with Élisabeth and Xavière in order to disarm the threat and negate the danger they represent. This is not to suggest that she does so in awareness but it seems clear that there is a shift in the balance of power in each case. Compensation may also play a part; if Françoise cannot have exactly what she desires from Élisabeth and Xavière, she can have something from someone close to them, someone important to them.[41] Françoise triangulates her intense relationship with Élisabeth by coming between Élisabeth and her brother, Pierre, and beginning an intense (initially sexual) relationship with him. Close reading of the text suggests that Élisabeth's relationship with Pierre is her primary relationship in the sense that it is his love and approval she craves both in the omitted chapters and throughout the novel.[42]

---

[38] Elizabeth Fallaize points out that there is also a narrative trio, Françoise-Élisabeth-Gerbert in *The Novels of Simone de Beauvoir* (London: Routledge, 1988) 27.

[39] See for instance, Fallaize, *Novels* 29-30; Jane Heath, *Simone de Beauvoir* (London: Harvester Wheatsheaf, 1989) 27; and most recently, Genevieve Shepherd, *Simone de Beauvoir's Fiction: A Psychoanalytic Rereading* (Bern: Peter Lang, 2003) 77-99 where she offers a number of different interesting psychoanalytic readings of this triangle.

[40] Toril Moi, "*L'Invitée*: An Existentialist Melodrama" in *Simone de Beauvoir. The Making of an Intellectual Woman* (Oxford: Blackwell, 1994) 110-24.

[41] In her discussion of Françoise's inability to actualise her desire for Xavière, Sarah Fishwick argues convincingly that Françoise's relationship with Gerbert should be read in many respects as a compromise. See Sarah Fishwick, *The Body in the Work of Simone de Beauvoir* (Oxford: Peter Lang, 2002) 209.

[42] See *L'Invitée*, p. 271: "Etait-elle capable d'aimer? [...] Il y avait eu Pierre. S'il lui avait donné sa vie, peut-être n'y aurait-elle jamais eu en elle ces divisions ni ces mensonges. Peut-être pour elle aussi le monde aurait été plein et elle aurait connu la paix du coeur." "Was she capable of loving? [...] There had been Pierre. If he had devoted his life to her, perhaps she would never have have grown up with these discords or these lies within her. Perhaps for her, too, the world would have been complete and she would have known peace in her heart." (SCS 214)

Interestingly, in the published novel, Élisabeth even thinks of Françoise as the woman Pierre loves, defining Françoise in relation to him (I 87). There is no doubt that initially at least, Pierre is in some way instrumental in Françoise's relationship with Élisabeth. At the first dress-rehearsal she attends, where she is to meet Pierre for the first time, Françoise sees him as the key to knowing and understanding Élisabeth.

Similarly, Françoise triangulates her intense relationship with Xavière by coming between Xavière and her lover Gerbert and becoming his lover too. In both cases Françoise allies herself with the newest member of the triangle to persecute the first. In both cases Françoise sublimates an intense relationship with a woman, turning to a man with whom they are close. In both cases splitting occurs; one element is designated all good, the other all bad.[43]

It has clearly emerged that in the story told in *L'Invitée,* Françoise's relationships with Élisabeth and Xavière are sites of power struggles. To sum up, in her relationship with Élisabeth there is a clear power reversal between the discarded chapters and the published novel; Élisabeth no longer exercises power over Françoise. Françoise has "won"; it never was a question of friendship for her. There is a series of power reversals in Françoise's relationship with Xavière too. Françoise's initial assumption of supremacy is forced to give way in the face of Xavière's refusal to be annexed.[44] This reversal of power is epitomised by the two afternoons less than one year apart that Françoise and Xavière spend at the Moorish café. During the first, Françoise is in control. She is delighted that Xavière belongs to her and, from her point of view, only exists thanks to her (I 23). During the second afternoon, Xavière unmistakably takes control and manipulates Françoise into agreeing to bring about her reconciliation with Pierre (I 426-28). Françoise is aware of what Xavière is doing and allows her self to be manipulated, "docile au désir de Xavière" (I 429). Subsequently, for Françoise, her secret affair with Gerbert and her collusion with Pierre to dupe Xavière as to his true feelings for her, are proof of her victory: "J'ai gagné, pensa Françoise avec triomphe" (I 467).[45] At this

---

[43] Although the Françoise-Xavière-Pierre trio is intended to be based on reciprocity and equality, Françoise finds herself excluded/persecuted. Xavière has no voice but her behaviour suggests that her experience of the trio was not dissimilar. In the final chapters of the novel, Françoise clearly sides with Pierre to persecute Xavière.

[44] This military diction is used in the free indirect discourse relating Françoise's thoughts in the Moorish café: "Ce qui l'enchantait surtout c'était d'avoir annexé à sa vie cette petite existence triste." (I 23) "What especially delighted her was to have annexed this insignificant, pathetic little being into her own life." (SCS 11)

[45] "'I've won', thought Françoise triumphantly." (SCS 379)

point, it does not matter to Françoise that Xavière is unaware that she has been defeated. Only later, when faced with Xavière's version of events, does she understand that for her to win, Xavière must admit defeat, that "il n'y avait pas de victoire possible sans son aveu" (I 495).[46] The murder is Françoise's final bid to grasp back power.

These power struggles are played out on the level of narration too.[47] *L'Invitée* can be read as a battle for narrative authority. In his discussion of the ending of *L'Invitée,* Maurice Merleau-Ponty points out that "once we are aware of the existence of others, we commit ourselves to being, among other things, what they think of us, since we recognize in them the exorbitant power to *see us*".[48] Françoise's sense of identity is intimately threatened by others' views of her. Her extreme fear of the power of representation is a constant in the text. There is a vivid example in the unpublished chapters. The adolescent Françoise who prides herself on her prowess at school is caught cheating. Her version of events – that she has only tried to save time – is superseded by Mlle Vaisson's account that she has copied her translation; the verdict, accentuated because it appears between speech marks, seems to resonate in the text: "Françoise Miquel a copié sa version". Françoise is appalled: "Et soudain c'était devenu une faute hideuse qui resterait marquée sur sa figure pendant des années; ça existait à jamais [...]" (DCI 288).[49] Françoise swears she did the translation herself and begs her teacher to believe her. She cannot bear the idea that Mlle Vaisson believes she is capable of lying. When she tells Françoise that it is a matter for her conscience: "Françoise la suivit des yeux avec une haine étonnée; elle allait à travers les couloirs du lycée, elle continuait tranquillement à vivre, avec au coeur, cette pensée hostile et obstinée sur laquelle on n'avait du dehors aucune prise; c'était effrayant et presque monstrueux" (DCI 290).[50]

Early in the published novel, Françoise tells Gerbert that she is terrified at the idea that she can be reduced to nothing more than an image in

---

[46] "There could be no possible victory without her confession." (SCS 402)

[47] This point is also addressed by Fallaize in *Novels,* 35.

[48] "Metaphysics and the Novel", in *Critical Essays on Simone de Beauvoir,* ed. Elaine Marks (Boston: Hall, 1987) 41.

[49] "And suddenly it had become a hideous fault that would stay branded on her face for years; it existed forever [...]."

[50] "Françoise watched her leave, astonished at the hatred she felt. She would walk down the school corridors, she would go on living happily, with that hostile and stubborn thought in her heart, which no one from outside could do anything about; it was frightening and almost monstrous."

someone else's head (I 18).[51] As the novel reaches its climax, Françoise is horrified when Gerbert tells her Xavière's version of her break-up with Pierre, namely that Pierre still loves her passionately and that she has rejected his love for Françoise's sake because she is fiercely jealous. In a striking echo of the unpublished text, we read: "Françoise aurait voulu cacher sa figure" (I 490), she wanted to hide her face. As she goes upstairs to their flat, she imagines Xavière crouching behind the door in her nest of lies, waiting to grab hold of Françoise and force her into her story, "se saisir de Françoise et la faire entrer de force dans son histoire" (I 491). Françoise holds back from confronting Xavière with the truth (her truth) but Xavière steals the key to Françoise's desk and reads her letters from Pierre and Gerbert. Françoise finds the letters scattered on the carpet: "Son amour pour Gerbert était là devant elle, noir comme la trahison. [...] Xavière vivait. La trahison de Françoise vivait" (I 497).[52] Françoise's earlier triumph is reversed as Xavière turns her innocent love for Gerbert into a sordid betrayal; Xavière's interpretation of events is very different from Françoise's: "Vous étiez jalouse de moi parce que Labrousse m'aimait. Vous l'avez dégoûté de moi et pour mieux vous venger, vous m'avez pris Gerbert" (I 498-99).[53]

Françoise is horrified to see the woman she is in Xavière's eyes. It is as if she is nothing more than a character in Xavière's fiction. Her distress and disbelief are underlined as she repeats Xavière's words: "'J'ai été jalouse d'elle. Je lui ai pris Gerbert.' [...] 'J'ai fait cela. C'est moi'" (I 499).[54] She cannot bear the idea that Xavière will define her as culpable: "Chaque matin renaîtrait cette femme détestée qui était désormais Françoise. Elle revit le visage de Xavière décomposé par la souffrance. Mon crime. Il existait pour toujours" (I 500).[55] The tortured, fragmented syntax and the sudden shift from the first person to external narration replicate Françoise's distress. She understands that her identity depends on her grasping narrative supremacy and eliminating Xavière and with her the hated woman that Françoise now

---

[51] She also maintains that she does not care what others think of her; this is not borne out by the text. For example, on the previous page, she is clearly concerned about what Gerbert thinks of her (I 17).

[52] "Her love for Gerbert was there before her, black as treason. [...] Xavière was alive. Françoise's treason lived." (SCS 403-4)

[53] "You were jealous of me because Labrousse was in love with me. You made him loathe me and to get better revenge, you took Gerbert from me." (SCS 405)

[54] "'I was jealous of her. I took Gerbert.' [...] 'I did that. It was I.'" (SCS 406)

[55] "Each morning this abhorred woman, who was henceforth Françoise, would be reborn. She recalled Xavière's face contorted with pain. 'My crime.' It was going to exist forever." (SCS 406)

was (I 500). Equally contorted and disrupted syntax marks her defiance and resolve to wipe out Xavière and, with her, Françoise's own guilt:

> C'était une longue histoire. Elle fixa l'image. Il y avait longtemps on essayait de la lui ravir. Rigide comme une consigne. Austère et pure comme un glaçon. Dévouée, dédaignée, butée dans les morales creuses. Et elle avait dit: 'Non.' Mais elle l'avait dit tout bas; c'est en cachette qu'elle avait embrassé Gerbert. 'N'est-ce pas moi?' Souvent elle hésitait, fascinée. Et maintenant, elle était tombée dans le piège, elle était à la merci de cette conscience vorace qui avait attendu dans l'ombre le moment de l'engloutir. Jalouse, traîtresse, criminelle. On ne pouvait pas se défendre avec des mots timides et des actes furtifs. Xavière existait, la trahison existait. Elle existe en chair et en os, ma criminelle figure. Elle n'existera plus. (I 500-501)[56]

As Françoise looks at her reflection in the mirror, others' definitions of her are told in a series of asyntactic sentences. A question in the first person breaks into the text. The delayed past participle, "fascinée" reproduces Françoise's hesitation as the text seems to falter. Xavière's definition of Françoise, a stark enumeration, erupts into the text. Syntax poses the existence of Xavière and the existence of Françoise's betrayal as equivalent since two clauses are simply placed in the same sentence with no conjunction ("Xavière existait, la trahison existait"). The displacement of the subject to the end of the final sentence of the paragraph heightens ambiguity and strengthens the identification Xavière, betrayal, guilt. The following one-sentence paragraph is decisive. Xavière, the betrayal and Françoise's guilt ("elle") will be extirpated in one move, just as their fate is decided in one short sentence: "Elle n'existera plus" (I 500-501). By killing Xavière, Françoise claims the right to determine who she is, to impose her narrative, her version of the truth.[57] To quote Elizabeth Fallaize, "she crushes the claim of another to narrate her story".[58]

Before addressing the question of narrative power, it is useful to clarify

---

[56] "It was a long story. She stared at her reflection. There had been a long enduring attempt to rob her of it. Inexorable as a duty. Austere and pure as a block of ice. Self-sacrificing, scorned, clinging obstinately to hollow morality. She had said, 'No.' But she had whispered it, she had secretly embraced Gerbert. 'Isn't that I?' She had often hesitated, spellbound. And now, she had fallen into the trap, she was at the mercy of this voracious conscience that had been waiting in the shadow for the moment to swallow her up. Jealous, traitorous, guilty. She could not defend herself with timid words and furtive deeds. Xavière existed; the betrayal existed. 'My guilty face exists in flesh and bone.' It would exist no more." (SCS 406-7)

[57] Harold Wardman discusses Françoise's desire "to be the omniscient narrator of her own life and of the lives of others" in "Self-Coincidence and Narrative in *L'Invitée*", *Essays in French Literature* 19 (1982) 87-103.

[58] Fallaize, *Novels* 36.

the narrative situation in *L'Invitée*. The story is told by a relatively covert external narrator in the third person, however Françoise's point of view is adopted throughout most of the novel; she is the focalizer in all but three and a half chapters.[59] The external narrator corroborates her vision and she is the source of the values and norms of the text. Élisabeth is focalizer in two and a half chapters but whilst her outsider's view of the trio necessarily differs from Françoise's, these chapters never fundamentally challenge or offer an alternative to the vision that dominates in the rest of the book. The same can be said of the single, short chapter focalised through Gerbert. As for Xavière, her perceptions do not directly shape the novel at all. Each chapter or part of a chapter recounts a certain stretch of time. Events and conversations are never summarised but related fully, as if in real time. The long dialogues which characterise the narrative allow readers to hear characters' voices directly. The use of free indirect discourse (to relate speech and thought) as well as distancing readers from the characters' voices, also introduces ambiguity into the narrative situation as the source of certain comments cannot be determined with any certainty.[60]

There is no doubt of the power attributed to narrative in *L'Invitée*. As an adolescent, Françoise discovers that writing is a defence. The first entry in her diary makes clear what is at stake:

> Pendant que je marchais dans ces rues, il m'a semblé que je me retrouvais moi-même, moi qui m'étais depuis longtemps délaissée. Élisabeth s'aime plus que tout et moi, si je ne me préfère pas à tous les autres, il n'y aura personne pour me préférer. (DCI 309)[61]

Through writing her narrative she constructs herself: "C'était plaisant; au fur et à mesure que les lettres bleues apparaissaient sur le papier, il naissait une histoire qui était son histoire" (DCI 309).[62] She is enchanted to find that in her diary she is someone with a strong and coherent personality ("une personnalité forte et cohérente" [DCI 310]). This is not Françoise's actual experience of herself:

> Rien de ce qui arrivait à Françoise n'était tout à fait vrai; quelquefois, quand

---

[59] The narrative strategies in *L'Invitée* are analysed in detail by Elizabeth Fallaize in *Novels* 25-43.

[60] Beauvoir discusses the narrative techniques she uses in *L'Invitée* in *La Force de l'âge* 385, 391-93.

[61] "As I walked through the streets, I felt as though I found myself again, myself that I had neglected for so long. Élisabeth loves herself above everything and if I don't put myself first before everybody else, no one else will put me first."

[62] "It was pleasing; gradually, as the blue letters appeared on the page, a story was born which was her story."

elle regardait en arrière, elle apercevait quelque chose qui ressemblait à un acte, à une idée et les autres gens pouvaient s'y tromper; mais jamais elle ne se surprenait en train d'agir ou de penser. (DCI 311)[63]

The language used to describe the sense of alienation attributed to Françoise in the discarded chapters of *L'Invitée*, is strikingly similar to that used to describe Élisabeth both in Beauvoir's memoirs and in the published novel:

Rien de ce qui lui arrivait n'était jamais vrai. Parfois, en regardant au loin dans le brouillard, on apercevait quelque chose qui ressemblait à un événement ou à un acte; les gens pouvaient s'y laisser prendre: mais ce n'étaient que des trompe-l'oeil grossiers. (I 269)[64]

Narrative has the power to make real. The first dress-rehearsal she attends does not seem real to the adolescent Françoise and she leaves early, feeling shut out of a secret she can never know. It will be Élisabeth's narrative that transforms it into a wonderful evening, "un beau soir de générale" (DCI 316). Later, Pierre plays a crucial role in constructing Françoise's narrative: "Tant qu'elle ne l'avait pas raconté à Pierre, aucun événement n'était tout à fait vrai" (I 30); "Tous les moments de sa vie qu'elle lui confiait, Pierre les lui rendait clairs, polis, achevés, et ils devenaient des moments de leur vie" (I 30).[65] As Elizabeth Fallaise argues, Françoise effaces herself in favour of the verbalised "Françoise" she and Pierre create.[66]

Narrative that at first is explicitly used by Françoise as a defence then becomes a weapon. I am suggesting that in *L'Invitée,* narrative power is (ab)used to demonise and "destroy" both Élisabeth and Xavière. The portrait of Élisabeth is extremely negative. She is depicted as narcissistic, affected, weak and above all false. Françoise describes her feelings as false, her vocation as false and the whole of her life as false (I 36). She is clearly portrayed as demoniacal in her delirium as she fantasises about harming the Françoise-Pierre-Xavière trio. Her jealousy sustains her desire to make

---

63 "Nothing that happened to Françoise was ever quite real; sometimes, when she looked back, she would see something that looked like an action, an idea and others might be mistaken; but she never caught herself acting or thinking."

64 "Nothing that happened to her was ever real. Sometimes, far into the fog, it was possible to catch a glimpse of something that faintly resembled an event or an act; some people could let themselves be taken in by it, yet it was nothing but blatant deception." (SCS 213)

65 "Nothing that happened was completely real until she had told Pierre about it;" "Every moment of her life that she entrusted to him, Pierre gave back to her clear, polished, completed and they became moments of their shared life." (SCS 17)

66 Fallaize, *Novels* 37.

them suffer (I 104, 283). She sees this as a way of feeling truly alive. Her mental and emotional stability is repeatedly questioned. Her *mauvaise foi* is a given in the text. Remarkably, the portrayal in the chapters focalised through Élisabeth is equally negative. Even here, she is depicted as "une vivante parodie de la femme qu'elle prétendait être" (I 271).[67] Moreover, it is not only that Élisabeth's self image is negative and remains unquestioned. When focalization shifts to the external narrator the tone remains extremely critical. One such shift possibly occurs as Élisabeth greets the trio as they come to spend the evening with her; as she opens the door Élisabeth echoes Françoise's judgment of her as false – "Est-ce qu'ils savaient que tout était faux?" – and sees that Françoise is holding a bunch of anenomes, her favourite flower. The source of the malicious comment that at least Élisabeth had decided they were her favourite flower ten years earlier, is not absolutely clear but the use of Élisabeth's name suggests it is not her. It is most likely the narrator, as if any opportunity to have a dig at Élisabeth were too good to miss (I 272). This strongly supports the argument made by Elizabeth Fallaize that the values of the narrator and Françoise coincide to a great extent.[68]

The overwhelming weight of narrative disapprobation directed at Élisabeth might well prompt a sense of injustice. It is, however, possible to read against the overt, critical narrative stance of the text and discern a different Élisabeth, not one who is wholly good by any means but one who is not wholly bad either. For example, her *mauviase foi* is generally taken for granted yet there is textual evidence that she is perfectly lucid and honest with herself. Indeed, this makes her suffering more acute. Contrary to the strong impression that Élisabeth is fooling herself over her relationship with Claude, she is in fact aware that he will never leave his wife and that she has clung on to vain hopes through cowardice; she knows she would do anything to keep him because she feels she cannot live without him although pain and bitterness have killed her love for him (I 271). A second example concerns Élisabeth's professional life. A number of critics agree that Élisabeth is the portrait of a failed artist.[69] However, a close reading of the text reveals that Élisabeth is in fact a successful artist. Even with her low

---

[67] "[…] a living caricature of the woman she pretended to be." (SCS 215) This point is also made by Fallaize, *Novels* 39.

[68] Fallaize, *Novels* 39.

[69] See for instance Catherine Savage Brosman, *Simone de Beauvoir Revisited* (Twayne's World Authors Series 820, Boston: Twayne, 1991) 53 and Fallaize, *Novels* 38.

self-esteem, she describes herself as "une jeune artiste au bord de la réussite" (I 88). Her work is being talked about (I 237), her reputation is growing (I 271). Whereas Françoise has yet to complete the writing of her first book, Élisabeth has already exhibited her work and has played a major role in designing a theatre (I 269). The fact that she cannot enjoy her success is part of her tragedy. This is clear in the discussion she has about her work during the evening she spends at her flat with Pierre, Françoise and Xavière (I 274-75). Even then, although she calls her paintings imitations or false her confidence begins to grow as she shows the trio her work and she has an inkling that perhaps all artists feel they are nothing but daubers until their work becomes real because it is known. One of the most positive comments, if not the most positive comment, about Élisabeth's work occurs towards the end of this scene. Xavière is clearly bored with looking at paintings she does not understand and distracted by her, Pierre also loses interest and does no more than glance at Élisabeth's most recent canvas. The source of the positive appraisal – "C'était un tableau hardi et complexe qui méritait d'amples commentaires" – is not certain (Élisabeth or the external narrator) but it is unequivocal and quite exceptional (I 276).[70] What is interesting is that this more generous reading of Élisabeth is always latent in the text but is consistently outweighed by the dominant negative reading fostered by the narrative focalised through Françoise.

In fact the threat represented by Élisabeth is contained but not eliminated by this narrative. I have argued elsewhere that, although Simone de Beauvoir intended the narrative to foreground what separates Françoise and Élisabeth, shared lexis and imagery actually construct these characters as doubles.[71] Élisabeth is the mirror that reflects Françoise's darker self, revealing not what she might become but what she already is, those aspects of herself which she finds unacceptable: her murderous hate and jealousy; her mental and emotional instability; her *mauvaise foi*. Beauvoir's text exposes the essential affinity between Élisabeth and Françoise.

Narrative power is also (ab)used to demonise and destroy Xavière. There is no question that Xavière is constructed in the text as a hostile consciousness, a demoniacal, non-human figure whose very existence is a threat to Françoise's sense of self. As we have seen, Françoise first realises

---

70 "It was a daring and complex painting which called for considerable comment." (SCS 218)
71 Alison Holland, "Mirrored Characters in Simone de Beauvoir's *L'Invitée*: Françoise and Élisabeth," *Simone de Beauvoir Studies* 17 (2000 – 2001) 89-97.

the nature of the threat that Xavière represents after the incident in the
night-club. Throughout the text, a number of details contribute to the construction of Xavière as a menacing figure. In particular, repeated references
to her smile, which is not a smile but a maniacal rictus or grin ("rictus
maniaque"), accumulate in the text and contribute to the creation of a
threatening, demoniacal persona.[72] At one point, her smile is clearly
described in terms of vaginal imagery. It is depicted as dangerous, a wound
infected by jealousy: "Une passion de haine et de souffrance gonflait sa
face, où la bouche s'entrouvrait dans un rictus semblable à la blessure d'un
fruit trop mûr; par cette plaie béante, éclatait au soleil une pulpe secrète et
vénéneuse" (I 407).[73] Animal imagery associated with Xavière reinforces
the impression that she is demoniacal. Powerful images suggest slaughter
and cannibalism. The word "prey" reappears over and over in the text.
Shortly after the episode in the night-club, Françoise realises she has been
powerless against Xavière's hatred, her affection, her thoughts: "Elle les
avait laissées mordre sur elle, elle avait fait d'elle-même une proie" (I
364).[74] She feels impelled to run away from Xavière and her avid tentacles
that wanted to devour her alive (I 367).[75]

Xavière herself has no voice in the text or, to be more precise, no
access to narrative power.[76] Her voice is actually heard in dialogues,
through the filter provided by Françoise. Xavière is explicitly portrayed as
a spineless, jealous tyrant. With just a slight shift in persepective, readers
glimpse a young woman out of her depth, talked at more than talking,
sometimes even bullied by the older couple. Françoise herself cannot
simply reject Xavière's version of the end of her affair with Pierre, which
she hears first from Gerbert (I 489-90). In this story, Pierre still loves
Xavière but she has been forced to give him up because of Françoise's jealousy. Pierre is not there to reassure Françoise and doubts creep in; while
she discusses Pierre with Xavière "une voix chuchotait: il ne l'aime plus, il
ne peut plus l'aimer" (I 494).[77] Xavière's parallel narrative of Françoise's

---

[72] Toril Moi notes how Xavière's mouth is repeatedly emphasised and discusses references to her smile in *Beauvoir* 116.

[73] "A wave of violent hatred and suffering swelled her face. Her mouth was partly open in a smile, like a cut on an over-ripe fruit; and this open wound exposed to the sun a secret, venomous pulp." (SCS 328-29)

[74] "She had let them bite into her, she had turned herself into a prey."(SCS 293)

[75] For a more detailed discussion of these and other aspects of the portrayal of Xavière, see my "Identity in Crisis."

[76] Fallaize observes the absence of Xavière's point of view from *L'Invitée* in *Novels* 32.

[77] "A voice whispered, 'He doesn't love her anymore, he cannot love her anymore.'" (SCS 401) Françoise's doubts are understandable in view of Pierre's earlier betrayal. See p. 444. The point is not

betrayal which errupts in the final pages of the novel is startling (I 498-99). It was there all the time but camouflaged.

Critics have highlighted the way in which Beauvoir's later fiction focuses on the problematic nature of language.[78] I find a similar metacommentary on language running through *L'Invitée*. Toril Moi makes the point that Françoise never comments on the problematic nature of language.[79] However, this is not borne out by a close reading of the text. The relationship between truth, knowledge and language preoccupies Françoise. Whereas Elizabeth Fallaize argues that Françoise "has an unshakable belief in the power of words,"[80] I want to modulate her argument slightly and suggest that in fact, although Françoise's belief in and fear of the power of representation is constant, she progressively loses confidence in words and language.

Much of the writing in *L'Invitée* is hyperbolic and extravagant; I have referred to it elsewhere as a Gothic writing of excess.[81] For instance, Françoise's metaphysical crisis which is prompted by seeing Xavière burning herself in the night-club, is related not in philosophical language but in hyperbolic terms: "Françoise eut un haut-le-corps; ce n'était pas seulement sa chair qui se révoltait; elle se sentait atteinte d'une façon plus profonde et plus irrémédiable, jusqu'au coeur de son être. Derrière ce rictus maniaque, un danger menaçait, plus définitif que tous ceux qu'elle avait jamais imaginés" (I 354).[82] The threat to Françoise is beyond language, beyond thought even: "On ne pouvait pas s'en approcher même en pensée, au moment où elle touchait au but, la pensée se dissolvait; ce n'était aucun objet saisissable, c'était un incessant jaillissement et une fuite incessante, transparente pour soi seule et à jamais impénétrable" (I 354-55).[83] Beauvoir's writing is characterised by excess because only contradiction,

---

made explicit but Pierre is necessarily implicated in Xavière's story as he has not been frank about his feelings in his letters to her.

[78] For example, Toril Moi, "Intentions and Effects: Rhetoric and Identification in Simone de Beauvoir's 'The Woman Destroyed,'" in Toril Moi, *Feminist Theory and Simone de Beauvoir* (Oxford: Blackwell, 1990) 61-93; Fallaize, *Novels*.

[79] Moi, "Intentions" 77.

[80] Fallaize, *Novels* 37.

[81] Holland, "Identity in Crisis."

[82] "Françoise flinched. Not only did her flesh rise up in revolt, but the wound had injured her more deeply and irrevocably to the very depths of her being. Behind that maniacal grin, was the threat of a danger more positive than any she had ever imagined." (SCS 284-85)

[83] "Approach to it was impossible even in thought. Just as she seemed to be getting near it, the thought dissolved. This was no tangible object, but an incessant flux, a never ending escape, only comprehensible to itself, and forever occult." (SCS 285)

language pushed to the limit of meaningfulness, can begin to express the nature of the threat:

> C'était comme la mort, une totale négation, une éternelle absence, et cependant par une contradiction bouleversante, ce gouffre de néant pouvait se rendre présent à soi-même et se faire exister pour soi avec plénitude; l'univers tout entier s'engloutissait en lui, et Françoise, à jamais dépossédée du monde, se dissolvait elle-même dans ce vide dont aucun mot, aucune image ne pouvait cerner le contour infini. (I 364)[84]

The threat is like death and not like it, excessive and immeasurable.

As the novel reaches its climax, Françoise realises that language cannot remove the threat to her existence, "on ne pouvait pas se défendre avec des mots timides" (I 500-501). In the past she has used language to ward off the unthinkable, confident that language guarantees our existence and identity (I 146). As we have seen, at first, Françoise believes that language confers reality; as long as she has not told Pierre about something it is not quite real, "il flottait, immobile, incertain, dans des espèces de limbes" (I 30).[85] As Françoise's crisis deepens, language lets her down. Her belief that "dès qu'elle aurait expliqué les choses à Pierre, tout serait effacé" (I 195) is disappointed.[86] Likewise her hope that "si elle arrivait à enfermer dans des phrases son angoisse, elle pourrait s'en arracher"; "les mots ne la délivraient pas" (I 369).[87] As language becomes problematical, Françoise comes to see it as part of her predicament rather than as a solution. Françoise loses her trust in words (I 145). She wonders: "On se sert tant de mots; mais qu'y a-t-il au juste dessous?" (I 159).[88] Language itself – "des signes ambigus" – comes to be seen as inherently mysterious, ambiguous and duplicitous (I 160). "Derrière les mots et les gestes, qu'y avait-il?" wonders Françoise

---

[84] "It was like death, a total negation, an eternal absence, and yet, by a staggering contradiction, this abyss of nothingness could make itself present to itself and make itself fully exist for itself. The entire universe was engulfed in it, and Françoise, for ever excluded from the world, was herself dissolved in this void, of which the infinite contour no word, no image could encompass." (SCS 292) See earlier too: "Les mots ne pouvaient que vous rapprocher du mystère mais sans le rendre moins impénétrable." (I 162) "Words could bring you nearer the mystery, but without making it any less impenetrable." (SCS 128)

[85] "[…] it remained poised, motionless and uncertain in a kind of limbo." (SCS 17) Xavière accuses Françoise and Pierre of substituting language for life. She tells Pierre, "Vous aviez l'air de vivre les choses pour une fois, et pas seulement de les parler." (I 253) "You seemed to live things, for once, and not just to talk about them." (SCS 203) This aspect of Françoise's attitude to language is discussed by Elizabeth Fallaize in relation to the concept of Françoise and Pierre's indivisibility in *Novels* 37.

[86] "[…] as soon as she had explained things to Pierre, it would all be forgotten." (SCS 155)

[87] "[…] perhaps if she managed to encompass her anguish in words she might be rid of it." (SCS 296)

[88] "One uses so many words, and what exactly lies behind them?" (SCS 126)

(I 166).[89] And Françoise is forced into a position where she never knows what anything means: "Les phrases de Xavière étaient toujours à double sens" (I 294).[90] She is reduced to guessing (I 314).

Françoise murders Xavière in the final pages of the novel and although questions have been raised about this ending in terms of aesthetics, Françoise's guilt, the moral dimension of the story, is by and large not addressed.[91] I would like to suggest that this is because Beauvoir's text, her writing practice, exonerates Françoise. Or rather, no justification of the murder is necessary, the need to kill Xavière is self-evident. Interestingly, the working title of *L'Invitée* was *Légitime Défense,* self-defence. In terms of the Gothic economy of the text, the nature and scale of the threat Xavière represents make the murder inevitable.[92] The excess in the text makes it legitimate. As the culmination of the novel is reached, Beauvoir's command of the craft of writing is dazzling. The text reaches a crescendo with Françoise a Faustian figure in a life and death struggle with evil:

> [Françoise] traversa le couloir, elle titubait comme une aveugle, les larmes brûlaient ses yeux: 'J'ai été jalouse d'elle. Je lui ai pris Gerbert.' Les larmes brûlaient, les mots brûlaient comme un fer rouge. Elle s'assit au bord du divan et répéta hébétée: 'J'ai fait cela. C'est moi.' Dans les ténèbres, le visage de Gerbert brûlait d'un feu noir, et les lettres sur le tapis étaient noires comme un pacte infernal. Elle porta son mouchoir à ses lèvres. Une lave noire et torride coulait dans ses veines. Elle aurait voulu mourir. (I 499)[93]

The text has an hallucinatory quality. Disarticulated and convulsive syntax conveys Françoise's distress; the rhythm could almost be the rhythm of broken sobs. Repetition adds to the intensity of the text: "brûler", "larmes", "noir". The same motifs are found again a few lines later: "Elle ferma les yeux. Les larmes coulaient, la lave brûlante coulait et consumait le cœur" (I 500). The colours red and black so prominent here, have gathered symbolic weight throughout *L'Invitée,* adding to the doom-laden Gothic atmosphere of the

---

[89] "What was there beneath the phrases and the gestures?" (SCS 131)

[90] " Xavière's words always held a double meaning." (SCS 233)

[91] In *La Force de l'âge* Beauvoir is severe in her criticism of the ending of her book which she describes as clumsy, abrupt and implausible (FA, pp. 387-88).

[92] The need to murder Xavière is mentioned relatively early in the novel (I 376). See also p. 497 where Françoise again sees Xavière's death as the only way forward.

[93] "[Françoise] crossed the passage, staggering as though blind, and tears burned her eyes. 'I was jealous of her. I took Gerbert from her.' The tears, the words scorched like a hot iron. She sat on the edge of the couch, dazed, and repeated, 'I did that. It was I.' In the shadows, a black fire flickered round Gerbert's face, and the letters scattered on the carpet were as black as an infernal pact. She put her handkerchief to her lips. A black, torrid lava was coursing in her veins. She wanted to die." (SCS 406)

book. The colours resonate with hell and evil, fire and blood. It is Beauvoir's writing that succeeds in making everyday life topple over into tragedy.[94]

In the final pages of the novel, as Françoise is on the point of murdering Xavière, the threat of engulfment she represents is evoked again:

> En face de sa solitude, hors de l'espace, hors du temps, il y avait cette présence ennemie qui depuis si longtemps l'écrasait de son ombre aveugle; elle était là, n'existant que pour soi, tout entière réfléchie en elle-même, réduisant au néant tout ce qu'elle excluait; elle enfermait le monde entier dans sa propre solitude triomphante, elle s'épanouissait sans limites, infinie, unique; tout ce qu'elle était, elle le tirait d'elle-même, elle se refusait à toute emprise, elle était l'absolue séparation. (I 502-503)[95]

One long sentence builds up the menacing picture, clause upon clause. The syntax magnifies and mirrors Françoise's sense of submergence. At this point in the text, there is a distinct contrast between this long sentence connected to Xavière and a series of short sentences associated with Françoise after the murder: "Seule. Sans appui" (I 502); "Il n'y avait plus personne. Françoise était seule. Seule. Elle avait agi seule. Aussi seule que dans la mort" (I 503). Françoise's emancipation from Xavière is figured on a textual level. Her solitude being "enacted" by single-word sentences that stand alone.[96] To sum up, Beauvoir's writing – the rich and dense fabric of the text – at once puts Françoise's brutal and irrational act beyond moral judgment and keeps the ending from being the aesthetic disaster Beauvoir fears.

It has clearly emerged that women and language are at the heart of Beauvoir's enterprise in *L'Invitée,* her first published novel. Françoise's relationship with Xavière that ends in a murder, described by Beauvoir in her memoirs as the *raison d'être* of the book, is paralleled by her destructive relationship with Élisabeth. Language is at once form, theme and protagonist in the drama that is played out.

---

[94] One of Beauvoir's severest criticisms of the ending of *L'Invitée* was that it failed to do this (FA 387). Unfortunately the published translation of the relevant passage in *La Force de l'âge* is extremely misleading. It reads: "I failed to achieve a properly balanced integration between daily life and tragedy." (PL 340)

[95] "Face to face with her aloneness, beyond space, beyond time, stood this alien presence that had for so long overwhelmed her by its blind shadow: Xavière was there, existing only for herself, entirely self-centred, reducing to nothingness everything for which she had no use; she encompassed the whole world within her own triumphant aloneness, boundlessly extending her influence, infinite and unique, everything that she was, she drew from within herself, she barred all dominance over her, she was absolute separateness." (SCS 408)

[96] This effect is unfortunately not reproduced in the published English tanslation: "alone; unaided; relying now..." (SCS 408); "Alone. She had acted alone: as alone as in death." (SCS 408) An alternative analysis of such syntax is to read it as sentences that are fragmented and the fragments separated by full-stops. See Dahl's discussion of James Joyce's expressionistic sentences in "The Attributive Sentence Structure', pp. 449-50.

Works Cited

Beauvoir, Simone de. "Deux chapitres inédits de *L'Invitée*". Ed. Francis, Claude and Fernande Gontier. *Les Écrits de Simone de Beauvoir: La vie – L'écriture,* Paris: Gallimard, 1979. 275-316.

_____. *L'Invitée.* Paris: Gallimard, 1943.

_____. *She Came to Stay.* Trans. Yvonne Moyse and Roger Senhouse, London: Fontana, 1982.

_____. *La Force de l'âge.* Paris: Gallimard, 1960.

_____. *The Prime of Life.* Trans. Peter Green, Harmondsworth: Penguin, 1988.

Brosman, Catherine Savage. *Simone de Beauvoir Revisited.* Boston: Twayne, 1991.

Clarkson, Petrūska. *Gestalt Counselling in Action.* London: Sage, 1989.

Dahl, Liisa. "The Attributive Sentence Structure in the Stream of Consciousness Technique with Special Reference to the Interior Monologue used by Virginia Woolf, Joyce and O'Neill." *Neuphilogische Mitteilungen,* 68 (1967): 443.

Fallaize, Elizabeth. *The Novels of Simone de Beauvoir.* London: Routledge, 1988.

Fishwick, Sarah. *The Body in the Work of Simone de Beauvoir.* Oxford: Peter Lang, 2002.

Heath, Jane. *Simone de Beauvoir.* London: Harvester Wheatsheaf, 1989.

Holland, Alison. "Mirrored Characters in Simone de Beauvoir's *L'Invitée*: Françoise and Élisabeth." *Simone de Beauvoir Studies* 17 (2000-2001): 89-97.

_____. "Identity in Crisis: The Gothic Textual Space in *L'Invitée*." *Modern Language Review* 98 (April 2003): 327-34.

Merleau-Ponty, Maurice. "Metaphysics and the Novel." *Critical Essays on Simone de Beauvoir.* Ed. Elaine Marks, Boston: Hall, 1987. 31-44.

Moi, Toril. "Intentions and Effects: Rhetoric and Identification in Simone de Beauvoir's 'The Woman Destroyed'." Toril Moi. *Feminist Theory and Simone de Beauvoir.* Oxford: Blackwell, 1990.

_____. Simone de Beauvoir: *The Making of an Intellectual Woman.* Oxford: Blackwell, 1994.

Shepherd, Genevieve. *Simone de Beauvoir's Fiction: A Psychoanalytic Rereading.* Bern: Peter Lang, 2003.

Wardman, Harold. "Self-Coincidence and Narrative in *L'Invitée*." *Essays in French Literature* 19 (1982): 87-103.

3 "Ce sera bientôt l'aube": Narration and Lexis in *Le Sang des autres* and *Tous les Hommes sont mortels*

Sarah Fishwick

This chapter takes as its focus Beauvoir's second and third novels: *Le Sang des autres,* published in 1945 and *Tous les Hommes sont mortels,* published one year later in 1946. Both novels were written by Beauvoir during World War II and begun during the German Occupation of Paris. According to the second and third volume of her autobiographical *mémoires,* Beauvoir embarked upon *Le Sang des autres* in 1941 (FA 692) and *Tous les Hommes sont mortels* was commenced in 1943 (FC I 92). As numerous commentators on Beauvoir's fictional writings have noted, there are several points of contact between the two novels in terms of their form and content. While both texts explore the relationship between the individual and history and the existential "burden" of consciousness, it is perhaps on the issue of narrative structure that the points of contact are so marked. In both of these texts, Beauvoir employs a "shifting" gendered narrative perspective – "shifting" in the sense that the narrative is recounted *alternately* through the lenses of their two central protagonists, one male and one female. *Le Sang des autres* is composed of thirteen chapters, of which the odd-numbered chapters are focalised through the text's central male protagonist, a political activist named Jean Blomart, and the remaining even-numbered chapters are recounted from the perspective of the novel's heroine, Hélène Bertrand.[1] The vast majority of the narrative of *Tous les Hommes sont mortels* – comprising the five central parts or chapters which make up the "core" of Beauvoir's text – is focalised through Fosca, the novel's immortal hero. However, a substantial prologue, focalised through the novel's principal female protagonist, a twenty-eight year old aspiring actress named Régine, precedes Fosca's narrative, thus allowing Beauvoir to introduce the reader to the woman to whom Fosca will later recount the adventures of his life. Yet, the recounting of Fosca's adventures

---

[1] Gérard Genette has argued that it is possible to differentiate between narrative voice *(voix/Qui parle?)* and the consciousness through which the narrative is focalised *(perspective/Qui voit?).* What Genette's theorisation illuminates is that whilst it is possible for the narrator and the focaliser to be one and the same person, the protagonist whose "point-of-view" directs the narrative is not necessarily the narrator. See Gérard Genette, *Figures III* (Paris: Seuil, 1972) 203.

from his birth in Northern Italy in the thirteenth century through to his involvement in the 1848 French Revolution, which take up the five main sections of the novel, do not form a continuous, uninterrupted narrative. Fosca's first-person narrative is punctuated by short sections of text – sections which are signalled by a break in the text which constitutes Fosca's narrative and which begin on each occasion on a fresh page.[2] These short-lived, but highly revelatory sections of the narrative are clearly focalised through Régine but not narrated by her. The novel ends as it begins with a section of text which once again is recounted from Régine's perspective. Labelled "Épilogue", this section of text is far shorter than the lengthy "Prologue" which opens the novel.

These novels, then, are clearly marked by the experimentation with narrative strategies with which Beauvoir was preoccupied in this early phase of her career as a writer of fiction – a preoccupation which is fore-grounded by Beauvoir herself in her discussion of the genesis of *Le Sang des autres* featured in *La Force de l'âge*. Beauvoir writes:

> Je ne voulais pas que ce roman ressemblât au précédent [*L'Invitée*]. Je changeai de tactique. J'adoptai deux points de vue, celui d'Hélène, celui de Blomart, qui alternaient de chapitre en chapitre.[3] Le récit centré sur Hélène, je l'écrivis à la troisième personne, en observant les mêmes règles que dans *L'Invitée*. Mais pour Blomart, je procédai autrement. Je le situai au chevet d'Hélène agonisante et il se remémorait sa vie; il parlait de soi, à la première personne, quand il adhérait à son passé, à la troisième quand il considérait à distance la figure qu'il avait eue aux yeux d'autrui: feignant de suivre le fil de ses souvenirs, je pouvais prendre beaucoup plus de libertés que dans *L'Invitée*. (FA 621)[4]

Taking as its starting point Beauvoir's avowed interest in experimenting with textual strategies in embarking upon the writing of *Le Sang des autres*

---

[2] In his discussion of *Tous les Hommes sont mortels,* Terry Keefe has usefully described these short sections, which are focalised through Régine, as "brief tailpieces to each chapter". See Terry Keefe, *Simone de Beauvoir* (London: Macmillan, 1998) 89. Though these "tailpieces" appear on a fresh page in the French original, this is not the case in Euan Cameron's 1995 English translation of the text.

[3] It must be emphasised – as Beauvoir goes on to note in this quotation – that the narrative of her first-published novel, *L'Invitée* (1943), whilst being recounted entirely in the third-person, is also focalised through a number of *different* protagonists. Although the majority of the novel is narrated from the perspective of Beauvoir's heroine, Françoise, some sections are mediated through a male protagonist, Gerbert, and others through Françoise's female friend, Élisabeth.

[4] "I did not want this novel to resemble its predecessor, so I altered my tactics. I wrote from two viewpoints, those of Hélène and Blomart, in alternate chapters. The parts of the narrative centred on Hélène I wrote in the third person, observing the same rules as I had in *She Came to Stay*. But for Blomart I proceeded rather differently. I placed him at the dying Hélène's bedside, and made him reflect in retrospect on his life. When he spoke of himself, his own bygone activities, I made him use the first person, changing to the third when he was required to survey, at a distance, the impression he

in the early 1940s, this chapter will examine the effects produced by the narrative structures of Beauvoir's second and third published works of fiction. It will also examine some of the key features of Beauvoir's deployment of lexis and grammar in these novels with a view to illustrating how Beauvoir uses stylistic techniques to underscore features of and patterns established by the structural and temporal composition of these récits.

Having already briefly outlined some of the complexities which characterise the narrative structures of these two novels, the following section of my discussion is concerned with a number of key characteristics shared by the narratives in terms of their formal features. My discussion of these formal features is guided throughout by an interest in what the implications of those features have for Beauvoir's representation of gender in these texts. In both novels, Beauvoir uses sections – or, in the case of *Le Sang des autres,* chapters – of the narrative which are focalised through a central female protagonist to "frame" the corresponding hero's largely confessional narrative. What is more, in both *Le Sang des autres* and *Tous les Hommes sont mortels,* the sections of the narrative which are focalised through their respective heroines are relayed in the third- and not in the first-person, unlike the sections of these narratives which are recounted from the perspective of their respective heroes. As Terry Keefe points out in his 1983 discussion of *Le Sang des autres,* there are occasional instances contained in the even-numbered chapters of this novel which see Hélène's first-person voice surface for a short period (165). For example, in Chapter 2: "Elle ramena la bicyclette à sa place et traversa la cour en courant. Tant pis pour mon amour-propre [...]" (57) and in the same chapter: "Elle avait envie de se jeter à son cou. Ma bicyclette; elle est vraiment à moi; tout à l'heure je partirai par les rues, je traverserai tout Paris; je suis sûre qu'elle roule si bien. Il lui semblait que toute sa vie était transfigurée" (60).[5] However, in comparison with the number of instances of first-person narration which feature in the male-focalised, odd-numbered chapters, these manifestations of Hélène's first-person voice are minimal.

---

had made upon other people. By pretending to follow the thread of his memories I could take far more liberties than had been possible in *She Came to Stay.*" (PL 543–44) Beauvoir also alludes to her belief that *Le Sang des autres* was technically innovative in her discussion, featured in *La Force des choses* of the critical response to the novel following its publication in September 1945. Beauvoir writes: "Techniquement, j'avais eu l'impression d'innover; les uns m'en félicitèrent, d'autres se plaignirent du 'long tunnel' qui ouvre le récit [...]." (FC I 60)

5 "She wanted to throw her arms around his neck. 'My bicycle, it is really mine! By and by I'll go through the streets, I'll go right across Paris, I'm sure it runs perfectly'. It seemed to her that her whole life was transfigured." (BO 46)

That both narratives are marked by such a discrepancy is something which goes to further reinforce the reader's sense that a hierarchy of narrators/ focalisers is at work within each text – one which would appear to be organised according to the gender of the protagonists concerned. It is also the case that the technique of embedded flashback (or analepsis) is employed by Beauvoir in both novels.[6] Further, in *Le Sang des autres* Jean's retrospective narrative weaves flashbacks with episodes which have taken place much later in time in relation to the events in the remoter past with which the flashback begins. The technique of flashback is used by Beauvoir as a means to elucidate the often-harrowing chain of events that have led to the situation – recounted in the "first" temporal level of the narrative – in which her heroes and heroines find themselves. The deployment of this temporal structure in *Le Sang des autres* as a means of linking both present dilemmas and future accountability with past experience is highlighted by Beauvoir in her autobiographical commentary on the novel:

> Je respectais l'ordre chronologique; mais, par moments, l'actualité brisait l'évocation des jours anciens, J'y emmêlai aussi, en les soulignant par des italiques, les pensées, les émotions qu'éprouvait Blomart au cours de la nuit. […] Toutes les dimensions du temps se trouvaient rassemblées dans cette veillée funèbre: *le héros vivait au présent, en s'interrogeant à travers son passé sur une décision qui engageait son avenir.* (FA 621; emphasis added)[7]

In addition, the narratives attributed to Jean and Fosca are recounted during the night. In *Le Sang des autres* Jean's night-time vigil – or what Beauvoir terms his "veillée funèbre" – in which he watches the life of his lover Hélène, slowly ebb away, spans a single night. Similarly, much of Fosca's autobiographical narrative, which forms the bulk of the text of *Tous les Hommes sont mortels* and is recounted in the presence of Régine, is relayed during the night. Though the narrative present of *Tous les Hommes sont mortels* does not span a single night, unlike that of *Le Sang des autres,* temporal indicators in Beauvoir's text point to the fact that, like the first-order narrative in *Le Sang des Autres,* Fosca's tale of immortality ends in daylight. In Beauvoir's dramatisation of the events which prompt Fosca to reveal his

---

[6] See Gérard Genette's discussion of *analepsis* or flashback in *Figures III.* For Genette, the flashback constitutes "un récit temporaire second, subordonné au premier […]" (90).

[7] "I retained a normal chronological sequence, though now and then present events broke in on the evocation of bygone time. I also inserted here and there, in italics, the thoughts and emotions which Blomart experienced during the night. […] All dimensions of time were united in this deathbed vigil; the hero lived through it in the present, while searching his past for clues to a decision that would affect the course of his future." (PL 544)

past to Régine, the text registers that it is still dark when Régine hastily leaves her apartment in order to look for her lover, whom, she realises on waking, has fled her apartment during the night: "Quand Régine ouvrit les yeux, il faisait à peine jour" (109). Beauvoir's text likewise indicates that the last of the five phases of Fosca's long narrative ends in full daylight over twenty-four hours later:

> Régine détourna les yeux. Il faisait grand jour; des paysans assis autour des tables mangeaient de la soupe et buvaient du vin blanc; dans le monde des hommes une nouvelle journée commençait; le ciel était bleu de l'autre côté de la fenêtre. (TH 525)[8]

The similarities between the two narratives do not end there. The figure of the *amoureuse* features prominently in both novels. In line with her account of the *amoureuse* (woman in love) featured in the second volume of *Le Deuxième Sexe,* Hélène and Régine are cast by Beauvoir as women who are engaged in a deluded quest to find self-validation in erotic submission to a sovereign male other (DS II 555). What is more, the *amoureuses* in question, Hélène in *Le Sang des autres* and Régine in *Tous les Hommes sont mortels,* are cast by Beauvoir in the role of "listener". That is, both female protagonists act as narratees for a male-authored tale which constitutes the dominant proportion of the narrative.[9] In *Le Sang des autres* Hélène lies dying in bed after becoming seriously injured in Resistance action while Jean, the novel's central (male) protagonist and Hélène's lover, sits at her bedside agonising over whether to give the go ahead for further acts of sabotage – acts which could lead to reprisals and the fatal wounding of scores of others. Hélène drifts in and out of consciousness during the narrative present in which Jean Blomart's third- and first-person narrative is relayed. While Hélène is a near-silent recipient of Jean's narrative, Régine of *Tous les Hommes sont mortels,* on the other hand, is an "overt" narratee.[10] She is a thoroughly conscious recipient of Fosca's lengthy first-person narrative and, what is more, we witness her pleas and interjections during the short sections of the narrative which break up Fosca's monologue. It is important to note, furthermore, that it is

---

[8] "Regina looked away. It was broad daylight; there were peasants seated around tables, eating soup and drinking white wine. In the world of men, a new day had begun. On the other side of the window, the sky was blue." (AMM 403)

[9] On the positioning of Hélène and Régine as narratees by Beauvoir in these texts, see Catherine Savage Brosman, *Simone de Beauvoir Revisited* (Boston: Twayne, 1991) 58, 65.

[10] For a useful discussion of narratees, see Shlomith Rimmon-Kenan, *Narrative Fiction: Contemporary Poetics* (London: Routledge, 1983) 103-4.

Régine who urges Fosca to begin recounting the events which have befallen him so far in his life:

> – Mais pourquoi? dit-elle. Expliquez-moi.
> – C'est impossible. Il faudrait tout vous raconter.
> – Eh bien! racontez, dit-elle. Nous avons le temps, n'est-ce pas, nous avons tout le temps?
> – A quoi bon? dit-il.
> – Faites-le pour moi, Fosca. Ce sera peut-être moins terrible quand je comprendrai. (TH 113)[11]

Yet, while Hélène is a protagonist in the action depicted in both the framing and framed sections of the narrative which make up *Le Sang des autres*, Régine only participates in the action represented in the first-level or framing narrative of *Tous les Hommes sont mortels*.[12] A further distinction is noteworthy with respect to Beauvoir's depiction of women as "sounding boards" for male-authored narratives. While the insights gained by the reader into the role of narratee fulfilled by Régine in *Tous les Hommes sont mortels* are filtered through the consciousness of Régine herself, in *Le Sang des autres* the role of narratee as it is acted out by Hélène is focalised through the male protagonist from whom the embedded narrative emanates.

In her 1995 analysis of *Le Sang des autres*, Alex Hughes has argued that the structural organisation of Beauvoir's text makes for a "linear, goal-oriented narrative structure" in which Beauvoir's chronicling of Jean's "dilemmas and decisions" prepares the reader for the decisive "moment of metaphysical resolution/choice" with which the text reaches its conclusion.[13] At the same time, Hughes points out, a close examination of Beauvoir's text reveals the presence of a host of recurrent images and motifs – motifs connected with blood and food amongst others – which lend the text a distinctively "circular", "obsessional" quality. For Hughes, this circularity is at odds with the otherwise predominantly linear structure of the narrative; one that proceeds from hesitation towards the apparent resolution

---

[11] "'But why? Explain it to me'.
'It's impossible. I'd have to tell you everything.'
'Very well' she said. 'We've got time, haven't we? We've got all the time in the world'.
'What's the point?' he asked. 'Do it for me, Fosca. Perhaps it will seem less terrible when I understand'". (AMM 79)

[12] On the distinction between intradiegetic narratees (those who participate in the action of the framing story) and extradiegetic narratees (those who are external to the action relayed), see Seymour Chatman, *Story and Discourse in Fiction and Film* (New York: Cornell University Press) 254.

[13] Alex Hughes, *Beauvoir: Le Sang des autres* (Glasgow: University of Glasgow French and German Publications, 1995) 54–5.

of the dilemmas with which the hero has been grappling throughout the text (Hughes 56-7). As a result, Hughes concludes, *Le Sang des autres* is characterised by "an unsettling pull between goal-oriented cohesion and repetitive, disruptive circularity" (58). In the following section of my analysis, I shall argue that the *circularity* detected by Hughes in her discussion of Beauvoir's recourse to a number of motifs in *Le Sang des autres* is also a prominent feature of Beauvoir's deployment of style in general in both *Le Sang des autres* and *Tous les Hommes sont mortels*. A central focus of this chapter will be a detailed exploration of Beauvoir's use, in these novels, of lexical items linked to the binaries of light/dark, birth/death and movement/immobility. This exploration is undertaken with a view to revealing the extent to which Beauvoir weaves lexical and grammatical "patterns" within these texts. These patterns, which are effected through techniques involving repetition, mirroring and play with tenses, I shall argue, have consequences for Beauvoir's staging in these novels of instances of male narration and the positioning of women as recipients of male-inflected narratives.

A number of existing critical commentaries on *Le Sang des autres* and *Tous les Hommes sont mortels,* such as that offered by Terry Keefe in his 1996 study of Beauvoir's fiction and Elizabeth Fallaize's discussion of *Le Sang des autres,* have asserted that in these novels the male narrator-focaliser constitutes the dominant narrative force in the text.[14] Such an assessment would appear to implicitly suggest that the portions of these texts that are mediated through female protagonists are of secondary importance to those phases of each narrative which are focalised through Beauvoir's heroes. The key justifications given for such an assessment are that, first, the sections which are recounted from the perspective of a female protagonist concerned take up a smaller proportion of the text of each novel and, second, that these female-focalised sections merely act as a "frame" or supporting vehicle for the central male-narrated strand of the text. The fact that in both *Le Sang des autres* and *Tous les Hommes sont mortels,* the sections of the narrative that are focalised through male narrator-focalisers take up a far greater portion of the text of each novel – more than four hundred pages in the case of Fosca's narrative in *Tous les Hommes sont mortels* – than those sections focalised through Hélène and Régine respectively certainly gives weight to this critical assessment. Yet, Beauvoir's own autobiographical discussion of *Le Sang des autres* would seem

---

14 See Elizabeth Fallaize, *The Novels of Simone de Beauvoir* (London, Routledge, 1988) 45, 47 and Keefe, *Beauvoir* 61.

to suggest that Hélène's chapters play far less subsidiary a role in that novel than may appear to be the case. Beauvoir writes in *La Force de l'âge:* "L'histoire [d'Hélène] occupait une grande place dans le livre" (619). Further, with respect to *Tous les Hommes sont mortels,* Fallaize has highlighted an important consequence of Beauvoir's casting of a female protagonist in the role of narratee:

> Fosca's narrative dominates the novel in terms of themes and in terms of sheer weight of pages (constituting roughly three-quarters of the text). However, structurally speaking, Fosca is a character in a text which focuses on Régine; it is for her that Fosca's story is told. (82)

In her 1996 discussion of *Tous les Hommes sont mortels,* Barbara Klaw, has usefully expressed the discrepancy to which Keefe and Fallaize refer – between lengthy male-narrated central "core" (or what might be described as "columns" of narrative) and a much shorter female-focalised "frame" – in terms of a focus in Beauvoir's early writing on "narrative competition". Klaw goes on to assert that Beauvoir's third novel "combines the theme of narrative competition with a focus on the ways men and women differ in their use of language".[15] For Klaw, it is the technique of gendered focalisation and the use of an embedded narrative that allows Beauvoir to "[highlight] the distinction between the discourses of man and woman" and the unequal power relations which underpin the gendering of those discourses (467). Beauvoir's deployment of a relatively short, intermittent female-focalised embedding narrative and a much longer male-authored embedded narrative, Klaw maintains, far from reinforcing the authority of masculine historical narratives, and implicitly male supremacy, actually calls the assumed authority of such narratives into question. Klaw comments:

> [...] although Fosca tells his own story for over 400 pages, it is through Régine that readers see his current situation. His version of the past remains forever embedded in her view of the present. (484)

The discussion which follows focuses too on Beauvoir's foregrounding in *Le Sang des autres* and *Tous les Hommes sont mortels* of a hierarchised relationship between (male) *narrator* and (female) *narratee.* Like the discussions of *Tous les Hommes sont mortels* offered by Fallaize (1988) and Klaw (1996), it seeks to reinstate Beauvoir's heroines at the heart of critical analyses of

---

[15] Barbara Klaw, "Subverting the Dominant Order: Narrative as Weapon in Simone de Beauvoir's *Tous les Hommes sont mortels*", *Studies in Contemporary Literature* 20.2 (1996) 467.

these texts. Focusing on Beauvoir's representation in these texts of instances of confessional storytelling by male protagonists – instances around which the narratives of both novels are organised – as well as her textual insistence on the inescapable march of time, my analysis will demonstrate the degree to which Beauvoir's utilisation of lexis in conjunction with these central themes allows both texts to reflect upon on the ostensibly subordinate narrating position in which their heroines are cast.

A central theme elaborated by Beauvoir within the narratives of *Le Sang des autres* and *Tous les Hommes sont mortels* is the passing of time and consequently the weight of "conscious" existence brought to bear upon individuals by that relentless cycle. The circularity which underpins the temporal structure of both narratives functions to further accentuate Beauvoir's textual emphasis on the ineluctable march of the days and the seasons and the profound impact of the realisation of this circularity on her heroes and heroines. As I observed earlier, Beauvoir's use of an embedded or second-order narrative in both of these texts serves to elucidate the origins of the torment to which the central protagonists in the first-order or framing narrative have succumbed, as well as to explore the burden of responsibility brought by consciousness with which her protagonists continually grapple. What is more, as Beauvoir's autobiographical account of *Le Sang des autres* indicates, the guilt and indecision to which Jean is prey – the twists and turns of which are charted in the framing sections of the narrative – allow Beauvoir to defer the revelation of Jean's eventual decision regarding the proposed attacks until the very close of the novel. Beauvoir comments: "[…] je créai un *suspense:* à l'aube donnerait-il, ne donnerait-il pas le signal d'un nouvel attentat?" (FA 621; emphasis added). Further, Beauvoir's plotting of the novel is such that not only is our reading of the text propelled by a desire to discover what Jean's final decision will be but also by our anticipation of Hélène's tragic demise with which the novel seems sure to draw to a close.

In Beauvoir's depiction of Jean's night-time "journey" from despair to clarity and resolution – through hesitation, rage and guilt – the inevitable coming of the dawn (*l'aube*) serves both as a temporal marker which anticipates the delivering of Jean's decision and a motif for the relentlessness with which time follows its cyclical course. In the fictional universe mapped out by Beauvoir in this novel, night-time represents a period of hesitation and reflection, heralding a pressing search for clarity – the regaining of which will coincide with the symbolic coming of light brought by the dawn. The alliance of the birth of the dawn with a perspective marked by clarity and decisiveness rather than confusion is facilitated by the Latin root of the French noun *aube* (*alba*) which designates whiteness. In the opening section of the narrative of *Le Sang des autres,* Beauvoir makes reference to a number of everyday household substances – notably, wash powder, soup and (Madeleine's) cigarettes – the aromas of which are said to permeate the nocturnal air inside the flat in which Jean and his friends wait out the night. The stale, pungent aromas emitted by these substances evoke symbolically the anguish and confusion which threaten to engulf Jean. Moreover, as well as a quest for clarity, the night represents a period of preparation for inevitable death since, as the reader is continually reminded by Beauvoir's text, the dawn will bring the death of Hélène, a feminine figure who is repeatedly cast by Beauvoir as the beloved *female other who will not see the dawn.* Beauvoir's use of language repeatedly marries references to Hélène's final few hours with the passing of the night and the coming of the new day. The clauses concerned take on the quality of a terse and mournful refrain in which references to the long-anticipated *aube* act as a motif for that which Hélène has effectively sacrificed in relinquishing passive inauthenticity and choosing to participate in Resistance action. A close examination of these sentences reveals that their impact stems from the repetition of elements – not only within the sentences themselves – but also of lexical items which have been employed from the very outset of the narrative in conjunction with the demise of Hélène. In the following two extracts, Beauvoir links two main clauses, repeating the chosen verb whilst varying the tenses from clause to clause or sentence to sentence. In the following example from the opening chapter of the novel, the pronominal verb *s'éteindre* (to pass away) is employed in the simple future and is then followed by a construction made up of the future tense form of *être* and the past participle of *éteindre* (to put out, extinguish): "elle va s'éteindre, elle sera éteinte à l'aube" (SA 12). Here, the reiteration of forms of *s'éteindre/ éteindre* serve to convey the inevitability of Hélène's passing. Likewise, much later in the novel, Beauvoir's evocation of Hélène's imminent death turns on her use of the verb *passer* (to pass). Here, the verb appears in both sentences, with Hélène (designated as *Elle*) as the subject of the future-tense verb in the first sentence and the night (*la nuit*), whose end draws ever closer, as the subject of the verb in the second and described by the past participle *passé[e]* (over): "Elle ne passera pas la nuit. Et la nuit est presque passée" (SA 305). The symmetry suggested by the grammatical arrangement of elements across both sentences – an approximate symmetry that is based on the repetition of two forms of the lexeme *passer* and the noun *nuit* – produces a kind of mirroring effect which successfully conveys, once again, the terrifying nearness of Hélène's death.[16] A similar emphasis on that which will be ushered in by the coming of the new day is also evident in *Tous les Hommes sont mortels,* a narrative, which, as I noted earlier, also reaches its conclusion in daylight after an agony-inducing night-time journey. The delivering of Fosca's testimony mapped out by the framing narrative of *Tous les Hommes sont mortels* not only sees the novel's heroine listen to a story that lasts a good many hours but also sees the couple undertake a night-time walk in which they make their way towards a village inn aptly named *Le Soleil d'Or* (The Golden Sun):

> Ils continueraient à marcher jusqu'au village; toutes les portes étaient barricadées, les volets fermés: pas une lumière, pas un bruit. Devant la porte du *Soleil d'Or,* il y avait un banc de bois peint en vert. Ils s'assirent. On entendit à travers les persiennes le ronflement égal d'un dormeur. (359)[17]

In common with Jean of *Le Sang des autres* as he sits at Hélène's bedside, Régine and Fosca's night-time discussion sees them located within hearing distance of someone who sleeps (*un dormeur*). While a reflective Jean sits and waits for the dawning of a new day in the framing narrative of *Le Sang des autres,* in the framing narrative of *Tous les Hommes sont mortels* Beauvoir stages an episode in which Régine and Fosca sit outside an inn whose name connotes the golden brightness brought by the new day (*Le Soleil d'Or*).

The *veillée funèbre* which forms the focus of the action of the "narrative present" in *Le Sang des autres,* is not the first night-time vigil at Hélène's bedside recounted in the novel. In Chapter 5, Jean learns from Hélène's friend Yvonne the news that Hélène has had a clandestine abortion following a one-night stand (an encounter that was apparently prompted by Jean's earlier rejection of her). Yvonne urges Jean to spend the night watching over

---

16 Roland Carter defines the term "lexeme" as 'the abstract unit which underlies some of the variants [that can be] observed in connection with "words". Thus BRING is the lexeme which underlies different grammatical variants; "bring", "brought", "brings", "bringing" which we can refer to as word-forms. Lexemes are the basic, contrasting units of vocabulary in a language. Roland Carter, *Vocabulary: Applied Linguistic Perspectives* (London: Routledge, 1998) 7.

17 "They continued to walk until they reached the village. All the doors were locked, the shutters closed; not a sound, not a light. In front of the *Soleil d'Or* was a green wooden bench. They sat down. Through the shutters, they could hear the rhythmic sound of someone snoring." (AMM 272)

Hélène: "– Alors, il faudrait que quelqu'un passe la nuit auprès d'elle" (123). The narration of the events of the night following the termination of Hélène's pregnancy, focalised through Jean in flashback mode, provides an episode in the second-order narrative which mirrors the deathbed scenes which form the substance of the action of the first-order narrative and which prompt the relaying of Jean's fragmented chronicle of his life. At a number of crucial points in the narrative, then, Hélène is depicted by Beauvoir as a woman who *sleeps* in the presence of a tormented and guilt-ridden male lover. So, while Beauvoir's dramatisation of the relaying of Fosca's story in *Tous les Hommes sont mortels* casts Régine as *la femme qui écoute,* in the framing narrative of *Le Sang des autres* Hélène is positioned as *la femme qui dort.* Hélène's status as a kind of sleeping beauty figure who lies tragically wounded is repeatedly flagged up by Beauvoir's use of lexis. In Chapter 3, for example, Madeleine asks: "Elle dort toujours?" and Jean replies: "Elle n'a pas cessé de dormir" (69). On the same page, Hélène wakes for a very short time and utters the words "J'ai dormi." Jean's narrative records that she then closes her eyes once again, something which prompts a lapse into interior monologue as Beauvoir's narrative flags up Jean's pleas for her not to go back to sleep: "Non. Ne te *rendors* pas. *Réveille-toi* pour de bon, *réveille-toi* à jamais" (70; emphasis added). While Hélène drifts in and out of a sleeping state, Beauvoir's text repeatedly casts those others present in the flat while Jean waits by Hélène's bed as *les vivants;* individuals who will live long enough to see the night draw to an end and the new day break: "Ils étaient *vivants.* Pour *eux,* cette nuit aurait une fin: il y aurait une aube" (11; emphasis added). In the opening phase of the novel, we learn that Laurent, a member of Jean's Resistance group, will sleep through the night, like Hélène (*la femme qui dort*), but unlike Jean (*l'homme qui veille*). In the same section, Jean gives Laurent instructions to come and see him as soon as the latter wakes the following morning. Here, Beauvoir's use of the present participle of *réveiller* underscores the fact, not only that Laurent is among those – unlike Hélène – who will see the new day but also that the dawn in question will require Jean to deliver his final decision on the matter of the proposed acts of sabotage: "Écoute, viens me voir en te réveillant [...] j'ai besoin de réfléchir" (12). The line which divides those who will find brief respite during the night and those who will continue their vigil is emphasised once more by Beauvoir in the following lines from Chapter 1: "Laurent va aller *se reposer.* Mais *nous restons là toute la nuit*" (12; emphasis added). The distinction between the *restful* and the *restless* is also a central focus of the section of narrative, focalised through Jean, which opens the third chapter of the novel. Once again, Beauvoir's dramatisation of Jean's conversation with Madeleine foregrounds Jean's dawn meeting with Laurent:

> Il y a une chambre de l'autre côté de la porte; toute une maison; une rue; une ville. Et des gens, *d'autres gens qui dorment ou qui veillent.*
> – Laurent a été *dormir*?
> – Oui, il [Laurent] viendra te voir *à six heures.* (69; emphasis added)[18]

Thus, Beauvoir's narrative repeatedly sets up a contrast between the precariousness of Hélène's life and the heightened conscious state of those who are getting ready to mourn her passing. While Hélène is "at this last link of the fatal chain" (*au bout de la chaîne fatale*) (SA 12, BO 8), ironically Jean's narrative – one which will "fill in the gaps" for the reader in terms of how Hélène came to be fatally wounded – is only at its beginning. In the opening phase of Chapter 7, Jean's narrative flags up, once again, the chasm which divides the living from the dying. The irony inherent in the insurmountable gap that exists between his own mournful deliberations on Hélène's imminent death and Hélène's *living out* of that death is not lost on Jean: "J'existe, moi qui songe à la mort. C'est elle qui meurt. *Moi je vis*" (193; emphasis added). At a time when Beauvoir's depiction of setting in this episode situates Jean – in spatial terms – in very close proximity to Hélène, Beauvoir's use of lexis, on the other hand, flags up that which estranges Jean from Hélène. The emphasis on that which divides Jean from Hélène is achieved in the extract cited above by means of Beauvoir's simultaneous use of synonymy and antonymy.[19] The synonymous present-tense verb forms "exist" (*existe*), "think" (*songe*) and "live" (*vis*) point to Jean's heightened sense of his own consciousness while the juxtaposition of these three verbs with a fourth verb, also in the present tense, which denotes the action of dying (*meurt*), flags up the existential chasm which separates narrator and narratee.

---

18 "There is a room on the other side of the door, a whole house, a street, a town, and other people: other people who sleep or watch.
'Has Laurent gone to get some sleep?'
'Yes, he'll come and see you at six o'clock'" [...]. (BO 53)
19 The discussion featured in this chapter draws on John Lyons' discussion of synonymy contained in *Linguistic Semantics: An Introduction* (Cambridge: CUP, 1995) 60–65. A further useful discussion of synonymy is offered by D. A. Cruse in *Lexical Semantics* (Cambridge: CUP, 1986) 265–94. On antonymy, see John Lyons, *Introduction to Theoretical Linguistics* (Cambridge: CUP, 1968) 460–470.

The circularity produced by the frequent movement in both of these novels between a linear first-order narrative and a segmented retrospective second-order narrative, together with fictional retellings of actual historical events and frequent allusions to the inevitable march of time allow Beauvoir's narratives to explore on a number of different levels the relationship between the individual and history. What is more, in both *Le Sang des autres* and *Tous les Hommes sont mortels* Beauvoir employs narrative structure and lexis to establish a clear link between the related notions of time/ history and story/journey. The following quotation from the first chapter of *Le Sang des autres* highlights the inevitable circularity of the days and the seasons but at the same time, by means of direct reference to events which are contained on the pages of literary and historical narratives, the author makes a connection between time/history and textual narrative: "Les saisons passaient, les paysages changeaient, dans les livres dorés sur tranche de nouvelles aventures se déroulaient" (14).[20] The reader's sense of the parallel being established here between *journeys through time/history* and *textual journeys* is heightened further by Beauvoir's use in this sentence of the verbs *passer, changer* and *se dérouler;* verbs of movement which echo the steady unfolding of those journeys which form the focus for Beauvoir's fictional explorations of the interaction between the individual and history elaborated in these two novels. Moreover, Jean's narrative, in Chapters 7 and 13 amongst others, makes direct reference to the strikes made by the clock. Counting down the hours until 6am, Beauvoir's text repeatedly emphasises the journey towards the dawn mapped out by the movement of the clock. As four o'clock strikes, Jean's narrative registers that the streets are still deserted but as the clock strikes five, a number of cafés light up as their proprietors prepare for a new day of business:

> Il y aura *une aube. Quatre coups.* Aux carrefours déserts, l'aiguille des horloges *tourne* […]. (193; emphasis added)[21]

> Un rai de lumière filtre à travers les persiennes. *Cinq heures.* Les premières portes s'ouvrent. […] Autour des gares quelques cafés s'allument. (305; emphasis added)[22]

---

[20] "Season succeeded season, the countryside changed, new adventure stories were published in books with gilt edges, but nothing changed the even murmur of the machines." (BO 9)

[21] "There will be a dawn. Four chimes. At the corner of the deserted streets the hands of the clocks move round […]." (BO 151)

[22] "A ray of light filters through the Venetian blinds. Five o'clock. The first doors are opening. […] Round the railway stations, lights go up in some of the cafés." (BO 236)

Il regarda la fenêtre. Le jour était né. Les minutes appelaient les minutes, se chassant, se poussant l'une l'autre, sans fin. Avance. Décide. A nouveau *le glas sonne,* il sonnera jusqu'à ma mort. (310)[23]

In the third extract, the near-synonymy that exists between the present participles *chassant* (chasing) and *poussant* (pushing), together with Beauvoir's repetition of two forms of the lexeme *sonner* ("sonne" and "sonnera") serve to impress upon the reader the sense of urgency felt by Jean in the face of time's relentless march and his perception of the weight of the responsibility that lies on his shoulders. *Tous les Hommes sont mortels,* as I indicated earlier, also draws to a close with the realisation that it is daylight: "Il faisait grand jour" (525). As is the case in *Le Sang des autres,* the new day – and the end of the narrative proper – are heralded by the ringing of a bell: "Ce fut quand l'heure commença de sonner au clocher qu'elle poussa le premier cri" (528; emphasis added). Many of the direct references to the ineluctable passing of time made in these novels occur in the framing sections of each narrative – focalised through Jean in *Le Sang des autres* and Régine in *Tous les Hommes sont mortels.* This is hardly surprising given that it is from these very "frames" – and the constant shifts between a first- and second-order narrative prompted by them – that the narrative circularity common to both texts principally (but not exclusively) stems. In *Tous les Hommes sont mortels,* Fosca's own seemingly interminable and tumultuous journey through history, related solely by him in the embedded flashback, is echoed and underscored by Beauvoir's textual insistence in the framing narrative on Régine and Fosca's night-time journey on foot. In the following citation from the short section of narrative which follows the first segment of Fosca's tale, Beauvoir foregrounds real and figurative acts of journeying by means of repeated references to the *route* which Régine and Fosca intend to follow, the reiterated references to the action of walking effected by the use of the verb *avancer* and its near-synonym *marcher,* as well as the evocation of the perpetual twists and turns of Fosca's journey through history:

Elle [Régine] désigna *la route:*
– On peut toujours *suivre cette route,* n'est-ce pas? Elle rit.
– Le cœur bat, et *un pied avance après l'autre. Les routes n'ont pas de fin.*
Ils *marchèrent, un pied avançant après l'autre.* (227–8; emphasis added)[24]

---

23 "He looked at the window. The day had dawned. The minutes were calling the minutes, chasing, driving each other forward, without end. Go on … go on. Decide. Once more the bell tolls, it will toll until my death." (BO 240)
24 "She pointed to a road. 'There's nothing to stop us taking this road, is there?' She laughed. 'Your heart beats, and one foot follows the other. Roads go on forever.' They began walking step by step down the road." (AMM 170)

Once again, Beauvoir's rendering of this episode sees her repeat lexical items and patterns, making small amendments to their form as the narrative proceeds. In his dialogue with Régine, a despairing Fosca (*l'homme qui raconte*) seeks to convey to Régine the full enormity of the burdensome existence to which he has condemned himself in consenting to immortality; Fosca lives a never-ending consciousness that inspires increasing indifference in him, in which *un pied avance après l'autre*. This is immediately followed by a section of third-person narrative – focalised through Régine – in which Beauvoir employs a further form of the lexeme *avancer*. The couple are shown to continue walking, this time "un pied *avançant* après l'autre" (228; emphasis added). Here, the adverbial phrase previously employed by Fosca is repeated, with the sole exception that the present tense verb *avance,* becomes a present participle. This repetition of wordforms serves to foreground the repetitiveness and meaninglessness that have come to characterise Fosca's existential journey. Beauvoir's use of vocabulary in the following extract, taken from the fractious conversation which occurs between Fosca and Régine in the short section of first-order narrative which follows the *second* instalment of Fosca's testimony, turns on a parallel between the act of journeying and the perpetual cycle of history/time:

> Ils *avaient marché* très longtemps [...], la *nuit* était tiède sous le couvert des arbres. [...] Elle s'assit et dit:
> – Ne *continuez* pas c'est inutile. Ce sera jusqu'au bout de la même *histoire,* je le sais.
> – La même *histoire,* et chaque *jour* différente, dit Fosca. Il faut que vous l'entendiez.
> – Tout à l'heure, vous ne vouliez pas la *raconter.* (318; emphasis added)[25]

Here, the idea of sameness flagged up by the text's repetition of the adjective *même* (same) is curiously pointed up by the instance of antonymy, or more precisely complementarity, produced by the juxtaposition of *même* with the feminine form of the adjective *différent* (different). What is further noteworthy in the extract cited above is that, as in *Le Sang des autres,* Beauvoir, by means of her allusions to Fosca's long and repetitive tale (*la même histoire*) makes an additional connection between the metaphorical

---

[25] "They had been walking for a very long time and they were deep in the forest. The night was warm beneath the cover of the trees. [...] She sat down.
' Don't go on', she said. 'There's no point. It will be the same story right until the very end. I know it.'
'The same story, and every day different,' said Fosca. 'You have to hear it all.'
'A little while ago you didn't want to tell it to me.'" (AMM 241–42)

journeying made possible through fictional and semi-fictional narratives and the anxiety-inducing journey of the conscious individual through time. Allusions to the warm night (*la nuit*) spent under the cover of the forest and the circular cycle of the days featured in the above extract from *Tous les Hommes sont mortels* echo and recall Beauvoir's depictions of Jean's anguished night-time reflections on his responsibility towards others which are a central feature of the male-focalised chapters of *Le Sang des autres*. "Story" (*histoire*) and the present-tense verb "unfold" (*se déroule*) repeatedly appear as collocates in Beauvoir's 1945 novel – something which further reinforces the inextricable link between personal narrative and history already established by Beauvoir in the opening chapter of the novel.[26] One such example of this can be found in Chapter 11: "*La voix parle et l'histoire se déroule. Mon histoire. Et toi tu te tais, tes yeux demeurent fermés. Ce sera bientôt l'aube*" (277; emphasis added).[27] In the following quotation from Chapter 1, the juxtaposition of the noun *histoire* and the verb *se dérouler* signal, once again, Beauvoir's textual preoccupation with the relationship between telling and living:

> Je la regarde, depuis des heures je la regarde et derrière ses paupières fermées, je ne vois rien; autour de moi, ce sont mes souvenirs qui se pressent; c'est mon *histoire* qui se *déroule*. (45)[28]

In *Tous les Hommes sont mortels,* as Terry Keefe has previously commented, the reader is continually reminded that Fosca's autobiographical narrative is a *story* (89). As Régine comes to the realisation that she cannot attain through Fosca the validation that she so badly craves, her request – issued at the end of the prologue – that he tell her the full story of his past turns to anguished pleas for him to *finish* the story of his interminable existence as soon as possible. Yet, the sense of weariness and dejection which besets both protagonists is made all the more vivid for the reader since that very reader, like Régine, wonders how this tale of onerous immortality can ever draw to a close: "*L'histoire* est presque finie, dit Fosca. – Finissez, dit-elle.

---

[26] Katie Wales has usefully clarified the term "collocation" (or collocability) as follows: "[Collocation] refers to the habitual or expected co-occurrence of words, a characteristic feature of lexical behaviour in language, testifying to its predicability as well as its idiomaticity". Katie Wales, *A Dictionary of Stylistics,* Second Edition (Harlow: Pearson Education, 2001) 67.

[27] "The voice speaks and the story unfolds. My personal history. And you – you are silent, your eyes remain closed. Soon it will be dawn." (BO 215)

[28] "[…] I look at her, for hours I have been looking at her, and behind her closed eyelids I can see nothing; about me press my own memories – it is my own personal history which unfolds." (BO 34)

Finissons-en" (441; emphasis added). While Jean is preoccupied with telling his story, Régine longs for its end.

Aside from illuminating Beauvoir's own preoccupation in these novels with the interconnecting themes of the paths marked out by history and personal testimony, an examination of Beauvoir's deployment of lexis in *Le Sang des autres* and *Tous les Hommes sont mortels* allows us to see both novels as texts in which their central female protagonists are cast as women who become progressively immobilised by their encounters with men. It is not the case that Hélène and Régine are depicted throughout these narratives as women who are dangerously poised on the threshold between life and death, narcissistic longing and anguished knowledge. The second chapter of *Le Sang des autres,* narrated from Hélène's perspective rather than Jean's, presents an ironic counterpoint to the darkness and despair which characterises the novel's opening chapter. In a flashback to a time prior to her first meeting with Jean, the reader is introduced to a vibrant and energetic Hélène, poignantly the same Hélène whose imminent death we have witnessed Jean preparing himself for in the previous chapter. In this second chapter, Beauvoir's focus is, once again, on the relentless march of time. Yet, ironically, the end of the day recounted in this chapter and the promise of a new one, to which Beauvoir's text refers, is a day, unlike that invoked in the first-order narrative, that Hélène will unquestionably see: "Voilà. Elle était arrivée *au bout de sa journée. Demain, une autre journée recommencerait* toute pareille" (47; emphasis added).[29] In *Le Sang des autres* and *Tous les Hommes sont mortels,* Beauvoir's uses a series of verbs of physical movement in association with her female protagonists. The following examples are just a selection of those employed in *Le Sang des autres* in conjunction with a pre-deathbed Hélène: "elle *descendit* l'escalier" (47), "elle *se précipita*" (49), "elle *s'approcha* de la maison" (173), "Hélène *sauta* sur le quai et *courut* vers un employé" (209; emphasis added). All of these verbs of (often rapid) physical movement serve to convey Hélène's impulsiveness and vitality. It is further telling that in Chapter 6, the narrative, mediated through Hélène, registers that it would be a mistake for her to arrive at her destination earlier than planned: "Il ne fallait pas *marcher trop vite,* ce serait affreux si elle *arrivait en avance*" (173; emphasis added). The same is true of Beauvoir's depiction of Régine in *Tous les Hommes sont mortels:* "Elle *descendit* les marches […]" (13),

---

[29] "That was that: she had come to the end of the day: there would be another day tomorrow and it would be the same thing all over again." (BO 36)

"Elle *traversa* le studio" (37), "Elle *franchit* la porte cochère et *traversa* la cour du vieil immeuble [...]" (81), "Régine *sauta* du taxi et *monta* rapidement l'escalier" (85; emphasis added). In common with a number of the verbal structures used by Beauvoir to describe the manner in which Hélène moves freely around the spaces she inhabits, several of the examples cited above in conjunction with Régine feature verbs which are followed by direct objects or objects of prepositions which denote spaces, channels or thresholds. For example, Régine is described as she crosses a courtyard (elle [...] traversa *la cour*), jumps from a taxi (Régine sauta *du taxi*) and goes through the street door (Elle franchit *la porte cochère*). However, a feature of Beauvoir's dramatisation of Régine's encounters with Fosca point to Régine's increasing sense of immobility in his presence: "Un instant Régine *resta immobile* sur le seuil de la chambre [...] puis elle renferma la porte et s'avança au milieu du studio" (70; emphasis added). Later, when she thinks she has lost Fosca's attention, Régine becomes hesitant and stands motionless at the door of the studio: "Elle ouvrit la porte et elle *resta clouée* sur le seuil du studio" (85; emphasis added). In Beauvoir's staging of both of these episodes, the text registers not only that Régine is unable to move – signalled in these examples by the repeated past historic form of the verb *rester* (to stay), the adjective *immobile* (motionless) and the past participle *clouée* (nailed to the spot) – but that she stands paralysed on a threshold (*le seuil*), caught between two spaces. As Beauvoir's narrative progresses, the author's use of lexis clearly suggests that Régine is unable to move through spaces and across thresholds with the ease that she had once enjoyed. Moreover, while Hélène passes away at the end of *Le Sang des autres*, in *Tous les Hommes sont mortels* the knowledge brought by Fosca's story leaves Régine exhausted, defeated and beset by anguish. As the novel draws to a close, Régine is cast as no longer capable of bodily movement:

> Elle fit un pas, et *s'arrêta, clouée* sur place; il avait disparu, mais elle *demeurait* telle qu'il l'avait faite [...]; elle était trop *fatiguée*. Elle écrasa ses mains contre sa bouche, elle inclina la tête, elle était *vaincue* [...]. 'Ce n'est que le commencement', pensa-t-elle, et elle *restait immobile* comme s'il eût été possible de ruser avec le temps, de l'empêcher de poursuivre sa course. Mais ses mains *se raidissaient* contre ses lèvres *contractées*. (528; emphasis added)[30]

---

[30] "She took a step and stopped, nailed to the spot. He had disappeared, but she remained as he had made her [...]. She was too tired. She held her hands tightly to her mouth, her head slumped forward. She was defeated. [...] 'And it's only the beginning,' she thought. She stood motionless, as if it were possible to play tricks with time, prevent it from following its course. But her hands grew taut against her quivering lips." (AMM 405–6)

Here, a whole host of verbs and adjectives connoting bodily paralysis are employed by Beauvoir in conjunction with her anguished heroine. Her lips and hands are wrought with tension, indicated by the use of a form of the verb *se raidir* (to stiffen) and the action of "crushing" her hands against her mouth (*elle écrasa ses mains contre sa bouche*) as well as the adjective "contracted" (*contractées*). Once again, Régine is metaphorically "nailed" (to the spot) (*clouée [sur place]*) and immobile. Further, the past historic form of the verb *rester* appears once again as a collocate of *immobile* and serves to reinforce Beauvoir's earlier use of the verbs *s'arrêter* (to stop) and *demeurer* (to stay), with which *rester* is quasi-synonymous.

Earlier on in my discussion of the circularity which characterises the narrative structure of *Le Sang des autres* and *Tous les Hommes sont mortels,* I suggested that one of the ways in which Beauvoir's narratives underscore that circularity is by means of temporal indicators and an insistence on the related motifs of night and day. We saw the way in which Beauvoir's incorporation into her texts of a host of lexical items connected with the dawn (*l'aube*) or the coming of a new day (*la nouvelle journée*) facilitates her textual examination of the responsibilities imposed by history and the impact of (male-authored) personal narratives on (female) others. Lexical items connected with night and day form just one subset of a whole group of lexical items featured in these novels which invoke notions connected with light and sight. In his 1975 discussion of Beauvoir's fictional writings, Robert D. Cottrell highlights that "[s]ight is the primary sense in Beauvoir's world" and, as his analysis suggests, the narratives of *Le Sang des autres* and *Tous les Hommes sont mortels,* amongst others, point to Beauvoir's textual peoccupation with vision.[31] I would argue, however, that lexical items connected with light/sight tend to be deployed in association with female rather than male protagonists in these two texts. In *Le Sang des autres* one way in which Beauvoir's text flags up the precariousness of Hélène's existence is by means of repeated references to her eyes. In making frequent references to Hélène's eyes, Beauvoir deploys the technique of synecdoche whereby invocations of Hélène's eyes stand in for Hélène herself.[32] Emblematic throughout Beauvoir's writing of the conscious self and the

---

[31] Robert D. Cottrell, *Simone de Beauvoir* (New York: Frederick Ungar Publishing, 1975) 69.

[32] For a useful gloss on the distinction between synecdoche and metonymy with respect to the French language, see Hilary Wise, *The Vocabulary of Modern French* (London: Routledge, 1997) 146–7.

objectifying gaze, in *Le Sang des autres,* Hélène's eyes operate as a barometer for her physical deterioration and her progression towards death. In the opening chapter of the novel, Jean's narrative informs us that the eyes of she who will not see the dawn are shut: "Les yeux sont fermés" (12). Beauvoir's text goes on to record Jean's angst-ridden monitoring of Hélène's eyes with such frequency that these references heighten the reader's anticipation of her death in the same manner as the periodic references to chiming of the hours as the countdown to the new day continues. For example, in Chapter 3: "Elle ouvre les yeux [...] elle referme les yeux" (69–70) and in Chapter 6: "Et toi tu te tais, tes yeux demeurent fermés" (277). In the opening section of the final chapter of the novel, Jean's narrative registers that Hélène has opened her eyes and is looking at him: "Elle avait ouvert les yeux. Elle le regardait" (305), yet Hélène soon loses consciousness. As Hélène slides further and further towards death, her eyes, once again, become a focus for Jean's anguish:

> Elle ouvrit les yeux; il la prit dans ses bras. Ces yeux ouverts ne voyaient plus [...]. Ces yeux sont encore un regard, un regard figé qui n'est plus un regard de rien. (308–9)[33]

It is telling that in life – as opposed to near-death – Hélène is associated not with an inability to see but instead with light and brightness. In the second-order narrative of *Le Sang des autres,* Hélène is repeatedly associated with sources of light and shiny objects that are emblematic of her zest and impetuosity. These include a gleaming bicycle and sources of light such as lamps and fireplaces. The description of the bicycle, which is stolen by Hélène, featured in Chapter 2 turns on a lexical set connected with fire/light composed of adjectives of differing intensity such as *neuve* (brand new), *flambante* (flaming), *nickelé* (polished), *propre* (clean) and the verbs *étinceler* (to sparkle) and *briller* (to shine):

> La bicyclette était toujours là, neuve, flambante avec son cadre bleu pâle et son guidon nickelé qui étincelait contre la pierre morne du mur. (47)[34]

> Elle ouvrit la porte qui donnait sur la cour; le guidon, les pare-boue brillaient

---

[33] "She opened her eyes and he took her in his arms. Those open eyes no longer saw. [...] Those eyes still have a look, a frozen look, a look which no longer sees anything." (BO 239)

[34] "The bicycle was still there, brand new, with its pale-blue frame and its plated handlebars which sparkled against the dull stone of the wall." (BO 36)

dans l'ombre […] Si lisse, si propre, si gaie: à la fois fragile et robuste […]. Il y
aurait ce rond de lumière qui me précéderait dans les rues silencieuses […]. (48)[35]

Further, the opening paragraphs of Chapter 4 see Hélène curled up in front
of a fire as she and her friend Yvonne roast chestnuts: "Hélène s'étira: elle
était roulée en boule devant la *cheminée* et les *flammes* lui *rôtissait* le visage […].
Elle [Hélène] plongea les pincettes dans les *cendres brûlantes*" (99; emphasis
added). While Beauvoir's depiction of Hélène's sparkling pale blue bicycle
sets that bicycle up against a drab stone wall and the shadowy courtyard, in
similar fashion, the author's evocation of the fireside episode contrasts the
burning flames of the fire which roast Hélène's face (*rôtir*) and the drab grey-
ness of the day outside: "Une journée molle et grise s'écrasait contre les
vitres de la chambre" (99; emphasis added). In an episode that contains ironic echoes of Jean's night-time vigil beside a dying Hélène in the first-order
narrative, the beginning of Chapter 12 sees Hélène positioned beside a lamp
as she gives herself a manicure and waits for the end of the day: "Elle était à
demi couchée sur le divan, elle avait tiré les rideaux et allumé la lampe de
chevet: comme ça on pouvait croire que la journée allait bientôt finir; mais
elle savait bien que ça n'était pas vrai" (291).[36]

Motifs of light are likewise a recurrent feature of Beauvoir's representation
of Régine in *Tous les Hommes sont mortels*. However, in her 1946 novel,
Beauvoir's focus is on the eyes of others who gaze at Régine rather than
Régine's own eyes. As Klaw has highlighted, the opening paragraphs of *Tous
les Hommes sont mortels* dramatise the curtain call of a theatrical performance
in which Régine has a starring role. As she takes the audience's applause in a
brightly-lit auditorium, Beauvoir's references to the light of admiration that
Beauvoir's heroine detects in the eyes of audience members who applaud her
points up for the reader Régine's ambitious pursuit of the limelight:

> Le rideau se releva; Régine s'inclina et sourit; sous les *lumières* du *grand lustre*,
> des *taches roses* papillotaient au-dessus des robes multicolores et des vestons
> sombres; dans chaque face, il y avait des *yeux*, et au fond de tous ces *yeux*,
> Régine s'inclina et souriait […]. (13; emphasis added)[37]

---

[35] "She opened the door which gave onto the courtyard; the handlebars and the mudguards gleamed
in the shadow. […] So smooth, so clean, so bright, both delicate and strong […]. 'I'll go everywhere I
want. I'll come home late at night. Only a pool of light will go ahead of me in the silent streets […].'"
(BO 37)

[36] "She was half-lying on the divan; she had drawn the curtains and lit the bedside lamp; in this way,
she could believe that the day would soon come to an end, but she knew perfectly well that it was not
true." (BO 226)

[37] "The curtain rose again. Regina took her bow and smiled. Beneath the glare of the brilliant lights
pink spots flickered over the multicoloured dresses and dark suits. In every face there were eyes, and
reflected in each pair of eyes was Regina, bowing and smiling." (AMM 1)

The closing chapter of *Le Sang des autres* charts Hélène's physical death as it is mediated through Jean's consciousness, while in the "Epilogue" of *Tous les Hommes sont mortels* Régine undergoes a symbolic death as she desperately struggles to come to terms with the realisation that she cannot attain uniqueness through the love of an immortal. Beauvoir's use of lexis and imagery in the closing sections of these *récits* flags up the loss of or estrangement from light which immediately threatens each of her heroines. In the case of *Le Sang des autres,* once again, Beauvoir's dramatisation of Hélène's death is centred on her eyes: "Elle respire encore une fois; *les yeux se voilent; le monde se détache d'elle* […] un rictus tire le coin de ses lèvres *il n'y a plus de regard. Il* abaissa les paupières sur *les yeux inertes*" (309; emphasis added). Beauvoir's use of metaphor and lexis here points to the rapid paralysis of Hélène's eyes; her eyes become veiled over (*les yeux se voilent*) and the narrative records that under her eyelids her eyes are "inert" (*inertes*). In *Tous les Hommes sont mortels,* Régine's anguish is signalled in Beauvoir's text by metaphorical references to a bright, burning light which "vibrates" inside her head: "Dans sa tête vibrait *une grande lumière brûlante,* plus *aveuglante* que la nuit" (527; emphasis added). Not only is it a "burning" light (*lumière brûlante*) but it is one that is "more blinding than the night" – a hyperbolic statement which is built on a contradiction since the night is conventionally understood as blinding by virtue of an absence rather than a predominance of light. Beauvoir's rendering of Régine's symbolic demise conveys the paralysis and indecision which afflict her on Fosca's departure – a fear-induced paralysis metaphorically represented as a game of cat and mouse with the light: "Il ne fallait pas crier; et pourtant, si elle criait, il lui semblait que quelque chose arriverait; peut-être cette trépidation lancinante se figerait, la *lumière s'éteindrait*" (527; emphasis added).[38] Perhaps not unsurprisingly, given the circularity that can be detected within the narratives of the two novels which have formed the focus of this chapter, Beauvoir's use of lexis in this quotation from the epilogue to *Tous les Hommes sont mortels* in many ways brings us right back to Jean's *veillée funèbre* depicted in the framing narrative of Beauvoir's 1945 novel. While in *Le Sang des autres,* forms of the lexeme *s'éteindre* (to go out; to pass away) appear as collocates of the pronoun *elle* (designating Hélène) and the noun *l'aube,* in the quotation cited above from *Tous les Hommes sont mortels* a further form of the lexeme *s'éteindre* appears as a collocate of the noun *la lumière* (light).

---

[38] "She had to stop herself from screaming. And yet if she screamed, it seemed to her that something would happen. Perhaps that painful trembling would cease, perhaps the light would go out." (AMM 405)

That this is the case suggests that the trajectories mapped out for Hélène and Régine by Beauvoir in many ways constitute parallel journeys. That the bodily inertia/state of death that engulfs Hélène and Régine is played out in the final pages of each novel renders the parallel set up by Beauvoir's texts between personal journey and story/narrative all the more vivid for the reader. Both women are taken on a journey from the "darkness" of inauthenticity to a state of enlightenment, brought about by their gradual recognition of the burden of history. However, in Beauvoir's textual universe, with the dawn of enlightenment comes paralysis and the realisation of inescapable death.

The detailed textual analysis of Beauvoir's 1945 and 1946 novels undertaken in this chapter reveals that the author's thematic preoccupations are matched by a close attention to the particular effects created by narrative structure and lexical play. The circularity mapped out by Beauvoir with respect to narrative composition and lexical patterning facilitates and underscores Beauvoir's textual exploration of the interconnectedness of history and personal testimony, of existential journeys and journeys of the imagination through narrative. What is more, Beauvoir's staging of instances of male-directed storytelling in each of these novels and the involvement of female protagonists in the unfolding – and, in the case of *Tous les Hommes sont mortels,* in the interpretation of those personal narratives – places the female narratee and, implicitly, the real-life reader at the heart of responses to those narratives. That structural, lexical and grammatical patterns are deployed in the service of dominant thematic preoccupations lends these fictional productions richness and cohesion – ironically a cohesion that a number of critics have judged to be sadly lacking from *Tous les Hommes sont mortels* in particular.[39] As my discussion has shown, Beauvoir makes ample use of synonymy, antonymy and techniques involving the repetition and mirroring of lexical and grammatical forms. Yet, despite the frequent points of contact between these texts, *Tous les Hommes sont mortels* marks an important departure from the narrative composition of *Le Sang des autres* with respect to the status accorded to its central female protagonist. While the female narratee featured in the framing narrative of Beauvoir's 1945 novel lies prone in a state of semi-consciousness poised on a threshold between life and death, *Tous les Hommes sont mortels* is noteworthy by virtue of its casting of a female protagonist in the role of an active, even demanding – though no less flawed – narratee.

---

[39] Keefe, *Beauvoir* 178.

Works Cited

Beauvoir, Simone de. *Le Sang des autres*. Paris: Gallimard, 1945.

_____. *Tous les Hommes sont mortels*. Paris: Gallimard, 1946.

_____. *Le Deuxième Sexe*. Paris: Gallimard, 1949.

_____. *La Force de l'âge*. Paris: Gallimard, 1960.

_____. *La Force des choses*. Paris: Gallimard, 1963.

_____. *The Blood of Others*. Trans. Yvonne Moyse and Roger Senhouse. Harmondsworth: Penguin, 1964.

_____. *The Prime of Life*. Trans. Peter Green. Harmondsworth: Penguin, 1965.

_____. *All Men are Mortal*. Trans. Euan Cameron. London: Virago, 1995.

Brosman, Catherine Savage. *Simone de Beauvoir Revisited*. Boston: Twayne, 1991.

Carter, Roland. *Vocabulary: Applied Linguistic Perspectives*. London: Routledge, 1998.

Chatman, Seymour. *Story and Discourse in Fiction and Film*. New York: Cornell University Press, 1978.

Cottrell, Robert D. *Simone de Beauvoir*. New York: Frederick Ungar Publishing, 1975.

Cruse, D.A. *Lexical Semantics*. Cambridge: Cambridge University Press, 1986.

Fallaize, Elizabeth. *The Novels of Simone de Beauvoir*. London: Routledge, 1988.

Genette, Gérard. *Figures III*. Paris: Seuil, 1972.

Hughes, Alex. *Beauvoir. Le Sang des autres*. Glasgow: University of Glasgow French and German Publications, 1995.

Keefe, Terry. *Simone de Beauvoir. A Study of her Writings*. London: Harrap, 1983.

_____. *Simone de Beauvoir*. London: Macmillan, 1998.

Klaw, Barbara. "Subverting the Dominant Order: Narrative as Weapon in Simone de Beauvoir's *Tous les Hommes sont mortels*." *Studies in Contemporary Literature* 20 (2) (1996): 467-90.

Lyons, John. *Introduction to Theoretical Linguistics*. Cambridge: Cambridge University Press, 1968.

_____. *Linguistic Semantics: An Introduction*. Cambridge: Cambridge University Press, 1995.

Rimmon-Kenan, Shlomith. *Narrative Fiction: Contemporary Poetics*. London: Routledge, 1983.

Wales, Katie. *A Dictionary of Stylistics*. Harlow: Pearson Education, 2001.

Wise, Hilary. *The Vocabulary of Modern French*. London: Routledge, 1997.

4 The Case of Henri Perron: Writing and Language in Crisis

Susan Bainbrigge

The decision to focus on the character of Henri Perron in *Les Mandarins* might appear a surprising choice in a book devoted to the study of women and language in the fiction of Simone de Beauvoir. The character of Anne Dubreuilh would seem a more obvious point of reference given her extensive internal monologues which offer the reader access to her innermost thoughts, and which can be compared with the depictions presented of her via other characters, as Elizabeth Richardson Viti does in Chapter 5. Anne's language of death and the ways in which she describes her crises of identity stand out as a particularly rich resource for this type of analysis. Indeed, Heath has argued that "Anne is the most acutely anxious (to the brink of suicide) about her sense of identity".[1] This is certainly the case. However, it could also be argued that Henri Perron's sense of identity and his understanding of his role in society is also shaken. In this chapter, Henri's development as a character will be traced through analysis of his discourse, in particular his reflections about himself, his relationships, his writing, and his politics. His relationship to, and analysis of language will be examined through close textual analysis with particular attention paid to the recurring references in his narrative to "liberté", "bonheur", "vérité", "Histoire", and "histoires".

If Beauvoir stated, "On ne naît pas femme, on le devient", she also wrote in *Tout Compte fait* that "On ne naît pas homme, on le devient": one is not born a man, one becomes one. To what extent does *Les Mandarins* depict different stages of Henri's "becoming" in changing socio-historical circumstances? The character of Henri presents the opportunity for Beauvoir to explore the relationship between writing and action, past and present, public and private, men and women, self and other. In particular, his identity as a writer suggests that he enjoys a privileged relationship to language. However, before moving on to consider his use of language in more detail, Beauvoir's decision to explore the role of the *writer* through a male rather than a female character first needs to be considered.

---

[1] Jane Heath, *Simone de Beauvoir* (Hemel Hempstead: Harvester Wheatsheaf, 1989) 98.

Beauvoir maintained the need to express herself via different genres, and through both her male and female characters. She wrote in *La Force des choses,* for example, that she did not recognise herself any less in *Le Deuxième Sexe* than in *Les Mandarins,* and argued that this diversity was necessary to her in her writing.[2] Indeed, Beauvoir's justification for choosing both male and female narrators in this work, and for the writer to be male, is revealing as far as gender stereotyping is concerned: if Anne had been a writer, Beauvoir argues, she would have been considered a special case, but by giving a man this occupation, his character was more likely to be read as "universal" (FC I 360). What is more, Beauvoir also stated in *La Force des choses* that she had recounted negative aspects of her experiences via Anne (fear of death and nothingness, the shame of forgetting, the scandal of living, and so on),[3] and through Henri the joy of living and the pleasure of writing ("la joie d'exister, la gaieté d'entreprendre, le plaisir d'écrire" [FC I 365]), arguing that Henri was just as much a character based on her as Anne, if not more so.[4] Thus it would appear fruitful to study in detail the way in which language is used to reflect the changing realities of both narrators in this work. Beauvoir's comment that Anne is the negative to Henri's positive ("elle me fournissait le négatif des objets qui se découvraient à travers Henri sous une figure positive" [FC I 360]) suggests that Henri is not plagued by doubt and fear.[5] However, this is not necessarily the case: his positive outlook on the world is dramatically shaken after the experiences of the Second World War. In a scene early in the novel Henri finds himself contemplating his changed circumstances as he sits writing in Portugal. He questions whether he knows any more what happiness and

---

[2] "Mes essais reflètent mes options pratiques et mes certitudes intellectuelles; mes romans, l'étonnement où me jette, en gros ou dans ses détails, notre condition humaine. Ils correspondent à deux ordres d'expérience qu'on ne saurait communiquer de la même manière. Les unes et les autres ont pour moi autant d'importance et d'authenticité. Je ne me reconnais pas moins dans *Le Deuxième Sexe* que dans *Les Mandarins*; et inversement. Si je me suis exprimée sur deux registres, c'est que cette diversité m'était nécessaire". (FC II 62)

[3] See FC I 365.

[4] In her autobiography, Beauvoir also denied the suggestion that Henri was based on Camus, and went on to reaffirm again her own identification with the character: "et la plupart du temps, ce sont mes propres émotions, mes propres pensées qui l'habitent" (FC I 366).

[5] See also her comments from a lecture delivered in Japan in 1966 entitled, "Mon expérience d'écrivain": "J'ai donné à Henri le sens d'une action à faire, le goût de la vie, le goût de l'engagement: il est un homme parmi les hommes qui est heureux de l'être, qui veut se battre parmi eux. [...] Le point de vue d'Anne conteste celui de Henri: souvent Anne trouve que Henri est fou de tant s'agiter pour des choses terrestres, alors qu'on mourra: mais inversement Henri trouve qu'il est facile de se dire qu'un jour on mourra, et d'échapper par là à l'engagement, à l'action. Finalement, je ne donne raison ni à l'un ni à l'autre", in *Les Écrits de Simone de Beauvoir* (Paris: Gallimard, 1979) 444.

pleasure, words he considers to be "old words", really mean ("Il ne savait plus bien ce que voulait dire les vieux mots: bonheur, plaisir" [LM I 154]). This crisis of meaning sets the scene for Henri's crises throughout the novel; these, broadly speaking, could be said to encompass a crisis of language (of words not being able to communicate a given reality, or to be subject to multiple and sometimes conflicting significations) and a crisis of values (in terms of a questioning of the role or even the importance of the intellectual or writer). Elizabeth Fallaize notes that, "although the 'old humanism' of the intellectual is severely strained in the novel, many of its values survive, though not as absolutes".[6] The way in which these strains manifest themselves through the language and actions of Henri will be the focus here. Henri's humanist, universalist ideals are certainly made clear in early descriptions of him in the novel. Although he does not see himself as a particularly gifted or ambitious writer or activist he believes in the role that he might play as a writer in striving for a greater good: "Un homme comme tout le monde, qui parlerait sincèrement de lui, il parlerait au nom de tout le monde, pour tout le monde" (LM I 82).[7] This universalist stance is tested throughout the novel.[8]

Some examples of the ways in which Henri, against the backdrop of the Liberation and the renewed debate on the role of the intellectual that characterised the post-war period, struggles to come to terms with his role(s) as writer, intellectual, friend, and lover will now be examined. First of all, Henri's moral framework is tested by a series of ethical dilemmas – he is torn, for example, over whether to publish information about the Salazar regime in Portugal in the journal *L'Espoir* at the risk of cutting off the journal's American sponsor. The question whether to make public reports that demonstrate the existence of Soviet camps is even more traumatic, and his decision to publish the reports culminates in his break with Dubreuilh, his long-standing friend and mentor. Finally, his reputation is seriously tarnished when he provides a false testimony to protect his lover Josette, a testimony which effectively silences the experiences of two young women who had

---

6 Elizabeth Fallaize, *The Novels of Simone de Beauvoir* (London and New York: Routledge, 1988) 97-98.
7 "A man like everyone else, who spoke sincerely of himself, would speak in the name of everyone, for everyone." (M 68)
8 This can be compared with Beauvoir's comment about her own stance in *La Force des choses*: "Pour parler de moi, il fallait parler de nous, au sens qu'avait eu ce mot en 1944". (FC I 361) The importance of the collective stance is often emphasised in her work as a revolt against bourgeois individualism, a stance that was sharpened after the author's own experiences of the Second World War.

been denounced by a Gestapo informant (Mercier) and, as a result, spent a year in Dachau.[9] It could also be argued that Henri's behaviour towards Paule verges on the reprehensible, although Henri himself is on the whole oblivious to this potential charge.

To these key events may be added the more general malaise that underpins Henri's depiction of past and present, which is interlinked with his perception of himself as a writer. The past becomes a nightmarish leitmotif in the novel: Henri can neither escape nor ignore it. He wishes to write a novel that will represent a break from the past, and from any bourgeois affiliation, and to do so, he places an emphasis on the potential for change (his own "becoming") offered by the present and the future ("il tenait avant tout à redevenir un homme" [LM I 18]).[10] The past is described as a booby trap – "un attrape-nigaud" (LM I 469-70), and images of imprisonment and enclosure become associated in Henri's mind with his own past, whether in a political or a personal context. Henri warns others, such as Nadine, of the dangers of living in the past, and despairs when Paule rereads old love letters, telling her, "tu ferais mieux de ne pas t'ensevelir dans le passé et de vivre un peu plus dans le présent" (LM I p. 470). However, Henri also has his own demons to fight. Linked to his questioning of the relative merits of capturing the past or saving the present through the writing act is an uncertainty about the value to be attached to humankind:

> Récupérer le passé, sauver le présent avec des mots, c'est bien joli: mais ça ne peut se faire qu'en les racontant aux autres; ça n'a de sens que si le passé, si le présent pèsent lourd. Si ce monde n'a pas d'importance, si les autres hommes ne comptent pas, à quoi bon écrire? (LM I 235-36)[11]

Ultimately, the past becomes bound up with a feeling of guilt for having survived, and this guilt plays a role in his equivocal stance as far as writing is concerned. Henri's contemplations of his role as writer, reveal his increasing scepticism about the power of words to effect change. Indeed, it

---

[9] As Ursula Tidd has noted, in certain respects Henri "fails to fulfil his intellectual mission when he temporarily eschews probity and perjures himself to save the bourgeois Josette" (p. 8), in "Testimony, Historicity and the Intellectual in Simone de Beauvoir's *Les Mandarins*" (forthcoming). She also examines his dilemmas about speaking out and his abuse of testimony (pp. 12-19).

[10] The unwelcome presence of a childhood acquaintance, Louis, also serves to remind him of the difficulties in escaping the past. (LM II 122)

[11] "To recapture the past and preserve the present with words is all very fine. But it can be done only if there is someone to read them; there's no sense to it except if the past, if the present, if life counts for something. If this world has no importance, if other men mean nothing, what point would there be to writing?" (M 192)

is revealing that the title of his play about the Occupation is called *Les Survivants* (a title that Beauvoir had considered herself for her novel before settling on *Les Mandarins)*[12]. Furthermore, Henri's statement that friendship ("la cameraderie") belongs to another era, and his suggestion of resignedly following the crowd ("Il n'y a qu'à suivre la foule" [LM II 294]) reinforce his view that both the potential to act independently and also to be part of a community have been seriously compromised.

After the horrors of the Second World War, Henri asserts that writing is about showing others how one perceives the world ("montrer aux autres le monde comme on le voit" [LM I 425]), and yet he claims that he has failed in his task to do just that. He rapidly abandons his "roman gai" and is plunged into a crisis that culminates in his decision to abandon writing. His disenchantment with writing is revealed through his questioning of the extent to which language can communicate his reality, and what that reality precisely is: "Ma vérité: qu'est-ce que ça signifie au juste? Il regardait stupidement la page blanche. Plonger dans le vide, les mains vides, c'est intimidant!" (LM I 197).[13] Terrorised by the blank page, words fail him. The preoccupations of his new (politically engaged) reality provoke a far-reaching questioning of his value systems. In the chapters devoted to Henri's point of view, alternating first- and third-person narrative voices heighten the sense of an internal conflict and reveal Henri's doubts about his commitment to the writing project. In particular, the novel he plans to situate around 1935, he no longer has any desire to write; he no longer wishes to portray "un monde dépassé" and he no longer recognises the self he was in 1935 (LM I 196).[14] Thus, a vocabulary evoking a death of self, a past that bears no relation to the present, and an uncertainty about the nature of his reality all inform Henri's questioning of the writing project.

Henri's scepticism about writing is heightened by his own observations on the reception of his work. For instance, he begins to suspect that the success of his first novel is simply a result of a series of misunderstandings ("Henri finissait par penser qu'il devait son succès à des malentendus" [LM I 192]). To illustrate his point, he cites examples of the different ways in which his book has been interpreted: Lambert, for whom Henri serves as role

---

[12] See Fallaize, *Novels* 92.

[13] "My truth. But what does that really mean? He looked dully at the blank page. 'It's frightening, plunging into empty space with nothing to clutch at.'" (M 161)

[14] "Il voulait parler de lui: eh bien, il n'avait plus rien à voir avec ce qu'il était en 1935." (LM I 225) Paris and the Occupation are referred to as a dead world that has taken Henri's future. (LM I 263)

model and mentor, believes that he is attempting to glorify individualism through collective action whereas Lachaume, of communist sympathies, thinks that he is advocating the sacrifice of the individual to the collectivity (LM I 192). He laments the fact that the public seems to have loved a book that bears no resemblance to the one he thinks he has written. Fact and fiction become for Henri a shifting reality: his fictional world overlaps with his lived experiences (an interlinking that will provoke Nadine's disapproval), and when he becomes embroiled in Josette's "tale" he will liken his life to an unreal "décor de comédie" (LM II 318). The anticipation of the reception of his play takes on in his mind the gravitas of a trial with the audience playing the role of the jury. Henri depicts himself as the criminal convinced that he will be found guilty (LM II 117-18), and refuses to believe that a positive reception from the audience would be sincere anyway (LM II 120). Finally, the idea that writing could offer a means of capturing the truth of one's existence is suspected by Henri to be illusory – "un mirage" (LM I 152). Language thus becomes an increasingly fragile and unstable means of communication.

However, it is not just the reception of his work that fuels Henri's questioning. The way in which his own persona is, in his view, "distorted" by others also shakes his perception of self, often in humorous ways. Marie-Ange Bizet, the ambitious journalist who interviews him for an article, presents him in such a light that Henri describes the act of reading the article as akin to a process of self-discovery: "[…] devant ces lignes imprimées il retrouvait la foi naïve du paysan qui lit la Bible: comme si à travers ces phrases qu'il avait suscitées lui-même il avait pu enfin apprendre qui il était" (LM I 191).[15] She has transformed him into "un sous-Rastignac pour midinettes" (LM I 192), he claims scathingly, his words revealing his own antipathy to being compared to a lesser version of Balzac's ambitious young hero with the added indignity of the journalist's frivolous slant. More generally, by dint of the dual narrative framework, depictions of characters are open to multiple perspectives. Henri's viewpoint is counterbalanced by Anne's and often the latter sheds further light from an external perspective on Henri's situation.[16]

---

[15] "Yet reading those printed words, he felt a little of the naïve faith of a peasant reading the Bible. It was as if he had succeeded at last in discovering himself through words he himself had fathered." (M 156)

[16] Terry Keefe argues that, "the significance of the dual narrative lies as much in the greater range of places and circumstances that it allows Beauvoir to cover in the novel as in the presentation of different 'truths'", in *Simone de Beauvoir: A Study of her Writings* (London: Harrap, 1983) 197.

In fact, the labelling of Henri by others is extensive and offers further examples of the ways in which language is increasingly viewed as a distortive tool. At a point when their relationship is at its most strained, Lachaume calls Henri a fascist (LM II 160) and Henri is shocked generally by the hostile stance of the communists towards him, some of whom had previously been his friends (LM II 163). Where Louis comments on his "humanisme" with women (LM II 126), Nadine criticizes his frequenting of what she calls a "sale monde", notably Claudie de Belzunce's circle of friends (LM II 167). Henri himself is appalled to be approved of and fêted by this group (LM II 172) and imagines that others will see him as a "social-traître", a self-image that further reinforces his feelings of culpability with respect to the role he plays to protect Josette. Such depictions are accompanied by Henri's sense of horror when faced with these multiple reflections.

In addition, Henri's crises of faith are further sharpened by his negotiations of the relationship between public and private spheres, and between "History" and "stories". The fact that the French word "histoire" encompasses both the supposedly factual History and fictional "stories" gives further credence to Henri's equivocal stance. Initially for him the terms "Histoire" and "histoires" are disconnected: this explains why he feels that after the war he has nothing of value to say and that his experiences are not worthy of comment: "Qu'est-ce que les gens ont à foutre de ce que je pense, moi, ou de ce que je sens? dit Henri. Mes petites histoires n'intéressent personne; et la grande histoire n'est pas un sujet de roman" (LM I 375).[17] It is Dubreuilh who disabuses him of his belief by telling him that everyone has personal stories that may not be of any apparent particular interest, but that this is how we discover ourselves in our neighbours, and our stories, if well told, may have a universal significance. Furthermore, Henri's attachment to his privacy and his belief that his private affairs could be kept from the public sphere reveals his initially naïve stance (LM II 169). In fact, after the publication of Lachaume's critical article, Henri is shocked that there might be repercussions relating to his personal affairs. In response to his belief that it is immoral to divulge information about his private life, it is Vincent who reminds him that he has no private life any more: "Tu es un homme public; tout ce que tu fais tombe dans le domaine public: en voilà la preuve!"

---

[17] "'Why should people give a damn about what I think, what I feel?' Henri said. 'My little personal stories don't interest anyone, and history, the big story, isn't in my opinion a fit subject for a novel.'" (M 301)

(LM II 162). Henri's viewpoint is tempered further by events throughout the course of the novel; they reveal the constant intertwining of public and private spheres and a revised position emerges. After the reception of his play and in the light of his guilty conscience about his false testimony, he affirms to Josette that fame is also a humiliation ("La célébrité aussi est une humiliation" [LM II 130], his words suggesting that any public attention will have a negative side. This stance is echoed in later comments that also testify to Henri's realisation that his private affairs cannot escape the public gaze: "[…] d'avoir prétendu garder une vie privée alors que l'action exige un homme tout entier?" [LM II 333]). Finally, it is Dubreuilh again who reminds him that his false testimony serves as example of the fact that private morality does not exist, that it forms part of an outdated value system that no longer carries any meaning: "C'est que la morale privée, ça n'existe pas. Encore un de ces trucs auxquels nous avons cru et qui n'ont aucun sens" (LM II 343).[18] The overlap of public and private spheres now blurs the previously clear boundaries that Henri had established in order to protect himself, the wholesale rejection by Dubreuilh of any distinct private morality further informing Henri's stance.

Inevitably, Henri's personal affairs cannot escape scrutiny in the context of his perception of the relationship between public and private spheres. Indeed, Terry Keefe's description of *Les Mandarins* as "a richly illustrated rumination on the nature of love" serves as reminder that the novel is not concerned solely with post-war politics and ideology.[19] The virtues of a "room of one's own" are initially extolled by Henri in a desperate bid to escape the suffocating environment he has shared with his lover Paule (LM I 131, 189). Writing and relationships are presented as mutually exclusive and relationships with women are held at arm's length if they threaten to encroach on his personal autonomy. This is particularly the case with Paule (and raises questions to be considered in due course concerning his questionable "language of love"). However, it could be argued that as far as Henri's relationships with women are concerned, and in particular with Paule and Nadine, there is some ambiguity and confusion in the stance that is revealed via his discourse on love. Henri's status

---

[18] "[That] personal morality just doesn't exist. Another one of those things we used to believe in and which have no meaning." (M 645) Elizabeth Fallaize argues that Dubreuilh's argument "is too generalised for Henri; the key question for him is to know what Dubreuilh – as an individual – would have done in his place." (95)

[19] Keefe, *Beauvoir* 192

in the novel could be viewed by modern readers as rather ambivalent. On the one hand, he is depicted as a respected writer and intellectual. However, his reputation is tainted by the false testimony that he provides to protect his lover Josette. Furthermore, his misogynistic comments about women, and especially Paule, do not pass unnoticed by the reader.[20] As critics such as Elizabeth Fallaize have noted, Henri echoes dominant patriarchal discourses on heterosexual relationships representative of a particular socio-historical context.[21] And yet his discourse is also influenced by theories expounded in *Le Deuxième Sexe*. For example, Henri's insistence that Paule be more independent could be compared to Beauvoir's critique of the dependency of "l'amoureuse", who according to Beauvoir, "[...] en s'assumant comme l'inessentiel, en acceptant une totale dépendance, [la femme] se crée un enfer" (DS II 561).[22] Often Henri's misgivings are echoed by Anne, who baulks at comments made by Paule stressing their interdependence ("nous sommes un seul être", [LM I 295]). Love itself is the subject of speculation in the text in a way that echoes comments made in Beauvoir's theoretical text. In the relationship between Henri and Paule love is presented as an experience that is felt differently by the two partners. Beauvoir had already examined in *Le Deuxième Sexe* different interpretations of the word "love" and the resultant misunderstandings between the sexes which ensue:

> Le mot 'amour' n'a pas du tout le même sens pour l'un et l'autre sexe et c'est là une source de graves malentendus qui les séparent. Byron dit justement que l'amour n'est dans la vie de l'homme qu'une occupation, tandis qu'il est la vie même de la femme (DS II 546).[23]

---

[20] Fallaize notes that "The relationship with Paule places Henri in a particularly unsympathetic light" (112).

[21] She writes that, "The question of Henri's sexism is more difficult, but it seems quite likely that Beauvoir was simply endowing her character with traits she perceived in her male entourage, and which she did not identify at the time of writing as sexist. The fundamental thesis of *The Second Sex* that femininity is a social construct naturally implies that the same is true of masculinity, and Anne's remarks show that Beauvoir had taken this idea on board. However *The Second Sex*, whilst devoting a series of chapters to the socialisation of women, did not engage in an investigation of the construction of masculinity, and it is not really surprising to note Beauvoir's uncritical portrayal of sexist and stereotypical masculine traits in a positively coded male character" (113).

[22] "[...] woman, in assuming her role as the inessential, accepting a total dependence, creates a hell for herself." (SS 664) Beauvoir writes in detail in the third volume of her autobiography, *La Force des choses*, about the way in which she had imagined the character of Paule: "Je conçus Paule comme une femme radicalement aliénée à un homme et le tyrannisant au nom de cet esclavage: une amoureuse. [...] je savais combien il est dangereux pour une femme de s'engager tout de soi dans sa liaison avec un écrivain ou un artiste, buté sur ses projets: renonçant à ses goûts, à ses occupations, elle s'exténue à l'imiter sans le rejoindre et s'il se détourne d'elle, elle se trouve dépouillée de tout; j'avais vu quantité d'exemples de cette déchéance et j'avais envie d'en parler." (FC I 362) See also Fallaize 109.

[23] Note also that Henri asserts that it is impossible for a man to desire indefinitely the same body. (LM I 473)

This statement would appear to reinforce the distinction made between men's and women's behaviour in this context, with Beauvoir's emphasis falling on the ways in which social conditioning shapes differentiated male and female responses, her critique highlighting the particular dangers for women of assuming the dependent position of "l'amoureuse". Some of Beauvoir's concerns about women's complicity with their situation appear to be recycled via both Anne and Henri's thoughts on Paule, and terms such as "aveuglement" and "égoïsme" used by Henri (LM I 470) may be found in critiques of "mauvaise foi" and references to "l'amoureuse" in *Le Deuxième Sexe*. In the text these problems transcend questions of gender insofar as both Anne and Henri have difficulties with Paule, notably as far as communication is concerned: language is either viewed as being unequal to the task or subject to misinterpretation. Thus Anne's self-reproach is based on her inability to communicate with Paule ("'Je n'ai pas su lui parler, j'ai été maladroite', me dis-je avec reproche en la quittant" [LM I 296]). Henri's failure to communicate his message is highlighted when Paule fails to or chooses not to read the indictment of their relationship in the manuscript of the novel that Henri tentatively gives her to read, a reaction that is dramatically different from the reaction that Henri imagined (LM I 452, 468). This is a further example of the way in which language (here, in the context of personal relationships) is shown to be an inadequate tool in some situations, and open to multiple interpretations in others.

Furthermore, by the time Henri sets up home with Nadine towards the end of the novel, a shift in his thinking can be traced. At the end of the novel he no longer describes himself in terms of the entrapment that characterised his descriptions of both the political context of post-war Paris and the personal context of his relationship with Paule. As a new father, he articulates more realistic expectations but also revises once and for all his understanding of the meaning of happiness. In Henri's lexicon the term no longer has any meaning ("Heureux: le fait est que le mot n'avait plus de sens. On ne possède jamais le monde: pas question non plus de se protéger contre lui" [LM II 490]). This is understood to be linked to the fact that humankind can no longer lay claim to "possess" or control the world nor be protected against it. His commitment to marrying Nadine and to raising his child reveals an underlying logic peculiar to Henri, namely that he tries to reassure Nadine about his feelings for her, in the knowledge that she may have engineered the pregnancy to force his hand in marriage and argues that it is precisely the fact that he was never duped by her intentions that meant that he never felt entrapped by the relationship (LM II 431). In his revised conception of relationships he reveals the particular limitations of this one: he is not convinced that he can make Nadine happy and is unsure whether he is able to love her fully (LM II 432). His revised stance, a more muted "Oui, ce qu'on préfère à tout, on l'aime" (LM II 479)[24], as Elizabeth Fallaize has highlighted, signals the replacement of utopian ideals with an ethos of preference (97). For Henri, managing ("se débrouiller") now replaces any strict adhesion to any political or moral frameworks.

In fact, the conflict for Henri between freedom and happiness that initially appears in the context of rather stereotyped male-female relationships is developed to encompass a more general conflict between interdependence and imprisonment, in political, geographical and personal terms. Politically, Henri is bound by certain party political lines and discovers that he has limited room for manœuvre. Geographically, he longs to escape to pastures new after the imprisoning years of the Occupation, whether to Portugal or Italy. Personally, he fears enslavement in his relationships with women, particularly with Paule, and becomes embroiled in a catch-22 situation with respect to Josette ("Quoi qu'il fît, il aurait tort: tort s'il divulguait une vérité tronquée, tort s'il dissimulait, fût-elle tronquée, une vérité" [LM I 501]). In most of these cases he reaches a position of compromise or reconciliation by the end of the novel, whether with Dubreuilh regarding political engagement (they both agree that literature has a role to play but have less idealistic expectations),[25] or as regards his decision to remain in France (but beyond the confines of Paris) rather than go to Italy. However, his decisions are not taken lightly and continue to cause anguish to the author throughout the text.

Finally, it could be argued that Henri's self-perception (and the anguish that comes to characterise his situation, referred to in previous sections of this chapter) is thrown more sharply into relief through analysis of another key relationship, this time of a non-sexual nature. The relationship between Henri and Robert Dubreuilh forms a central axis of the narrative and offers a further means to explore Henri's situation, notably what differentiates the

---

24 See also his comments on Paule and Nadine: "Préférer le vide au plein, c'est ce qu'il avait reproché à Paule […]. Inversement, il n'avait jamais cherché en Nadine 'la femme idéale' […]." (LM II 462)
25 As Elizabeth Fallaize observes, "Literature and individual experience need not be abandoned, as long as the individual is not seen in isolation from a wider context" (97).

men from other men in the novel. If Henri in his relationships with women broadly reflects Beauvoir's thesis that "Il est le sujet, elle est l'Autre", his relationship with Dubreuilh presents a different dynamic in which Henri's sense of self is shaken. Indeed, at times it could be argued that he views himself as alienated "Other". Mary Orr has noted in her study of Flaubert and masculinity that, "in the public domain, success for men is a key term for establishing status, both within a same-sex hierarchy, and in relationships and their codification between the sexes. Failure is then to be avoided at all costs as social stigma, particularly damaging if one is male".[26] Although the sociohistorical context is very different, the sentiment holds as true for the male characters in *Les Mandarins* as it does for those in *Madame Bovary*. Henri constantly measures himself against Dubreuilh and often presents himself in unfavourable terms in his comparisons. Their unequal relationship can be traced back to the fact that the latter served as a mentor for the aspiring writer, as we learn in the interview that Henri grants to the journalist Marie-Ange Bizet (LM I 170).[27] In particular, in terms of their career success, Henri is envious of Dubreuilh's capacity for hard work and his productive writing career. Henri claims to have been unable to emulate his mentor; he refers in particular to having been reduced from human to machine-like status in his attempts to match Dubreuilh's strict regime. This description of the self as inhuman carries echoes of the depersonalisation and loss of purpose of an increasingly technological society (one capable of dropping atom bombs, for example). Henri emphasises his own limitations, and through his eyes, Dubreuilh becomes increasingly monster-like in his tenacious drive to write: "Ce monstre de Dubreuilh ne se laisse pas dévorer, dit Henri avec une espèce d'envie: il écrit autant qu'autrefois" (LM I 315).

The perception of owing a debt of gratitude combined with Henri's inferiority complex underlines his subsequent dealings with Dubreuilh. The former perceives the relationship to be an unequal one in which Dubreuilh, to his mind, is successful at manipulating him to get what he wants. This emerges, for example, in Henri's analysis of discussions they have about linking *L'Espoir* to the SRL (and the pressure that he feels Dubreuilh exerts on him), and in his frequent ruminations after conversations with Dubreuilh in which he is susceptible to self-doubt. In general

---

[26] Mary Orr, *Madame Bovary: Representations of the Masculine* (Bern: Peter Lang, 1999) 12.
[27] Comparisons could be made here with the unequal power balance between Anne and her husband that has its roots in their tutor/student relationship.

terms, Henri remains convinced of his friend's ability to have the upper hand: "Jusqu'à sa mort, Dubreuilh continuerait à prendre des supériorités sur son propre passé et sur celui des autres" (LM II 455). Dubreuilh appears to know Henri's mind better than Henri does, suggesting to him, for example, that he will not last more than a year in Italy (LM II 449). At the same time Henri admires Dubreuilh as a public figure and is anxious about falling out with him because of his status and the sense of security he has offered Henri in the past. Even the apparent demonstration of empathy from Dubreuilh and Anne when they learn of Henri's perjury reinforces his discomfort ("l'indulgence de Dubreuilh et d'Anne", [LM II 433]) when faced with their pity. Certainly, other characters, such as Lambert, are of the opinion that Dubreuilh's influence is pernicious ("Lambert commençait par déplorer une fois de plus la néfaste influence exercée par Dubreuilh: c'était sa faute si après un brillant départ Henri avait perdu tout talent" [LM II 450]). Paule complains too that Henri always gives in to Dubreuilh's demands (LM I 187).

Thus a portrait is painted of their relationship in which Henri is presented as a divided self in the manner of a number of Beauvoir's female characters (Anne in this text, Laurence in *Les Belles Images*), rather than the "homme total" to which he refers in the quotation below. A certain modesty and self-critique is evident in Henri's self-representation in which he situates himself not as a role model, as some of his devotees would like, but as a *petit bourgeois* writer juggling obligations and preferences: "Mais c'est idiot cette idée d'homme total. En fait, je suis un écrivain petit-bourgeois qui se débrouille tant bien que mal et plutôt mal que bien entre ses obligations et ses goûts: rien de plus" (LM II 488).[28]

However, given the fact that Henri is brought closer to Anne and Robert through his relationship with Nadine, might we question whether the dynamics of this relationship are more complex than at first glance? The reader learns earlier in the novel that Henri is attracted to Anne but it is not just the fact that she is an old friend, but also Dubreuilh's wife, that stops

---

28 "This idea of a total man is idiotic. Actually I'm just a petit-bourgeois writer who steers his course more or less well – and usually rather less well – between his obligations and his desires. That's all." (M 753) This echoes an earlier comment on writing in which Henri accepts its limitations but nonetheless identifies the challenge for the individual to bring their particular reality to writing ("chacun a un goût"): "[...] on ne peut pas tout dire, d'accord, mais on peut tout de même tenter de rendre le vrai goût de sa vie: chacun a un goût, qui n'est qu'à elle, et il faut le dire, ou ce n'est pas la peine d'écrire." (LM I 82)

him from pursuing her. Instead, he becomes involved with her daughter. Henri's closer contact with the Dubreuilh family through Nadine prompts the reader to wonder whether this serves as a means for Henri to regain some of his status or to seek approval by marrying their daughter. Or alternatively, could his position be viewed as one that ultimately threatens the father-daughter relationship? Both Anne *and* Henri define themselves in terms of their relationship with Dubreuilh. In fact Henri's relationship with Anne appears to be more equally balanced (and this is reflected by the alternating narrative voices that structure the story). Beauvoir writes that for both Anne and Henri, "demain est incertain" (FC I 368). As narrators they have more in common than might at first appear.

To conclude, Henri's development as a character, as evidenced through his negotiations with language, has not always been a focus for critics. Yet his experiences of otherness and alienation, his reflections on (and frequent self-condemnation of) the effects of his actions and changing responses in the light of this reflection tell us much about how he engages with himself, his contemporaries, his culture, and his era, and reveals the intricate interconnections between language, institutions, subjectivity and power. In *Les Mandarins* we gain an insight into many of the complex philosophical, cultural and political problems faced in the post-World War Two era, a questioning of identity in the making and the undoing of humanist certainties. We have seen that key terms such as "liberté", "bonheur", "vérité", Histoire" and "histoires" recur in Henri's narrative and reveal the underlying tensions between competing philosophies of living and the ways in which external circumstances shape his reponses. Henri's own conclusion on writing is based on the view that talking and acting are better than doing nothing ("Faire quelque chose, ne fût-ce que parler, c'était mieux que de rester assis dans son coin avec ce poids obscur sur le cœur" [LM II 486]; "On n'arrête pas une guerre avec des mots; *mais la parole ne prétend pas forcément changer l'histoire: c'est aussi une certaine manière de la vivre. Dans le silence de ce bureau, abandonné à ses cauchemars intimes, Henri sentait qu'il la vivait mal*" [LM II 486-87, my emphasis]). The suggestive references to "poids obscur" and "cauchemars intimes" in the preceding quotations give an intimation of the darker side of Henri's character that this chapter has endeavoured to highlight. I have suggested that Beauvoir's exploration of the human condition via Henri could also be viewed in terms of a masculine condition, not just in the light of his relationships and encounters with women but also in the context of his negotiations with men. The subject-other relationship at the heart of the thesis of *Le Deuxième Sexe* recurs as a key analytical model in this work, but is not restricted to the male-female binary opposition. If the character of Anne was initially cited as an obvious target for explorations of crises of identity, Henri's mirror narrative also offers scope for this type of analysis, especially as far as the relationship between language, writing and self-definition is concerned.

Works Cited

Beauvoir, Simone de. *Le Deuxième Sexe*. Vol. II. [1949] Paris: Gallimard, 1992.

_____. *The Second Sex*. [1953] Harmondsworth: Penguin, 1977.

_____. *La Force des choses*. Paris: Gallimard, 1963.

_____. *Les Mandarins*. Paris: Gallimard, 1954.

_____. *Les Écrits de Simone de Beauvoir*. Paris: Gallimard, 1979.

Heath, Jane. *Simone de Beauvoir*. Hemel Hempstead: Harvester Wheatsheaf, 1989.

Fallaize, Elizabeth, *The Novels of Simone de Beauvoir*. London and New York: Routledge, 1988.

Keefe, Terry. *Simone de Beauvoir: A Study of her Writings*. London: Harrap, 1983.

Orr, Mary. *Madame Bovary: Representations of the Masculine*. Bern: Peter Lang, 1999.

5

A Questionable Balance: Anne Dubreuilh and the Language of Identity Crisis

Elizabeth Richardson Viti

L*es Mandarins* holds a unique position in Simone de Beauvoir's *oeuvre* for a variety of well-known reasons, but it is of particular interest to feminist literary inquiry. Promoted as a quasi-autobiography, or what today we would call autofiction, the novel is Beauvoir's second last; however, it is the first to allow a female protagonist, Anne Dubreuilh, to speak for herself, to use "I". This is in sharp contrast to the book's second narrator, Henri Perron, for as Elizabeth Fallaize points out, although the two narrators are of broadly equal weight, Henri, a heterodiegetic narrator, is represented by an unspecified third person who remains outside the fictional structure and who cannot be confused with the author; Anne, a homodiegetic narrator, speaks in the first person and privileges this confusion.[1] Beauvoir herself suggested this conflation of the woman in the novel with the woman behind it when she claimed that, in addition to her memoirs, *Les Mandarins* was "my most important work about myself".[2] Thus, because Anne Dubreuilh undergoes an identity crisis during which she seesaws back and forth between two conflicting personae, it appears that Beauvoir was also calling into question her own sense of self. It is Anne's language that exposes this questionable balance.

When Anne first speaks as narrator – "Non, ce n'est pas aujourd'hui que je connaîtrai ma mort; ni aujourd'hui, ni aucun jour. Je serai morte pour les autres sans jamais m'être vue mourir" (LM I 41)[3] – her ruminations about death simultaneously underscore the manner in which she hesitates between two conflicting perspectives and lend perfect symmetry to *Les Mandarins*. It is she who closes the novel with a contemplation of suicide but who does an about-face when the sound of her daughter Nadine's voice saves her.[4] Her identity crisis clearly unresolved, Anne uses interior

---

[1] Elizabeth Fallaize, "Narrative Structure in *Les Mandarins*," *Literature and Society: Studies in Nineteenth and Twentieth Century French Literature*, Ed. C.A. Burns (Birmingham: John Goodman & Sons, 1980) 221.

[2] Deirdre Bair, *Simone de Beauvoir* (New York: Summit Books, 1990) 321.

[3] "No, I shan't meet death today. Not today or any other day. I'll be dead for others and yet I'll never have known death." (M 30)

[4] Yolanda Patterson, "Mothers and Daughters in Postwar France: Simone de Beauvoir's *Les Mandarins*," *Simone de Beauvoir Studies* 2 (1984) 51.

monologue as frequently as she does in the first chapter. More importantly, her last words are in the form of a question: "Qui sait? Peut-être un jour serai-je de nouveau heureuse. Qui sait?" (LM II 501).[5] This final note of doubt could not be more fitting because Anne questions herself incessantly throughout this interior monologue, undermining any notion that she is an entirely autonomous woman sure of her own identity. The reader has only to move through her opening reflections to encounter this phenomenon. She asks herself, for example, why death is once again haunting her dreams, prowling about (LM I 41), and in the course of her initial narration alone, Anne questions herself a stunning sixty times, wondering about everything from how others confront their ineluctable death (LM I 41) to whether her husband Robert's devotion to humanism will somehow be defeated (LM II 81). In addition, when not explicitly posing a question, Anne's syntactical formulae set up oppositions more often than would normally be the case. Thinking about the holiday celebration she just attended, she notes, "C'est fête cette nuit: le *premier* Noël de paix; le *dernier* Noël de Buchenwald, le *dernier* Noël sur terre, le *premier* Noël que Diégo n'a pas vécu" (LM I 43; emphasis added).[6] A few moments later Anne reflects, "*Les morts sont morts; pour eux, il n'y a pas de problèmes; mais nous les vivants,* après cette nuit de fête, nous allons nous réveiller; et alors *comment vivrons-nous?*" (LM II 47; emphasis added).[7] But the most crucial contradiction is the one in which Anne herself explicitly reveals her identity crisis: "Me voilà donc clairement cataloguée et acceptant de l'être, adaptée à mon mari, à mon métier, à la vie, à la mort, au monde, à ses horreurs. C'est moi, tout juste moi, *c'est-à-dire personne*" (LM I 49; emphasis added),[8] seconded later in the opening chapter with "*Je ne suis personne,* c'est facile à dire: *je suis moi.* Qui est-ce? Où me rencontrer?" (LM I 60; emphasis added).[9]

Furthermore, the novel's major characters reveal how tenuous Anne's identity is, and her husband Robert is first among them. Yolanda Patterson notes that Anne's "identity, like that of so many wives and mothers, has rested upon her certainty that she is indispensable to another human being, a

[5] "Who knows? Perhaps one day I'll be happy again. Who knows?" (M 610)
[6] "Tonight's a holiday, the first Christmas of peace, the last Christmas at Buchenwald, the last Christmas on earth, the first Christmas that Diego hasn't lived through." (M 32)
[7] "The dead are dead; for them there are no more problems. But after this night of festivity, we, the living, will awaken again. And then how shall we live?" (M 35)
[8] "There I am then, clearly catalogued and willing to be so, adjusted to my husband, to my profession, to life, to death, to the world and all its horrors; me, precisely me, that is to say, no one." (M 35)
[9] "I'm no one. It's easy of course to say 'I am I.' But who am I?" (M 43)

certainty which no longer exists for her".[10] Anne, who met Dubreuilh when he was her professor at the Sorbonne, explains how he replaced the God of her childhood and quelled her fear of death as soon as she fell in love with him (LM I 41). Now, however, Anne feels a sense of emptiness.[11] Perhaps she has outgrown the subtle hierarchy that exists in their partnership, the age disparity and the former parent/student relationship that dictate her use of *vous* with Robert while he always addresses her with the familiar *tu* and that impose a somewhat self-effacing stance in intellectual or political discussions. Clearly she now understands that her union with Robert is not complete, realizing that ultimately each person is alone and that her husband sees everything, not through her eyes, but through his own. From the beginning Robert has been the measure of all things, and Anne has lived with him as if they are one and the same person. "*Mais* soudain, je n'ai plus confiance en rien," declares Anne (LM I 70; emphasis added).[12] The conjunction *mais* demonstrates that the oppositions evident in Anne's opening interior monologue clearly implicate her husband. And although admittedly this word finds particular favor in the French language because of the ubiquitous *oui, mais* construct, it appears to be the case that Anne makes inordinate use of it, along with similar words of attenuation, in particular, *pourtant, peut-être* and *si*. But it is a few paragraphs later during her reflection on her spouse that Anne employs her favorite method of contradiction – the use of the conditional mood – whether present or past. Wondering if another woman could have just as easily been in her place had the timing of events been different, she thinks to herself: "M'*aurait-il aimée* un an plus tôt, quand il était encore pris corps et âme dans la bizarre politique?" (LM I 74; emphasis added),[13] adding that he could have just as easily chosen someone else. Anne goes on to say that up until then she had not been unhappy, *but* on the other hand, she had not been happy either (LM I 74). Robert seems to have saved her from her fundamentally contradictory nature – "Robert avait tiré du chaos un monde plein, ordonné, purifié par cet avenir qu'il produisait" (LM I 75)[14] – and protected her from loneliness while allowing her her solitude. But

---

[10] Yolanda Patterson, "The Dark Window: Woman, Family and Career in the Fictional Works of Simone de Beauvoir," *Simone de Beauvoir Studies* 1 (1983) 74.

[11] Patterson, "Dark Window" 77.

[12] "But suddenly, I've lost all confidence – in everything." (M 50)

[13] "Would he have loved me a year earlier when he was still taken up body and soul in political battles?" (M 52)

[14] "From chaos, Robert had drawn a full, orderly world, cleansed by the future he was helping to produce." (M 52-53)

this unambiguous existence is short-lived once Anne realizes that being Robert's wife is not sufficient (LM I 75).

Henri, the second narrator, adds to Anne's identity crisis: they are so similar in opinion (Anne and Henri both believe, in stark contrast to Robert, that the Soviet labor camps should be exposed) that they are largely incapable of providing different accounts of events. Indeed, there is an underlying sympathy between the two that appears briefly in the *réveillon* sequence which opens the novel and in which Henri throws his arms around Anne and dances with her. Their connection becomes even more evident when, separated from Robert by the street crowd celebrating the end of the war, Anne and Henri enjoy a momentary tête-à-tête when they stop for a drink together. Anne admits to Henri her lack of faith in the future and the overriding fear she feels at the moment, making this conversation as intimate as any she has with Robert. Anne thinks to herself that it is rare that she feels comfortable with Henri because there are too many people between them – Robert, Nadine, Paule – but this night she feels close to him (LM I 317). And although the conversation quickly turns to Robert, nonetheless, points out Jacqueline Lévi-Valensi, there is a sexual undercurrent.[15] However, Anne's use of the past conditional sets up one of her ever present contradictions. She admits to the intimacy of the moment but knows that it must be short-circuited: "L'intimité, la confiance de cette heure, nous aurions pu la prolonger jusqu'à l'aube: par-delà l'aube peut-être" (LM I 324),[16] and the repetition of the verb falloir makes clear that a return to normal life is necessary.[17] Moreover, Elizabeth Fallaize contends that because Beauvoir distributed her own character traits between Anne and Henri, their relationship is potentially incestuous in nature, and it is this perhaps that explains Anne's belief that an affair between the two would be taboo.[18] Fallaize also suggests a conflation of Henri and Beauvoir herself: "In an evident desire to ward off any attempt to treat her novel as a *roman à clef,* Beauvoir has Henri explain to Nadine that his book is nothing of the sort."[19]

But it is Anne's relationship with the women of *Les Mandarins* which

---

[15] Jacqueline Lévi-Valensi, "Remarques sur une séquence des *Mandarins,*" *Roman 20-50: Revue d'étude du roman du XXeme siècle* 13 (juin 1992) 107.

[16] "We could have prolonged the intimacy of that hour until dawn, perhaps even beyond the dawn." (M 210)

[17] Lévi-Valensi 108.

[18] Fallaize, "Narrative Structure" 230.

[19] Elizabeth Fallaize, *The Novels of Simone de Beauvoir* (London: Routledge, 1988) 98.

most notably blurs the boundaries of her identity. Anne's relationship with her eighteen-year-old daughter is a case in point. Portrayed as a "parasitical responsibility eating away at the very core of a woman's identity," motherhood threatens Anne's sense of self.[20] Nadine's birth, the result of Robert's longing for a child, not his wife's, appears to have interrupted Anne's search for an identity and provokes one of the many contradictions so crucial to who Anne is: she simultaneously resents Nadine and feels guilty about this resentment.[21] Ironically, though, it is the mother/daughter relationship which makes the two women so similar. In fact, Nadine, wittingly or unwittingly, dictates much of what her mother does.[22] Anne's decision to sleep with Scriassine is in large part a reaction to Nadine's frequently quoted comment that her mother is too reserved ever to take off her *gants de chevreau,* her kid gloves. It is a choice made after so little contact with this man that Anne's one night stand brings to mind her daughter's ability to jump from one man's bed to another, and briefly makes Anne as sexually aggressive as Nadine. Later, when Anne appears unsuccessful in her attempt to get into bed with Lewis Brogan, Anne remarks, "Que d'histoires pour ne pas arriver à se faire baiser!" (LM II 36),[23] echoing Nadine's language register when Henri refuses to spend the weekend with her: "Vous avez […] une petite cervelle au bout de la queue" (LM I 262).[24] Of course, the most salient similarity between Anne and Nadine is each woman's marriage and ensuing motherhood. Like her mother, Nadine marries a man substantially older than herself who will be the mentor that Anne's husband was to her. Furthermore, because he is a writer and a politically active intellectual as well as Robert Dubreuilh's closest friend, Henri is the one partner she could have chosen who most closely resembles her father and, thus, her mother's choice of mate. Nadine appears to repeat a manifestation of the Oedipus complex that emerged in Anne's own psychoanalysis. Moreover, when Nadine becomes pregnant, it is to force Henri's hand and compel him to marry her rather than for her own fulfillment. Like her mother she has a daughter whom she treats as Anne treats her, that is to say, with conscientious attention – not maternal devotion.

---

[20] Patterson, "Dark Window" 89.
[21] Patterson, "Dark Window" 44.
[22] Patterson, "Dark Window" 43.
[23] "What a to-do about not getting kissed!" (M 339) The reader should note that this translation does not capture the vulgar register used in the French.
[24] "You have […] a little brain at the tip of your pecker." (M 172)

However, much more crucial to the resemblance between Anne and Nadine is the same identity crisis, exposed in both contradictory behavior and speech. Nadine tells her mother that she is probably the type of woman made to be married but quickly contradicts this thought when she adds that no man would be foolish enough to marry her (LM I 338). Only too familiar with this dynamic, Anne recognizes these contradictions and points them out, telling her daughter that as soon as a man is taken with Nadine her daughter refuses to believe it. She also understands this tension in her daughter's behavior toward her. Speaking about the favors she extends Nadine, a pair of new pumps that Anne gave her to wear, for example, although both of them were planning on going out that evening, Anne puts her finger, once again, on a contradiction, noting that her daughter was not truly appreciative and yet reproached herself for this ingratitude (LM I 96). Moreover, to convince Nadine to do something, Anne must always feign the opposite attitude. She thinks it a good idea that Nadine travel through France while Lambert does a series of interviews and so she claims indifference (LM I 341). But the most painful contradictions are those that Anne experiences in herself with regard to Nadine: "*Peut-être l'aurais-je soulagée si* je l'avais prise dans mes bras en lui disant: 'Ma pauvre petite fille, pardonne-moi de ne pas t'aimer davantage.' *Si* je l'avais tenue dans mes bras, *peut-être aurais-je été* défendue" (LM I 96; emphasis added),[25] adding a few pages later that if she had loved her daughter more their relationship would have been different. Perhaps she would have known how to prevent Nadine from living a life of which she disapproves (LM I 100). For her part, Nadine seems to perceive instinctively their similar contradictory behavior. Explaining to her mother the way she acts with Lambert, Nadine says, "quand je sens qu'il a envie que je lui dise une chose, je dis aussitôt *le contraire*. Tu ne comprends pas ça?" Anne answers, "je comprends un peu" but then seals the like mother, like daughter dynamic when she immediately says to herself, "Je comprenais très bien" (LM II 94; emphasis added).[26] More significantly, Anne assumes that Nadine will have to maintain the same balancing act that she does because her goals for her

---

[25] "Perhaps I might have been able to comfort her if I simply took her in my arms and said, 'My poor little daughter, forgive me for not loving you more.' If I had held her in my arms, perhaps it would have protected me." (M 66)

[26] "'[...] when I feel he wants me to say one thing, I immediately say the opposite. Can you understand that?' 'A little.' I could understand very well." (M 372-3).

daughter indicate that she does not imagine "the life of a woman as other than a *delicate balance;* although she would like Nadine to have a respectable and interesting job, she is at least as interested in getting her out of the house, married, and settled".[27] Nadine displays an angry recognition of the constraints placed on women, mocking them but allowing them to limit her own life at the same time. Her story is a parody of her mother's.[28]

Anne's close friend, Paule Mareuil, merges with Anne as well, although, fortunately for Anne, the merger between the narrator and her negative double is never complete. Initially their similarity is perhaps less apparent. After all, Anne is comfortably married to a man who remains committed to her and is exercising her profession as psychoanalyst whereas Paule is clinging to Henri, a man who is trying to end the relationship, and for whom she has given up her own career as a singer. Furthermore, many critics have pointed out that Paule perfectly illustrates Beauvoir's chapter in *Le Deuxième Sexe* devoted to *l'amoureuse,* the woman who makes a cult of love and seeks her own identity vicariously through a man. However, Beauvoir notes in *La Force de l'âge* that in most of her novels she places a *repoussoir,* or foil, next to her heroine (FA 350), and as such, Paule illustrates the "danger que court une femme médiocre si elle lie sa vie à un créateur fanatique. [...] Exclue de partout, frustrée, humiliée, le coeur gros de rancune, elle s'empêtre dans des contradictions qui risquent de l'égarer définitivement".[29] It is these very contradictions that entangle Paule which prove that she and Anne have more in common than their friendship, and once Anne has encountered the American writer Lewis Brogan and fallen in love, the resemblance between the two women assumes real weight. Elizabeth Fallaize notes that Anne does not imitate Paule's mythifying discourse or refusal of the passage of time, but she finds other danger signs in Anne's relationship with Lewis: "Paule's narcissism and belief in the illusion of clothes"[30] occasionally tempt Anne, and Paule's bizarre interpretations of Henri's behavior are echoed in Anne's misunderstanding of Lewis's

---

[27] Carol Ascher, *Simone de Beauvoir: A Life of Freedom* (Boston: Beacon Press, 1981) 160
[28] Ascher 161.
[29] "[...] risks an ordinary, unremarkable woman runs by linking her life to that of an obsessional creative artist. [...] Frustrated, humiliated, always an outsider, her heart bursting with resentment, [Paule] found herself floundering in a sea of inconsistencies that bid fair to derange her wits altogether." (M 430)
[30] Louise Renée Kasper points out in that Anne wears black, widow's colors, not because she has lost Robert, but because she has lost his love. It is only when she falls in love with Lewis that her wardrobe actually takes on some color. "Orange Blossoms and Roses: Love Imagery in the First Chapter of *Les Mandarins,*" *Simone de Beauvoir Studies* 11 (1994) 15.

increasingly desperate signals that he cannot cope with her double life.[31] When Anne discovers that Lewis has lied about his editor demanding he interrupt their Mexican vacation to launch his latest book in New York, she explicitly compares herself to Paule, saying that now it is she who has lost her mind (LM II 258). Lewis accuses Anne of seeing things as she wishes (LM II 261-262), much as Paule does with Henri, and she desperately wants to prove to Lewis, as Paule hopes to prove to her lover, that he has more to gain than to lose in their affair (LM II 269). Even more striking, she tries to assuage her lover's feelings in a manner that is essentially word for word Paule pleading with Henri: "Je prendrai ce que vous me donnerez et je n'exigerai jamais rien" (LM II 269),[32] even echoing Paule in her insistence that Lewis is free to sleep with other women. Nonetheless, Anne convinces herself, as Paule does, that her relationship with her lover is unique. Anne believes herself to be a new woman thanks to Brogan (LM II 225), at essentially the same moment that Paule asserts that she is a *femme nouvelle* with regard to Henri.

On the other hand, Anne has the impression that her life no longer belongs to her, that she is obliged to live an image of herself of someone else's design[33] – much in the way that Paule modifies herself entirely to fit what she believes will make her most desirable to Henri. After her return to Paris following her initial Chicago interlude, Anne is deeply saddened by Lewis's first letter and thinks that spending time with Paule and sharing her sadness would allow her to forget her own (LM II 76). On a subsequent visit, Anne witnesses Paule's total breakdown after reading Henri's adamant telegram insisting that their relationship is over. Anne assures Paule, "'Tu guériras, il faut guérir. L'amour n'est pas tout ...' Sachant bien qu'à sa place je ne voudrais jamais guérir et enterrer mon amour avec mes propres mains" (LM II 207).[34] Appropriately, Anne uses the future tense when speaking to Paule but places herself in the conditional. This purge is a type of death that Anne wants to avoid, preferring to die literally rather than to lose the vivid sense of living which she experiences with Lewis. In another striking contradiction, Anne, the psychoanalyst, chooses to forego therapy because it would

---

[31] Fallaize, *Novels* 109.

[32] "I'll take what you give me and I'll never demand anything." (M 475)

[33] Mary Lawrence Test, "Simone de Beauvoir: le refus de l'avenir – l'image de la femme dans *Les Mandarins* et *Les Belles Images*," *Simone de Beauvoir Studies* 11 (1994) 25.

[34] "'You'll get well, you've got to get well. Love isn't everything ...' And I knew very well that in her place I would never want to get well and bury my love with my own hands." (M 439)

deprive her of a freedom that, in Beauvoir's world, she can use for change.[35] In fact, a role reversal seems to take place. Having finished her therapy, Paule now wants to be like Anne, telling her friend that she is right: dependence is vile (LM II 351). Ironically, it is now Paule who counsels Anne that she can start life over with her American lover and that she is simply living in Robert's shadow. She even goes so far as to encourage Anne to be psychoanalyzed again, and her advice to Anne is the very same advice that Anne gently suggests to Paule when she refuses to do anything but live for Henri: "Il n'y a rien de plus pernicieux que de vivre à l'ombre d'une gloire, [...] on s'étiole. Il faut que toi aussi tu te trouves toi-même" (LM II 355).[36] Finally, once Lewis no longer loves Anne, her near suicide privileges the clearest telescoping of Anne and Paule, particularly because it is the vial of poison that Anne retrieves from her friend's possession that she intends to use to take her own life.

Nonetheless, the trap into which Paule falls is one which Anne will avoid, however close the call, when faced with that fascinating and creative American Lewis Brogan.[37] One reason for this is that Anne lives her affair with Lewis in the margins of her real life,[38] a marginality realized through her incessant vacillation between conflicting characterizations of the love affair. She makes ample use of the attenuating conjunctions she privileges in her speech, poses endless questions, favors verbs which are overwhelmingly in the conditional mood, and quite simply, behaves in a contradictory manner. During their initial encounter Anne muses to herself that she knows virtually nothing about Brogan yet he does not seem at all like a stranger (LM II 16). Anne tells Lewis that she will come back, but then immediately asks herself what would be the point (LM I 18), and when Brogan asks her to return to Chicago, she tells herself that she would not return and would instead seek out other male companionship (LM II 21). However, three months later when Philipp Davies, the son of her friend Myriam, is unable to join Anne in New York City, she calls Lewis to ask if she might visit him again. Anne hangs up the phone and thinks to herself how simple everything would be: they would talk briefly in a dimly lit bar. Brogan would then invite her to relax at his place where they would sit next to one another on his bed listening to Charles Trenet before

---

[35] Ascher 213.

[36] "There's nothing more injurious than living in the shadow of someone else's glory, [...] one wastes away. You, too, have got to find yourself." (M 525)

[37] Test 22.

[38] Test 24.

Brogan finally took her in his arms. It probably would not be an extraordinary evening, but he would be happy and that would be enough to satisfy her (LM II 25). Of course, nothing proves to be simple: the dimly lit bar where Anne thought they would have an intimate conversation is temporarily replaced by a brightly lit cafeteria where Lewis chats at length with three friends he has run into in the street; Brogan does not ask her to rest at his place so Anne naps in a hotel room; when they finally do return to Brogan's apartment any notion of stretching out on his bed to listen leisurely to Charles Trenet is lost, and instead, Anne strips off her clothes and jumps into bed. Most significant, a night that she thought would be similar to the one spent with Scriassine, that is to say, absent of any real desire, begins instead her most memorable sexual experience (LM II 27).[39]

The contradictions multiply and grow in intensity as the relationship develops. Anne describes herself and Lewis as a beautiful couple but, on the other hand, tells herself that they are not a legitimate one and could never be (LM II 42). She asks herself why she has even come to Chicago because she clearly cannot stay (LM II 44). This balancing act in which Anne hesitates, never commits to one position or another, is even clearer when Lewis declares his love. Anne cries without knowing "si c'était parce qu'il m'aimait, ou parce que je ne pouvais pas l'aimer, ou parce qu'il cesserait un jour de m'aimer" (LM II 46).[40] She wants to tell Lewis that she would have been able to love him but that she could not because of Robert, Nadine, her work and Paris. All of that was true and yet only one day had been necessary for it to become false (LM II 52). Anne goes back and forth in her mind about whether she should extend her Chicago stay for ten or fifteen days: "Je télégraphierais à Paris... Et après? Il faudrait bien finir par m'en aller. [...] Il ne s'agissait encore que d'une *aventure de voyage:* si je restais, ça deviendrait un *véritable amour,* un impossible amour, et c'est alors que je *souffrirais.* Je *ne voulais pas souffrir"* (LM II 54; emphasis added).[41] Nonetheless, her about-face is immediate and she asks Lewis if it would be possible for her to stay a week or two longer if she so wished (LM II 55).

---

[39] Asa Moberg points out that Scriassine is synonymous with male conquest and consequently his first name, Victor, is no accident. Furthermore, she goes on to say, his last name is intuitively linked to a scream, "cri" in French, suggesting someone in pain or inflicting pain. "Sexuality and Brutality – Contradictions in Simone de Beauvoir's Writings about Sexuality," *Contigent Loves: Simone de Beauvoir and Sexuality,* ed. Melanie C. Hawthorne (Charlottesville: University Press of Virginia, 2000) 104.

[40] "[...] not knowing whether it was because he loved me or because I couldn't love him, or because one day he would stop loving me." (M 345)

[41] "I'd cable Paris... and then what? Sooner or later I'd have to leave. [...] It still wasn't much more than a shipboard affair; but if I stayed, it would become a true love, an impossible love, and that's when I'd suffer. I didn't want to suffer." (M 349)

This is followed by the most moving love scene of the novel (LM II 55) after which Anne contradicts herself again and tells Lewis that she loves him. Furthermore, she passes in review a crucial hypothetical: "'Et pourtant, me dis-je, si Philipp était venu à New York, je *ne serais pas* ici.' [...] Je *n'aurais pas revu* Lewis, notre amour *n'aurait pas existé*" (LM II 57; emphasis added),[42] noting that this thought was just as disconcerting as trying to imagine never having been born or being someone else.

But Lewis himself is a contradiction, the antithesis of all that Anne knows. And, as many critics have pointed out, Deirdre Bair and Barbara Klaw among them, this is the very reason that Beauvoir found Nelson Algren, the model for Lewis Brogan, so attractive, something that Beauvoir herself admits in *La Force des choses*: "Quant à moi, j'avais besoin de distance pour engager mon coeur. [...] Algren appartenait à un autre continent" (FC II 14). Thus, similar to Algren, Lewis Brogan is the Other by virtue of his nationality and the English language, the only one he speaks, as well as his spartan lifestyle and the Chicago underworld that he loves to frequent. Anne confronts further differences during her second trip to the States when she realizes that Lewis has a mind of his own: "Brusquement je m'avisai que je n'étais pas seule à penser notre histoire: il la pensait aussi, à sa manière à lui (LM II 228-229).[43] Later, she seriously misreads her lover when he announces the change in their travel plans which will force them to go to New York. Anne initially thinks that Lewis has not mentioned this before to avoid ruining their vacation and is hurt when she discovers that he has fabricated this excuse to abort their holiday. More often, Anne is at a loss to understand who Lewis really is, which appears impossible to her because she loves him so much (LM II 257). While at the Murray's Lewis appears increasingly temperamental and he and Anne argue after she stays up until three in the morning talking with her host and other guests. Lewis makes an unflattering comparison between Anne and Eleanor Roosevelt, saying he would like to beat some sense into Anne. Anne assuages her stunned feelings with the conditional mood but quickly contradicts herself: "Il ouvrirait les yeux, il dirait: 'Je vous aime, ma petite Gauloise.' Et justement, non, il ne le dirait

---

42 "'And yet,' I said to myself, 'if Philipp had come to New York, I wouldn't be here ...' I wouldn't have seen Lewis again and our love wouldn't have existed." (M 351)
43 "Abruptly, I realized I wasn't alone in thinking about our problems; in his own way, he, too, was thinking about them." (M 452)

pas" (LM II 283),[44] hoping that this contradiction will, as usual, create a unique space for her. Lewis follows with an about-face of his own. He assigns his bad moods to a desire to be alone in Chicago with Anne, contradicting his earlier claim that he wanted to be with friends.

Before her final trip to Chicago Anne tries to protect herself against Lewis's vagaries. She attempts to project the end of this relationship with certitude, that is to say with the future tense, but she is unable. Once or twice she tries to tell herself, "'Un jour cette histoire finira et je me retrouverai avec un beau souvenir derrière moi, autant en prendre tout de suite mon parti.' Mais je me suis révoltée. Quelle dérisoire comédie!" (LM II 363).[45] Anne's preoccupation with age, on the other hand, provokes thoughts of a permanent end – and the future tense. Disgusted by older women (women who are her age, that is to say, thirty-nine!) seducing younger men at Claudie's reception, Anne remarks that when she loses Lewis she will immediately renounce any notion of still being a woman. She does not want to resemble these female predators (LM II 373). But when Paule, who wants to have a blouse made for Anne, asks her where the fabric she brought back from her trip abroad is, Anne seesaws back and forth between her life in Paris and life with Lewis. Suddenly she no longer knows where she is, there or elsewhere (LM II 268). However, it is this marginality, this *ailleurs,* or elsewhere, that allows Anne to sustain her balancing act: "avec ma peau je touchais la preuve qu'entre le bonheur évanoui et ma torpeur d'aujourd'hui il y avait un passage: il pouvait donc y avoir un retour" (LM II 369).[46] And when Anne puts on her new blouse she tells herself that six months from now she would not have aged a great deal; she would see Lewis again and he would still love her (LM II 369). But true to form she immediately contradicts herself, saying that she must have lost her mind to allow her fate to depend on someone else (LM II 376).

When Anne returns to Chicago for the third time the contradictions between what is real and what is not, between the future tense and the conditional mood, are dramatically more pronounced. Stopping over in New York, Anne examines herself in her hotel room and thinks about what

---

[44] "He would open his eyes, he would say, 'I love you, my little Gauloise.' But no, he wouldn't say it." (M 483)

[45] "'One day this affair will end and I'll be left with a beautiful memory; I might just as well make up my mind to it right now.' But I rebelled. What a ridiculous farce!" (M 529-30)

[46] "With my skin I was touching the proof that there was a road between vanished happiness and my present torpor, therefore, there *could* be a return." (M 533)

Lewis would do when he saw her. To her mind, the sexual tension would be as overwhelming as ever, but when she arrives in Chicago, although they make love, it has none of the intensity of their earlier lovemaking. Worse, Lewis tells Anne he no longer loves her. Anne wants to believe it is her new clothes and expensive perfume that make her less desirable, although ultimately she understands that the loss of love is impossible to explain. And yet Anne clearly vacillates between hope and despair which her contrasting use of the future and the conditional make evident. Because she has not resigned herself to this scenario, when she contemplates returning immediately to France she uses the conditional: "le taxi qui m'emporterait roulait quelque part dans la ville" (LM II 388).[47] However, she quickly moves to the future tense and its certainty: "Tant que je verrai Lewis, tant qu'il me sourira, je n'aurai jamais la force de tuer en moi notre amour" (LM II 389).[48] Once in his summer cottage on Lake Michigan, Anne tells herself that Lewis has not truly stopped loving her, but rather, he is just willing it to be the case, pointing out the contradiction between making a decision and actually carrying it out. On the other hand, Anne does not want to find herself among those women who lie to themselves, like Paule for example, and when that night Lewis makes love to her without a word, without a kiss, it is back to the future, so to speak. Anne accepts the fact that Lewis no longer loves her but is, nonetheless, determined to have a pleasant summer: "Je suis sûre que nous passerons un bel été" (LM II 395).[49]

Of course the underlying and ultimate contradiction in Anne's identity crisis is the dramatic distinction between the two men in her life, her husband and her lover. Familiarity has produced within the Anne/Robert couple the same twinship that critics often assigned to Beauvoir and Sartre,[50] a similarity which only serves to accentuate Lewis' otherness. Anne and her husband have not made love for five years, and her lengthy abstinence, her long wait for sexual pleasure, privileges her love affair with the American writer. What is more, in contrast to Robert, Lewis seems to ignore Anne's intellectual accomplishments altogether. He tells her, after she has brilliantly discussed the relationship between psychoanalysis and Marxism one evening, that for him she is something entirely other than an intellectual

---

[47] "The cab that would take me away was cruising somewhere in the city." (M 545)

[48] "As long as I see Lewis, as long as he smiles at me, I'll never have the strength to kill the love within me." (M 545)

[49] "I am sure we'll have a lovely summer together." (M 548)

[50] Serge Julienne-Caffié, "Variations on Triangular Relationships," Hawthorne, *Contingent Loves* 45.

(LM II 274). Anne appreciates Lewis' astonishment at her professional renown, but even more, his gentle mockery of it because it underscores his exclusive interest in her as a woman. Simply put, Lewis accentuates Anne's break with the competent, aggressive, assertive, independent, emancipated woman; she becomes feminine and somewhat submissive, something only hinted at in her generous and solicitous behavior with Robert.[51] Thus, it is only in the Anne/Lewis relationship, never the Anne/Robert couple, that the reader senses Anne's physical and emotional abandon: with Lewis she is all body and emotion and with Robert she is pure intellect. Yet, ironically, it is Robert's very existence which allows Anne her passion for Lewis. She can lose herself in another world and another identity because she is sure that her world with Robert will be there upon her return, not necessarily out of devotion to Anne, but because of habit and a certain indifference. Immersed in his work, Robert appears to encourage Anne's trips abroad while Lewis reproaches Anne the manner in which she has arranged to live two different lives (LM II 228).

Furthermore, each man serves as a mirror for Anne, revealing to her a conflicting image of the woman they both love. For his part, Robert reflects the unhappy intellectual truth of Anne's own mortality for it is he who reveals the secret of the mirror that time passes, everyone ages and eventually must die.[52] Lewis, on the other hand, reflects short-lived physical pleasure and uncovers for Anne the woman who "is nothing more than this I who admires herself in the desiring gaze of the other, 'a pure marvel'".[53] However, when Lewis no longer loves her, Anne and her identity are at their most vulnerable. While at a fair in Parker, where she is spending the summer with a lover now indifferent to her charms, Anne looks around at the crowd and realizes that no one speaks her language, a language that she herself has forgotten, as well as her memories of France and even her own image: "il n'y avait pas un miroir chez Lewis qui fût à hauteur de mes yeux; [...] c'est à peine si je me rappelais qui j'étais, et je me demandais si Paris existait encore" (LM II 399-400).[54] But, not surprisingly, shortly before her return to France, she glances in a hotel mirror on the way to dinner with

[51] Jean Leighton, *Simone de Beauvoir on Woman* (Rutherford, New Jersey: Fairleigh Dickinson Press, 1975) 99.

[52] Test 24.

[53] Béatrice Slama, "Simone de Beauvoir: Feminine Sexuality and Liberation," *Critical Essays on Simone de Beauvoir,* ed. Elaine Marks (Boston: G.K. Hall 1987) 227.

[54] [...] there was no mirror in Lewis's house which I could look into at eye-level; [...] I hardly remembered who I was, and I wondered if Paris still existed." (M 551)

her old friends Myriam and Philipp (LM II 419). Anne sees herself from head to toe for the first time in weeks and notes how pleasant it is to rediscover her image, making this scene emblematic of reassuming her fundamental identity. Rather than the body, it is the intellect that prevails, an intellect that "has been left in Paris, where she will quite sensibly return to the safety of her chaste marriage and 'her world'".[55]

Nonetheless, this return to a sexless marriage comes at great cost to Anne: the role that female sexuality plays in her identity crisis cannot be underestimated. Indeed, Anne Dubreuilh is Beauvoir's response, as is Françoise Miquel of L'Invitée, to those critics who find the feminist writer more cerebral than sensual.[56] And they are legion. Asa Moberg complains that there are too few physical details in Beauvoir's descriptions of lovemaking.[57] Céline Léon claims that Beauvoir never does anything more than present a Sartrian view of the female body: the breasts that Anne is delighted to rediscover are rarely more than "fleshy proliferations that, in the fullness of their gratuitous immanence, dread mirrors and caresses," adding that Beauvoir's women are really men and men who are none too healthy.[58] Carol Ascher believes that it is "man's pleasure which is active, while the woman's is unmeasured, global, unlocalized,"[59] while Jo-Ann Pilardi notes that in the novels which follow Le Deuxième Sexe, Beauvoir never gives more than a fleeting glance at female erotic experience, when she had claimed in her study of women that female eroticism needed a spokeswoman.[60] In stark contrast, Béatrice Slama believes that Beauvoir took up this challenge and she points that no novel is more crucial to an understanding of the feminist's views on female sexuality, as well as sexuality and liberation, than Les Mandarins: "A woman writer had never before laid bare, as Simone de Beauvoir does in the face of shame and taboos, sexual relations between a man and a woman, experienced in this manner from the inside, from the viewpoint of a woman."[61]

---

[55] Ascher 174.
[56] Yolanda Patterson, Simone de Beauvoir and the Demystification of Motherhood (Ann Arbor: UMI Research Press, 1989) 138.
[57] Moberg 91.
[58] Céline T. Léon, "Beauvoir's Woman: Eunuch or Male?" Feminist Interpretations of Simone de Beauvoir, ed. Marguerite A. Simons (University Park: Pennsylvania State University Press, 1995) 143, 153.
[59] Ascher 174.
[60] Jo-Ann Pilardi, "Female Eroticism in the Works of Simone de Beauvoir," The Thinking Muse: Feminism and Modern French Philosophy, ed. Jeffner Allen and Iris Marion Young (Bloomington: Indiana University Press, 1989) 31.
[61] Slama 218, 226.

Fittingly, Anne's experience of female sexuality rests on a fundamental contradiction: she feels the pleasure of the "I" recognized by another while at the same time she puts her own sense of self in question when feeling reduced to pure object. She allows that it is man's desire which "marks the rhythm of the intermittences of woman's body".[62] At the same time, there appears to be an effort to overcome, to contradict, this dynamic. Anne describes a space where women are as libidinous as men, a space where female touch replaces the masculine gaze:[63] "J'embrassai ses yeux, ses lèvres, ma bouche descendit le long de sa poitrine; elle effleura le nombril enfantin, la fourrure animale, le sexe où un coeur battait à petits coups. [...] Je ne savais pas que ça pouvait être si bouleversant de faire l'amour. [...] Rien ne nous séparait plus" (LM II 55).[64] In her lovemaking with Lewis, Anne seems to be elaborating on an earlier lovemaking experience with Scriassine during which she refuses the imposition of a male sexual economy. She derides his desire for mutual orgasm, understanding that it would not make them any less separate, and makes an ironic comment about men having discovered synchronicity. Anne's sexual behavior contrasts sharply with that of Nadine, who comments that women are made to get laid, and that of Paule, who eventually collects as many lovers as she can find. For her part, Anne Dubreuilh struggles with the contradictions, the double bind, that is female sexuality, illustrating Beauvoir's belief that woman within patriarchy is an imperfect being, intellectually, metaphysically and psychologically, but certainly sexually. She is an intermediate creature between male and eunuch, only a partially sexed being because she is not a phallic creature.[65]

Consequently, when Lewis, the man who once made Anne feel like a flesh and blood woman, no longer finds her desirable (LM II 398), this contradiction, different from all previous contradictions, does not create an alternate space for Anne. This contradiction eliminates her altogether. Reading a letter from Robert, Anne realizes that because he is not insistent that she return to Paris, she has no reason to leave the United States, but she has no reason to stay either (LM II 407). Worse, she no longer knows

---

[62] Slama 226.
[63] Barbara Klaw, "Sexuality in *Les Mandarins*," Simons, *Feminist Interpretations* 213.
[64] "I kissed his eyes, his lips; my mouth went down along his chest. [...] I never knew that making love could be so overwhelming. [...] Nothing separated us any longer." (M 350) The translator eliminates altogether Beauvoir's reference to oral sex.
[65] Pilardi 24.

herself: "Je ne savais pas qui j'étais moi-même" (LM II 409).[66] On the other hand, when she is ready to leave the States once again, Anne returns to the conditional mood to underscore what the balancing act has meant, and means, to her: "Notre histoire m'avait coûté bien des larmes; pourtant pour rien au monde je *n'aurais consenti* à l'arracher de mon passé. Et c'était soudain une consolation de penser que même finie, condamnée, elle *continuerait* à jamais à vivre en moi" (LM II 424; emphasis added).[67] Nonetheless, walking the streets of Chicago, Anne holds back tears because she is compelled to use the permanence of the future tense – "je ne reviendrai pas" (LM II 425).[68] And the contradictions which have been crucial to her balancing act reappear, but this time they seem irreconcilable: "le monde est trop *riche,* trop *pauvre,* le passé trop *lourd,* trop *léger;* [...] mon amour est *mort* et [...] je lui *survivrai*" (LM II 425; emphasis added).[69] But the most unbearable contradiction for Anne is that the man who once loved her is Lewis yet, because he no longer loves her, he is not Lewis at the same time. Ironically, the only way that the two former lovers can painlessly pass their last moments together is to return to the balancing act, but one of a different kind: "Nous n'avons parlé ni du passé ni de l'avenir [...]. Comme nous ne demandions rien, rien ne nous était refusé" (LM II 427-428).[70]

Anne discovers that the ideal relationship, one in which there is total reciprocity between partners, is apparently only viable for a woman when she moves back and forth between two men. Unfortunately for Anne, this balancing act is impossible to maintain, although initially she believes that Lewis would privilege this possibility. While on the one hand she is the self-effacing woman caught up in *l'éternel féminin* with her lover, on the other hand, she refuses to marry him and have his children – just as Beauvoir had rejected these roles with Algren. It is only with Robert that she assumes these identities, and yet it is with Robert that she exercises the

---

66 "I didn't know who I myself was." (M 556)

67 "Our affair had cost me dearly in tears; and yet I would not have agreed to rip it from my past for anything in the world. And suddenly, it was a consolation to think that even ended, doomed, it would continue to love in me forever." (M 565)

68 "I would never return." (M 565) Although the translator uses the conditional mood, the French is clearly in the future tense.

69 "[...] the world is too rich, too poor, the past too heavy, too light; [...] my love had died and I would survive it." (M 565-6) Again, although the translator uses the conditional mood, the future tense is used in French.

70 "We spoke neither of the past, nor of the future [...]. Since we asked for nothing, nothing was denied us." (M 567)

freedom to have a contingent love affair. This equilibrium is challenged when Lewis asks Anne to give up her life in France because he is asking her to give up a part of herself. Anne wants to forego traditional female bifurcation and remain whole by meeting her physical needs in America and her intellectual needs in France. However, she ultimately must choose and when she chooses Robert and her life in Paris, she is declaring her preference for language and reason over passion.[71] This choice is reinforced when, at the novel's close, Anne reflects on the pain she would have inflicted on her family had she committed suicide. She is resuscitated by the logos:[72] "Ils me parlent, je suis vivante" (LM II 500).[73] Yet, it is this triangular dynamic that Anne maintains as long as possible with Lewis and Robert that best captures what Beauvoir calls in *Force of Circumstance* the "spontaneous, whirling quality of existence with its *contradictions*" (FC 342; emphasis added).

Unquestionably Anne's love affair with Lewis Brogan is the relationship most crucial to her identity crisis. All the rest fades into the background once their love takes hold, and ironically, Anne's detachment, which allows her to comment dispassionately on the history unfolding before her eyes or on the dispute between her husband and Henri, and, of course, on her patients' problems, disappears while she is in love with Lewis. But the love affair is all the more noteworthy for its intimate resemblance to events in Beauvoir's own life. The pages devoted to the couple, the Beauvoir/ Algren counterpart, are the least fictionalized in the novel. So important was the pair to Beauvoir that she wrote the end of the Anne/Lewis affair before she wrote anything else, and in fact, wrote all the passages devoted to the two before she attempted the remainder of the novel.[74] Dominique Audry considered the Anne/Lewis love affair one of the best fictional versions from a woman's perspective. For her, Anne and Lewis have a vitality that the other characters lack and she finds Lewis to be the most successful and believable male in *Les Mandarins*.[75] Beauvoir concurs when she reveals in *La Force des choses* that of all her fictional characters Lewis is the one who comes closest to reality (FC II 371). Simply put, Beauvoir celebrates her

---

[71] Carol Gagnon, "'Il doit quand même y avoir un pays où on puisse vivre': les thèmes de l'espoir et de la responsabilité dans *Les Mandarins*," *Simone de Beauvoir Studies* 16 (1999-2000) 109.

[72] Gagnon 110.

[73] "[…] they speak to me, I am alive." (M 610)

[74] Bair 425.

[75] Leighton 97.

own love affair through Anne's, whose experience with Brogan is what makes Anne so memorable. While Anne does not allow herself to live solely through the man she loves, she does illustrate "that love is a powerful force to be reckoned with and cannot always be subordinated to the more important claims of career, etc".[76] Thus, Anne reflects what was Beauvoir's need to be one with the beloved which contrasted with the need for autonomy that so dominated her life.[77] Furthermore, because as a woman turning forty, Anne asks herself if there is yet another opportunity for love in her life, she also mirrors Beauvoir's own fear of aging: "the way Simone de Beauvoir connects Anne's feelings about age with her love affair and her sense of loss afterwards has a real tragic density of feeling that is beautifully evoked and altogether lacerating."[78]

In short, Beauvoir's most vivid female characters, Anne primary among them, "exemplify all the peculiar difficulties, temptations and woes that women are heir to".[79] Moreover, Anne's identity crisis, with its many contradictions typical of a woman winding her way through the patriarchal minefield, illustrates effectively why it was impossible for Beauvoir to create a feminist role model among her fictional women. But these complexities and contradictions, points out Renée Wehrmann citing Toril Moi, only add to admiration for Beauvoir who, also, was torn by the double binds of living within patriarchy.[80] Indeed, feminist literary criticism has allowed us to understand the degree to which gender informs both reading and writing and to read with new appreciation the works of those women authors who wished to capture female experience legitimately. These efforts escaped traditional male criticism, and women readers today, informed by feminist literary theory, are dismayed to find Jacques Ehrmann writing in *Yale French Studies* in 1961 that the personal side of *Les Mandarins* fails to touch the reader and that it is only when politics take center stage that the novel has any conviction.[81] They are stunned by and find extraordinarily ironic the words of the notable French scholar, Henri Peyre. Writing in his foreward to Jean Leighton's *Simone de Beauvoir on Woman*, published in

---

[76] Leighton 88.
[77] Dorothy Clark, "Simone de Beauvoir and l'Amérique," *Simone de Beauvoir Studies* 9 (1992) 106.
[78] Leighton 91.
[79] Leighton 18.
[80] Renée Fainas Wehrmann, "Simone de Beauvoir Mirrored in *Les Mandarins*," *Simone de Beauvoir Studies* 2 (1984) 111.
[81] Jacques Ehrmann, "Simone de Beauvoir and the Related Destinies of Woman and Intellectual," Marks, *Critical Essays* 91.

1975 before feminist literary criticism was well established, he states that Beauvoir will not be remembered as either an existential philosopher or novelist because, on the one hand, she simply mouthed Sartre's opinions, and on the other hand, "she not once, strangely enough, presented a female character whom we might admire, or merely remember lastingly as a complex, winning, mature, true woman".[82]

On the contrary, Beauvoir imbues her fictional works with the authority of experience, and as a result, they provide a valuable dimension to our understanding of the dilemmas posed by the conflict between traditional gender roles and the quest for independence.[83] Lecturing in Japan, Beauvoir noted: "si je veux rendre *le vécu* d'une expérience, avec son ambiguïté, ces contradictions, avec ce côté indicible qui exige la création d'une oeuvre qui finalement se refermera sur le silence [...] je me soucie de souligner ces ambiguïtés, ces nuances, ces contradictions qui sont la raison même de mon livre".[84] Thus, the novel is itself a mirror that reflects back to the reader the feminine condition[85] and underscores the ultimate contradiction in any identity crisis: "Aucune saisie de l'être ne paraît possible; nous ne saurons subjectiviser l'extériorité d'autrui et nous restons victimes de l'image qu'autrui se fait de nous".[86] Beauvoir herself necessarily falls victim to this image others have made of her, and thus, the reader interprets Anne's identity crisis as that of the woman who created her as well. In fact, Jean Leighton believes that the feminist's choice not to make Anne a Beauvoirian role model suggests her own unresolved uncertainty about her independence, or her theory.[87] Beauvoir could not present Anne Dubreuilh, or that other quasi-autobiographical character Françoise Miquel, as wholly positive because she did not see herself that way,[88] but at the same time *Les Mandarins,* along with *L'Invitée* and *Le Sang des autres,* gave Beauvoir

---

[82] Leighton 7.

[83] Wehrmann 111.

[84] Jacques Zéphir, "Féminisme et littérature dans l'œuvre de Simone de Beauvoir," *Simone de Beauvoir Studies* 2 (1984) 14. "If I want to capture a lived experience, with its ambiguity, its contradictions, with this aspect so difficult to express which demands the creation of a work which itself will contain this silence [...] I am concerned with underscoring these ambiguities, these nuances, these contradictions which are the very reason for my book." (My translation)

[85] Test 20.

[86] Test 26-7. "No grasp of an individual seems possible; we can only understand others subjectively and we are victims of how others see us." (My translation)

[87] Leighton 84.

[88] Leighton 107.

a stronger sense of herself as writer, intellectual and woman.[89] In other words, Beauvoir, too, was caught up in contradictions. Not surprisingly, then, Beauvoir was primarily "concerned with dilemmas of existence and of moral conduct and social responsibility to which there is no single answer. It is here that her relentless probing, her blend of simplicity and lyricism are at their best".[90] More importantly, for some women writers, and I would add for some women in general, Simone de Beauvoir has become "a symbol, or symbolic mother, as one has it, a person with whom they engage in dialogue in a quest for their own identity".[91] This is the ultimate questionable balance, this never-ending interrogatory – not simply between Beauvoir and her fictional women, most notably Anne Dubreuilh – but between Beauvoir and her readers who themselves are seeking a certain equilibrium.

---

[89] Toril Moi, *Simone de Beauvoir. The Making of an Intellectual Woman* (Oxford: Blackwell, 1994) 248.
[90] Winegarten 116.
[91] Winegarten 121.

Works Cited

Ascher, Carol. *Simone de Beauvoir: A Life of Freedom*. Boston: Beacon Press, 1981.

Bair, Deirdre. *Simone de Beauvoir*. New York: Summit Books, 1990.

Beauvoir, Simone de. *Le Deuxième Sexe*. Paris: Gallimard. 1949.

_____. *La Force de l'âge*. Paris: Gallimard, 1960.

_____. *The Prime of Life*. Trans. Peter Green. New York: The World Publishing Company, 1962.

_____. *La Force des choses*. Paris: Gallimard, 1963.

_____. *Force of Circumstance*. Trans. Richard Howard. New York: Putnam, 1965.

_____. *L'Invitée*. Paris: Gallimard, 1943.

_____. *Les Mandarins*. Paris: Gallimard, 1954.

_____. *The Mandarins*. Trans. Leonard M. Friedman. New York: The World Publishing Company, 1956.

_____. *Le Sang des autres*. Paris: Gallimard, 1945.

Clark, Dorothy. "Simone de Beauvoir and l'Amérique." *Simone de Beauvoir Studies* 9 (1992): 103-107.

Ehrmann, Jacques. "Simone de Beauvoir and the Related Destinies of Woman and Intellectual." *Critical Essays on Simone de Beauvoir*. Ed. Elaine Marks. Boston: G.K. Hall, 1987. 89-94.

Fallaize, Elizabeth. "Narrative Structure in *Les Mandarins*." *Literature and Society: Studies in Nineteenth and Twentieth Century French Literature*. Ed. C. A. Burns. Birmingham, England: John Goodman & Sons, 1980. 221-232.

_____. *The Novels of Simone de Beauvoir*. London: Routledge, 1988.

Gagnon, Carol. "'Il doit quand même y avoir un pays où on puisse vivre': les thèmes de l'espoir et de la responsabilité dans *Les Mandarins*." *Simone de Beauvoir Studies* 16 (1999-2000): 100-113.

Julienne-Caffié, Serge. "Variations on Triangular Relationships." *Contingent Loves. Simone de Beauvoir and Sexuality*. Ed. Melanie C. Hawthorne. Charlottesville: University Press of Virginia, 2000. 34-54.

Kasper, Louise Renée. "Orange Blossoms and Roses: Love Imagery in the First Chapter of *Les Mandarins*." *Simone de Beauvoir Studies* 11 (1994): 13-18.

Klaw, Barbara. "Sexuality in *Les Mandarins*." *Feminist Interpretations of Simone de Beauvoir*. Ed. Margaret A. Simons. University Park: Pennsylvania State U Press, 1995. 193-221.

Leighton, Jean. *Simone de Beauvoir on Woman*. Rutherford, New Jersey: Fairleigh Dickinson Press, 1975.

Léon, Céline. "Beauvoir's Woman: Eunuch or Male?" *Feminist Interpretations of Simone de Beauvoir*. Ed. Margaret A. Simons. University Park: Pennsylvania State University Press, 1995. 137-159.

Lévi-Valensi, Jacqueline. "Remarques sur une séquence des *Mandarins*." *Roman 20-50: Revue d'étude du roman du XXeme siècle* 13 (June 1992): 103-109.

Moi, Toril. *Simone de Beauvoir: The Making of An Intellectual Woman*. Oxford, UK: Blackwell, 1994.

Moberg, Asa. "Sexuality and Brutality – Contradictions in Simone de Beauvoir's Writings about Sexuality." *Contingent Loves: Simone de Beauvoir and Sexuality*. Ed. Melanie C. Hawthorne. Charlottesville: University Press of Virginia, 2000. 84-116.

Patterson, Yolanda Astarita. "The Dark Window: Woman, Family and Career in the Fictional Works of Simone de Beauvoir." *Simone de Beauvoir Studies* 1 (Fall 1983): 69-102.

_____. "Mothers and Daughters in Postwar France: Simone de Beauvoir's *Les Mandarins*." *Simone de Beauvoir Studies* 2 (1984): 43-59.

_____. *Simone de Beauvoir and the Demystification of Motherhood*. Ann Arbor: UMI Research Press, 1989.

Pilardi, Jo-Ann. "Female Eroticism in the Works of Simone de Beauvoir." *The Thinking Muse: Feminism and Modern French Philosophy*. Ed. Jeffner Allen and Iris Marion Young. Bloomington: Indiana University Press, 1989. 18-34.

Slama, Béatrice. "Simone de Beauvoir: Feminine Sexuality and Liberation." *Critical Essays on Simone de Beauvoir*. Ed. Elaine Marks. Boston: G.K. Hall, 1987. 218-234.

Test, Mary Lawrence. "Simone de Beauvoir: Le refus de l'avenir – L'image de la femme dans *Les Mandarins* et *Les Belles Images*." *Simone de Beauvoir Studies* 11(1994): 19-29.

Wehrmann, Renée Fainas. "Simone de Beauvoir Mirrored in *Les Mandarins*." *Simone de Beauvoir Studies* 15 (1998-1999): 105-112.

Winegarten, Renée. *Simone de Beauvoir*. Oxford: Berg, 1988.

Zéphir, Jacques J. "Féminisme et littérature dans l'oeuvre de Simone de Beauvoir." *Simone de Beauvoir Studies* 2 (Fall 1984): 12-23.

6 Les Belles Images: Countering the Refusal of History

Ursula Tidd

*L*es Belles Images, published in 1966, is possibly Beauvoir's most under-rated novel in the sense that its feminist critique of post-structuralist notions of subjectivity, and language deployed within the context of 1960s consumer society has not yet been fully explored.[1] In *Tout Compte fait,* Beauvoir notes in her commentary on the reception of *Les Belles Images* that certain readers reproached her for having apparently abandoned her usual literary and philosophical concerns for the jet-setting romantic fictional territory of Françoise Sagan; others claimed that they were unable to identify with any of the characters – communist readers, for example, lamented the absence of a positive hero (TFC 173). The bourgeois consumer clones of *Les Belles Images* are, however, an ideal social group for Beauvoir's purposes of exploring the cost of erasing history, praxis and the real in an advanced capitalist, technological society beginning to embrace globalisation. Indeed, the feminist and broadly humanist critique of the consequences of advanced capitalism and emerging globalisation in *Les Belles Images* lends it a highly contemporary relevance.

The purpose of this chapter will be to analyse the ways in which Beauvoir critiques what she perceives as the mythological and reactionary ideological bases of post-structuralist thought and the increasingly globalised consumerism of the 1960s Parisian bourgeoisie, with a particular focus on the role of language in effecting the alienation and oppression of women. She was not alone at this time in casting a critical eye upon the developing consumer society in France for Georges Perec's *Les Choses: Une Histoire des années soixante* was published just a year before in 1965 and reviewed amid some controversy in *Les Temps Modernes* in December of that

---

[1] Exceptionally, a sophisticated discussion of Beauvoir's critique of language and of the impasses of the Lacanian Imaginary, especially for women, in the context of the bourgeois technocratic society of the 1960s can be found in Jane Heath, *Simone de Beauvoir* (Hemel Hempstead: Harvester Wheatsheaf, 1989) 119-142; Lynne Ketler Penrod examines the representation of consumer society in *Les Belles Images* through the lens of Jean Baudrillard's *La Société de consommation* in "Consuming Women Consumed: Images of Consumer Society in Simone de Beauvoir's *Les Belles Images* and Christiane Rochefort's *Les Stances à Sophie*" in *Simone de Beauvoir Studies* 4 (1987) 160-175.

year.[2] Although Perec's novel was hailed on the Left as an indictment of capitalist consumerism because it portrays the vacuous mind-set of his generation and its pursuit of an inauthentic notion of happiness through the accumulation of "things", Perec attempted to distance his rather classical work, indebted to Flaubert's *L'Education sentimentale* (1869), from sociologically orientated, Marxist readings.[3] Nevertheless, there is a common focus in Flaubert's *L'Education sentimentale,* Perec's *Les Choses* and *Les Belles Images* on the moral bankruptcy of a generation whose individuals have largely lost the capacity for ethical and political action.[4] Beauvoir's ideological critique in *Les Belles Images,* however, distinguishes itself in several ways from Perec's concerns in *Les Choses,* as will be briefly examined below.

Les *Choses,* set both in France and Tunisia, draws on the *Bildungsroman* tradition, thereby broadly following its Flaubertian antecedent. Its protagonists, Jérôme and Sylvie, aged twenty-four and twenty-two respectively, are psycho-sociologists who are working as market researchers. In this capacity, like Laurence of *Les Belles Images* in her work as an advertising copywriter, they are collaborative agents working within the capitalist system by analysing the preferences and promoting the products of consumer society. But in *Les Choses,* Jérôme and Sylvie are caught (unlike Laurence) in an aspirational trap: submerged in the fabricated tastes and superfluous yet desirable products generative of 1960s consumerism, they lack the financial means to consume those products themselves. Their conflation of "être" with "avoir" in their desire, first, for objects, second, for space (around those objects), sets them apart from Laurence of *Les Belles Images* whose dilemmas revolve more around the technocratic bourgeoisie's conflation of "être" with "paraître". Indeed, the pithy titles of *Les Choses* and

---

[2] See the consecutive and opposing reviews by A. Leclerc and H. Peretz in *Les Temps Modernes* XXI (December 1965) 1134-1139. It is also of interest here that in a bid to inject new blood into *Les Temps Modernes,* Beauvoir called a meeting in autumn 1964 which Perec attended, although he ultimately did not join the *Les Temps Modernes* group; for further details, see Georges Perec, *Les Choses. Une Histoire des années soixante* [1965] (Paris: Julliard, 1988) and David Bellos, *Georges Perec, A Life in Words* (London: The Harvill Press, 1999) 297.

[3] For further information, see Bellos 303-324.

[4] While clearly there are major differences of focus between *Les Belles Images* and *L'Éducation sentimentale,* not least relating to Beauvoir's attention to gender politics, their protagonists, acting as conduits for their generation, allow the ethical and the political to be displaced by the sentimental and the erotic. Of *L'Éducation sentimentale,* Flaubert explained, "Je veux faire l'histoire morale des hommes de ma génération; 'sentimentale' serait plus vrai'" ("I want to write the moral history, or rather the sentimental history, of the men of my generation; 'sentimental' would be more accurate"), see "Letter to Mlle Leroyer de Chantepie, 6 October 1964" in *Correspondence* V (Paris: Editions Conard, 1933) 158. More generally, Beauvoir exhibits a Flaubertian fascination in *Les Belles Images* for bourgeois clichés and is equally adept in her deployment of narrative irony at the expense of the bourgeoisie.

Les Belles Images suggest in their blunt immediacy that Perec's text is an exploration of a relationship to non-human objects and of human beings rendered objects, whereas the scepticism and irony implicit in Beauvoir's title – a common term, itself found in Perec's text – suggests a quest for identity and authenticity beyond the banal homogenous images of bourgeois affluence.[5]

Approximately ten years older than Jérôme and Sylvie of *Les Choses,* and similarly trained in the identification and manipulation of consumer desire, Laurence pursues a different quest for self. Jaded in her professional life by a surfeit of "les mots et les choses", in her personal life she already possesses the financial means to obtain "les choses" and the space to surround them.[6] The intermittently critical detachment of Laurence from her milieu of consumerist bourgeois clones, evident in the intercalation of third and first person narration, effects a shift in focus in Beauvoir's text, away from the pursuit of objects and spaces of consumer desire as explored in *Les Choses* (whose protagonists literally do not speak but are spoken by their milieu in an exclusively third person narration) towards the gendered subject's pursuit of an ethical relationship to language, time and action. In *Les Belles Images,* this relationship, explored mainly by Laurence, her daughter Catherine and friend Brigitte, is fragile and ambiguous and represented as antithetical to atemporal and unethical bourgeois consumerism. In *Les Choses,* however, the petty bourgeois characters are situated outside history: "ils n'avaient pas de passé, pas de tradition."[7] Even when Jérôme and Sylvie do become politically active during the Algerian War, they still do not feel personally implicated. Motivated instead by the pursuit of beautiful things, they nevertheless recognise that they are unlikely to be called up to fight in a war to acquire a Chesterfield settee.[8] In *Les Belles Images,* underpinned as it is by Catherine's two metaphysical questions: "Pourquoi est-ce qu'on existe?" and "Les gens qui ne sont pas heureux, pourquoi est-ce qu'ils existent?", the tentative exploration of

---

5 Perec, *Les Choses* 59.
6 The reference here to "les mots et les choses" echoes the title of Michel Foucault's *Les Mots et les choses, une archéologie des sciences humaines* (Paris: Gallimard, 1966), itself a combination of the titles of Sartre's recent *Les Mots* (Paris: Gallimard, 1964) and Perec's *Les Choses.* Foucault's text appeared in the same year as *Les Belles Images* and is satirised in Beauvoir's text, as examined briefly in this chapter.
7 Perec, *Les Choses* 52.
8 Perec, *Les Choses* 91.

the female subject's ethical relationship to language, time and action will entail a fracturing of a historical, mythological discourse and an ephemeral sighting of authentic possibilities of existence.[9]

In *Les Belles Images,* Beauvoir offers a critique of the "discourse" of the technocratic bourgeoisie, as she explains in *Tout Compte fait* (although her purpose of providing an ideological critique of this social group is largely lost in the rendition provided in the English translation of that text):

> J'ai repris un autre projet: évoquer cette société technocratique dont je me tiens le plus possible à distance mais dans laquelle néanmoins je vis [...] mon intention n'était pas de décrire l'expérience vécue et singulière de certains de ses membres: je voulais faire entendre ce qu'on appelle aujourd'hui son *"discours"*. (TCF)[10]

Beauvoir explicitly signals here her contemporary understanding of the term "discourse", evoking its wider post-structuralist sense in *Les Belles Images* rather than merely referring to the (sounds of the) language employed by the technocratic bourgeoisie. In this wider sense, "discourse" may be understood – echoing Michel Foucault's use of the concept – as an historically contingent mode of specifying effects of knowledge, power and truth.[11] So Beauvoir's phrase "ce qu'on appelle aujourd'hui son 'discours'" signals both her knowledge of contemporary post-structuralist thought and that the concept is not new (to her). Indeed, the ideological deployment of language to specify effects of knowledge, power and truth was powerfully demonstrated in Beauvoir's analysis of the operation of myth in *Le Deuxième Sexe* (1949), eight years before the publication of *Mythologies* (1957), Roland Barthes's mythological analysis of popular culture. Hence, Beauvoir's ideological critique in *Les Belles Images* can be read not only as a response to the patriarchal anti-humanism that she deplored in post-structuralist thought and bourgeois consumer society more generally, but also contra the view that she might have abandoned her characteristic concerns

---

[9] "Why do people live?" "But what about the people who aren't happy: why are they alive?" (LBI 20-21) This rendition of Catherine's questions in the published English translation using "live" and "alive" rather than "exist" diminishes their existentialist resonance.

[10] "I turned back to an earlier project dealing with this technocratic society. It is a society that I keep as much as possible at arm's length but nevertheless it is one in which I live [...] I did not intend to take certain given members of this society and describe their particular experience; what I wanted was to reproduce the sound of it." (ASD 137)

[11] I draw here on a valuable explanation of Foucault's use of "discourse" from ed. Caroline Ramazanoglu, *Up Against Foucault, Explorations of Some Tensions Between Foucault and Feminism* (London and New York: Routledge, 1993) 19.

in *Les Belles Images* as a development of her analyses of gender and myth in *Le Deuxième Sexe.*

In *Le Deuxième Sexe,* it is argued that the myth of woman and femininity act as an ideological strategy to erase the diverse existence and lived experience of actual women:

> [...] à l'existence dispersée, contingente et multiple des femmes, la pensée mythique oppose l'Éternel Féminin unique et figé; si la définition qu'on en donne est contredite par les conduites des femmes de chair et d'os, ce sont celles-ci qui ont tort. (DS I 383)[12]

As Lundgren-Gothlin argues, Beauvoir views the function of myth as essentially conservative and reactionary, produced by the empowered subject or subject group to justify and preserve the prevailing order by attributing essential, abstract qualities to those who they wish to subjugate.[13] Myth works by erasing the historically situated lived experience of the subject or group in question and replacing it by a historical, abstract essential qualities. In this way, myth replaces historically – contingent experience with a falsifying, death-dealing necessity. Crucially, myths are internalised by individuals and groups and act upon them to shape and distort their self-consciousness and lived experience.

In *Les Belles Images,* most aspects of the novel are represented as mythologised and hence generative of inauthenticity: gender; the subject's relationship to time; love; religion; psychoanalysis; objects. Mythology works by stripping speech and silence of their historical contingency and their disruptive potential, leaving a frozen, depoliticised, ahistorical speech which presents a seamless (but surface) reality without contradictions or conflicts.[14] Indeed, early in *Les Belles Images,* Laurence's father gestures towards technology's mythologising and dehumanising transformation of nature and the real: "Rien n'étonne plus personne. Bientôt la technique apparaîtra comme la nature même et nous vivrons dans un monde parfaitement inhumain".[15]

In both *Le Deuxième Sexe* and *Les Belles Images,* Beauvoir is close in her

---

12 "[...] against the dispersed, contingent, and multiple existences of actual women, mythical thought opposes the Eternal Feminine, unique and changeless. If the definition provided for this concept is contradicted by the behaviour of flesh-and-blood women, it is the latter who are wrong." (SS 283)

13 Eva Lundgren-Gothlin, *Sex and Existence, Simone de Beauvoir's The Second Sex* (London: Athlone, 1996) 175.

14 I refer here to Barthes's analysis of the operation of myth in "Le mythe, aujourd'hui" in *Mythologies* [1957] (Paris: Seuil, 1970), see especially 200-203, 215-6.

15 "Nothing amazes anybody anymore. Presently we shall look upon technical achievement as nature itself and we shall live in a totally inhuman world." (LBI 35)

use of myth to Barthes's mythological analysis of popular culture. As Atack argues in an illuminating analysis of the use of myth in *Le Deuxième Sexe:*

> As a mythologist, Beauvoir holds her own against Barthes, and indeed their analyses have much in common. [...] For both, the myth is a system of secondary meaning, which invests the object, and is certainly not deduced from it. For both, there is a moral agenda in the unmasking of the mechanisms and techniques of mauvaise foi. For Barthes, petty bourgeois culture denies its own historical and cultural nature, naturalising its cultural discourses in a fraudulent manner. For Beauvoir, the myth of Woman springs from the collective metaphysical flight from the realities of human existence and its indignities of accident, chance and contingency.[16]

In *Les Belles Images,* however, Beauvoir crucially retains her concept of a gendered subject from *Le Deuxième Sexe* who, although subjected to mythologising discourses, acts as a site of struggle and transformation. Authentic action, underpinned by clarity and moral courage, as will be argued below, is an ethical imperative in *Les Belles Images* – as in much of Beauvoir's writing – so that the subject might avoid the danger of slipping into inauthenticity and self-delusion.

In a 1966 interview with Jacqueline Piatier in which she discussed *Les Belles Images,* Beauvoir highlighted what she perceived as the ideological dangers of the loss of the subject, history and praxis, as adumbrated in Foucault's *Les Mots et les Choses,* post-structuralist thought and contemporary literature more generally:

> Mais cette littérature et Foucault en particulier fournissent à la conscience bourgeoise ses meilleurs alibis. On supprime l'histoire, la praxis, c'est-à-dire l'engagement, on supprime l'homme, alors il n'y a plus ni misère ni malheur, il n'y a plus que des systèmes. *Les Mots et les Choses* est pour la bourgeoisie technocratique un instrument des plus utiles.[17]

Post-structuralist thought, and Foucault especially, are represented here as providing the intellectual justification for the bourgeoisie's use of mythology to deny the human subject's ability to act upon history and even to

---

[16] Margaret Atack, "Writing from the Centre: Ironies of Otherness and Marginality," ed. Ruth Evans *Simone de Beauvoir's The Second Sex, New Interdisciplinary Essays* (Manchester: MUP, 1998) 49.

[17] "This type of writing and Foucault in particular provide bourgeois consciousness with its best alibis. History, praxis, that's to say, commitment, are eliminated, human beings are eliminated so there's no more poverty or misfortune, only systems remain. *Les Mots et les Choses* is one of the technocratic bourgeoisie's most useful tools." "Simone de Beauvoir présente *Les Belles Images*: An Interview with Jacqueline Piatier" in "Introduction to *Les Belles Images*," ed. Blandine Stefanson (London: Heinemann Educational Books, 1980) 60.

deny history itself. As such, Beauvoir argues that post-structuralist thought in the service of the bourgeoisie functions as an anti-materialist and reactionary ideology that eliminates the subject as a possible site of discursive struggle and resistance. She refers here implicitly to the concluding section of Foucault's *Les Mots et les Choses* in which the human subject is deemed to be a recent and possibly obsolete epistemological invention:

> L'homme n'est pas le plus vieux problème ni le plus constant qui se soit posé au savoir humain. En prenant une chronologie relativement courte et un découpage géographique restreint – la culture européenne depuis le XVIe siècle – on peut être sûr que l'homme y est une invention récente. [...] Au milieu de tous les épisodes de cette profonde histoire du *Même* – un seul, celui qui a commencé il y a un siècle et demi et qui peut-être est en train de se clore, a laissé apparaître la figure de l'homme. [...] C'était l'effet d'un changement dans les dispositions fondamentales du savoir. [...] Si ces dispositions venaient à disparaître comme elles sont apparues [...] alors on peut bien parier que l'homme s'effacerait, comme à la limite de la mer un visage de sable.[18]

In *Les Belles Images,* a caricatural grasp of Foucault's notion of the possible obsolescence of the human subject is attributed to the male technocrats: "Jean-Charles et Dufrène sont d'accord (ils ont les mêmes lectures), l'idée d'homme est à reviser, et sans doute va-t-elle disparaître, c'est une invention du XIXe siècle, aujourd'hui périmée" (BI 131).[19]

But in the context of Beauvoir's arguments in *Le Deuxième Sexe,* Foucault's notion of the obsolescence of the human subject would eliminate the possibility of women, at an individual and collective level, being ever able to act as autonomous, historically-situated subjects. Jean-Charles may mouth tabloid clichés such as "l'avenir est aux femmes" in an attempt to show that he is in touch with what he perceives as the contemporary social "trend" of feminism, but he is swiftly derided by Gisèle Dufrène who

---

[18] Foucault, *Les Mots,* 398. "Man is neither the oldest nor the most constant problem that has been posed for human knowledge. Taking a relatively short chronological sample within a restricted geographical area – European culture since the sixteenth century – one can be certain that man is a recent invention within it. [...] In the midst of all the episodes of that profound history of the Same – only one, that which begun a century and a half ago and is now perhaps drawing to a close, has made it possible for the figure of man to appear. [...] It was the effect of a change in the fundamental arrangements of knowledge [...] If those arrangements were to disappear [...] then one can certainly wager that man would be erased, like a face drawn in sand at the edge of the sea." Michel Foucault, *The Order of Things, an Archaeology of the Human Sciences* (London: Routledge, 1970) 386-387.

[19] "Jean-Charles and Dufrène were in agreement (they read the same periodicals): the idea of what constituted man was due to be overhauled and no doubt it would vanish; it was a nineteenth-century invention and now it was out of date." (LBI 79)

claims that "le féminisme aujourd'hui, c'est dépassé" (BI 139).[20] It is deeply
ironic that contemporary thought in the shape of Foucault's *Les Mots et les
choses* is forecasting the disappearance of the human subject and that feminism is dismissed as "dépassé" (and by a female character!) even before the
laws of the 1960s and 1970s which were to improve the material situation
of French women have even been passed.[21] Indeed, Beauvoir's damning
critique of post-structuralist thought in *Les Belles Images* which depicts it as
a mythologising evacuation of the real is acutely attentive to gender issues
and suggests that it constitutes a dishonest denial of the material oppression
of women throughout the world.

For this reason, the individualised revolt against patriarchal bourgeois
myth by Laurence, Catherine and Brigitte in *Les Belles Images* is crucial for
it constitutes a refusal of the elimination of the gendered subject, pro-
pounded implicitly (in Beauvoir's view) by post-structuralism. As demonstrated in *Le Deuxième Sexe,* the operation of myth entails oppressive
material consequences, and it is usually women who suffer them most.
Two examples from *Les Belles Images* of the function of everyday myth and
its effects on women will be considered here before moving to look in
more detail at Beauvoir's notion of the gendered subject as a site of struggle and transformation in *Les Belles Images.*

First, towards the end of Chapter 2, Laurence becomes anxious about
the effect of television images on Catherine, observing (in accordance with
her professional training) that: "on y montre parfois des scènes peu support-
ables; et, pour une enfant, les images sont plus saisissantes que les mots" (BI
110).[22] A recent image, observed by Catherine's Jewish friend Brigitte, is
that of young girls working in a Third World factory putting bits of carrot
on herring fillets. Laurence's initial response to Brigitte's moral concern
over this image of mind-numbingly repetitive and poorly paid labour is that
the girls concerned have been brought up to have different expectations. But
Laurence knows that this explanation is inadequate, as does Brigitte who,
throughout the text, provides a moral challenge to the mythologising claims
of adults, particularly to Jean-Charles's myth of the future as a time bringing

---

[20] "[…] the future belongs to women" and "feminism is terribly old hat nowadays." (LBI 83-4)

[21] For example, the laws legalising contraception (1967), abortion (1974), replacing paternal authority
by parental authority (1970), instituting equal pay for the same job or work of equal value (1972) and
allowing divorce by consent (1975).

[22] "Sometimes they showed almost unbearable scenes and for a child pictures were more striking than
words." (LBI 67)

abundance and prosperity for all. At this point, Laurence remembers Jean-Charles's earlier words which reveal his mythologising moral bankruptcy in the face of human suffering: "Hier il m'a dit: 'Évidemment les incidences humaines des concentrations, de l'automation sont parfois regrettables. Mais qui voudrait arrêter le progrès?'" (BI 102).[23] She then remembers Brigitte's words and the earlier inadequacy of Jean-Charles's response:

> "Toute la journée des ronds de carotte". Sans doute, les jeunes filles qui font un pareil métier, c'est qu'elles ne sont pas capables d'un travail plus intéressant. Mais ça ne rend pas les choses plus drôles pour elles. Voilà encore de ces "incidences humaines" qui sont regrettables. Ai-je raison, ai-je tort de si peu m'en soucier? (BI 112)[24]

Child labour (specifically that of girls) is represented here as an unfortunate but necessary side effect of the march of progress from which, as Laurence recognises dimly, only First World bourgeois technocrats like Jean-Charles will benefit. In this way, material poverty and oppression are made myth; in reality they sustain western progress – if indeed it can be viewed as progress – and any action to eradicate poverty and oppression is perpetually deferred. Appropriated by bourgeois myth, poverty and oppression become a not-so-"belle image," exemplified by the poster announcing "les deux tiers du monde ont faim" (BI 37) which triggers Catherine's metaphysical and moral questions.[25]

Moreover, it is significant that Brigitte, as a Jew, is attributed with this acute moral consciousness which powerfully influences Catherine and her mother, Laurence. Brigitte's Jewishness, in addition to her refusal of the traditional norms of femininity, her interest in "real" history and her motherless upbringing position her as an outsider within the novel (BI 72-4). Yet it is precisely her outsider status, her friendship for Catherine and her insistent moral gaze upon a social group whose members barely glance at each other which provide the crucial catalytic ingredients for change. Specifically, the subversive power of female friendship – which Laurence was prevented from experiencing in her childhood – is that it produces free

---

[23] "Yesterday he said to me: 'Of course, the human effects of high population density and automation are sometimes unfortunate, but who wants to hold up progress?'" (LBI 62)
[24] "'Rounds of carrots all day long.' No doubt if girls earned their living like that it was because they were incapable of doing more interesting work. But that did not make it any the more amusing for them. This was another of those regrettable 'human effects'. Am I right or am I wrong to mind it so little?" (LBI 68)
[25] "Two thirds of the world goes hungry." (LBI 25)

and open speech between girls and women which can then act as a powerful antidote to patriarchal mythologising discourse (BI 242). In this way,
female friendship emerges in Les Belles Images as a fragile ethical alternative
to patriarchal mythologising discursive systems.

A second example of the everyday function of myth and its effects on
women occurs later in the text after Laurence has crashed the family car
rather than run over a cyclist, thereby incurring a large bill for a new car in
the absence of adequate insurance. In the ensuing discussion, Jean-Charles
and Laurence argue over two essentially moral questions: first, whether to
send Catherine to a psychologist to "cure" her "sensiblerie" (sentimentality)
as her metaphysical and moral concerns are described by Jean-Charles and,
second, Laurence's decision to risk damaging the car rather than hitting the
cyclist. In terms of the latter question, Jean-Charles implicitly hierarchises
property and people in value so that Laurence's "crime" against property
is deemed worse than if she had hit the cyclist. Laurence then receives a
bouquet of red roses from Jean-Charles. Trained to recognise psychological and emotional manipulation, she observes to herself:

> Un bouquet, c'est toujours autre chose que des fleurs: c'est de l'amitié, de l'espoir,
> de la gratitude, de la gaieté. Des roses rouges: amour ardent. Justement non.
> Même pas un sincère remords, elle en est sûre; simple déférence aux conventions
> conjugales: pas de mésentente pendant les fêtes de fin d'année. (BI 191)[26]

Barthes uses the same example of red roses in Mythologies to explain how
red roses (as signifier) unite with passion (as signified) to produce the sign
of red-roses-as-passion.[27] It is henceforth impossible to dissociate the red
roses from the passion as the signifier is emptied and the sign is filled.
Beauvoir, however, in this instance, demonstrates the material effects on
women of the mythological abuse of this sign of romantic discourse: here,
that it is used by Jean-Charles to silence Laurence and to subjugate her to
ensure the restoration of the myths of family harmony and conjugal bliss.

To palliate her sense of gendered alienation in an increasingly globalised
and technological world, Laurence seeks refuge and self-affirmation in different types of love. Given the myth-producing type of job she does, it
would be not be feasible for her to seek self-affirmation in her professional

---

[26] "A bouquet is always something more than mere flowers – it's friendship, it's hope, gratitude, happiness. Red roses – glowing love. And that was just what it was not. Not even sincere regret, she was
sure of that: only a gesture towards the conventions of married life – no disagreements over
Christmas." (LBI 114-5)
[27] Barthes 197, 113.

sphere. Fairly inevitably, however, this quest for self in the private sphere is revealed to be doomed and delusionary in the three out of the four examples of love examined: conjugal (in her marriage with Jean-Charles); erotic (in her affair with Lucien); filial (in her relationship with her father). It is only in the case of maternal love that Laurence manages to express a fragile sense of autonomy in her final defence of Catherine at the end of the novel when she refuses to allow her to be treated by a child psychologist.

In her relationship with Jean-Charles, Laurence wonders why she is with him rather than with someone else (BI 89-90). Professionally highly successful, Jean-Charles is represented (in Laurence's interior monologue) as a prime instrument of bourgeois phallogocentrism, in his domination of conversation, reason and representation, bound as he is to supply Laurence with five or six explanations for Catherine's metaphysical "sensiblerie" before she has had time to think or speak (BI 31). Jean-Charles always has to triumph over any disagreement rather than attempt to understand his interlocutor (BI 182). Incarnating the values of the technocratic bourgeoisie, he is disturbingly in flight from his past (he avoids speaking about his family background) and abhors the unexpected – presumably because the unexpected and the contingent disrupt his mythologising phallogocentric project. Positioned as an ideological foil to Laurence's humanist father, Jean-Charles believes that technology and globalisation will cure all humanity's ills, including those of the starving child on the poster announcing that two thirds of the world's population is hungry (BI 37). Yet Jean-Charles, like so many others of his milieu, is interchangeable, and is, to some degree, a consumer choice as far as Laurence is concerned. For, in a bid to recover a romantic intimacy now replaced and commodified by expensive gifts in her relationship with Jean-Charles, Laurence has an affair with Lucien. But, like Emma Bovary, she finds in adultery only the platitudes of marriage, as Lucien seeks to possess her and their onetime passion becomes ritualised.[28] Conjugal and romantic love are represented in *Les Belles Images* as (literally) seductive myths which serve only to alienate Laurence further from an authentic experience of self. In the case of her mother, Dominique, who is abandoned by her wealthy partner Gilbert for a nineteen-year-old débutante, the loss of love signifies only the loss of social status and power: "socialement une femme n'est rien sans un homme" (BI 200).[29]

---

[28] Flaubert, *Madame Bovary* [1857] (Paris: Gallimard Folio, 1981) 376.
[29] "[…] socially a woman without a man counts for nothing." (LBI 119)

Yet love, as experienced between parents and children, seems to offer more possibilities to Laurence for her self-actualisation, although at other times (for example in her relationships with her parents) it can act as an abusive and mythologising force. It is significant, however, that Laurence's ultimate and fragile rebellion against patriarchal bourgeois mythology emerges from her experience of filial and maternal love, rather than from conjugal or erotic love. Early in the novel, Laurence reveals her idealisation of her father to the detriment of her mother: "c'est son père qu'elle aime le plus – le plus au monde – et elle voit Dominique bien davantage. Toute ma vie ainsi: c'est mon père que j'aimais et ma mère qui m'a faite" (BI 43-4).[30] Temporarily abandoning her Electra complex in adult life for her relationships with Jean-Charles and Lucien, she then returns to her preferred child state and to her father as the source of wisdom, integrity and love: "Elle regarde son père: pouvoir se recueillir comme lui. Ce qu'elle a cru retrouver chez Jean-Charles, chez Lucien, lui seul le possède: sur son visage, un reflet de l'infini. Etre à soi-même une présence amie, être un foyer qui rayonne de la chaleur" (BI 47).[31] Yet Laurence is not merely seeking in her father a source of parental love and approval but also a model of existing in the world, as a self-contained yet open presence to others. Her father appears to her to possess a humanity and an ethical relationship to the world that is absent from her social milieu of bourgeois technocrats. He also interprets the world of "words and things" for Laurence, thereby dispensing her from the need to think: "J'aimais retrouver devant cet alphabet le mystère enfantin du langage et que, comme autrefois, le sens des mots et des choses me vînt par lui" (BI 217).[32]

In her idealisation of her father and her frequent deference to Jean-Charles until the point of her final tentative self-recognition and rebellion, Laurence might be viewed throughout the text as in flight from her own psychic complexity – a flight facilitated by her patriarchal bourgeois mythologising environment which has trained her to accept her role as a "belle image". To explore the parameters of this flight from psychic complexity, it

---

[30] "[…] it was her father she loved best – best in the world – and she saw much more of Dominique. My whole life has been like that: it was my father I loved and my mother who formed me."(LBI 29)

[31] "She looked at her father: oh to be able to sink into oneself like that. He alone possessed what she thought she had found in Jean-Charles and Lucien: upon his face there was reflection of the infinite. To be delightful company for oneself: to be a hearth that sends out warmth." (LBI 31)

[32] "I liked gazing at that alphabet and rediscovering the childhood mystery of the language; and I was pleased that the meaning of words and things should come to me through him, as it had in former days." (LBI 130)

is useful to refer briefly to the work of the psychoanalyst, Christopher Bollas. In his *Being a Character, Psychoanalysis and Self Experience* (1992), Bollas argues that as the child comes into the presence of his or her own mind, he or she embarks on a disturbing journey of psychic development which is in part devolutionary in its dismantling of pre-Oedipal and Oedipal structures.[33] The child is then faced with a terrifying psychic complexity, according to Bollas, from which he or she retreats in order to survive. This retreat from – as Bollas terms it – "having a mind" involves a regression into the soothing (because literally "familiar") experiences of coupledom, family life or group allegiance:

> Given the ordinary unbearableness of this complexity [...] the human individual partly regresses in order to survive, but this retreat has been so essential to human life that it has become an unanalysed convention, part of the religion of everyday life. We call this regression "marriage" or "partnership", in which the person becomes part of a mutually interdependent couple that evokes and sustains the bodies of the mother and the father, the warmth of the pre-Oedipal vision of life, before the solitary recognition of subjectivity grips the child. Ego development is thus a transformative regression. [...] To go forward in life, we go back, back to the places of the mother and the father, where we can evoke these figures as inevitably comforting and practically as defensive alternatives to a madness always latent in groups: to the groups of social life and more so to the group that is mental life.[34]

Such a regression into coupledom, family life and group membership is not without its terrors but, argues Bollas, it furnishes us with a belief in the veracity of a single vision of reality (for example, a psychoanalytical view [of the family romance, for example], a political doctrine, or a religious belief) which is unconsciously soothing and a powerful antidote to the anxiety of confronting our own psychic complexity.[35] In *Les Belles Images,* Laurence's urgent need to escape her psychic complexity can partly be explained by the anxiety and psychic disarray caused by her earlier mental breakdown, the result, she claims, of a conflict between her feelings for her father and her feelings for Jean-Charles:

> Je ne retomberai pas. Maintenant je suis prévenue, je suis armée, je me tiens en main. Et d'ailleurs les vraies raisons de ma crise, je ne les ignore pas et je les ai dépassées: j'ai explicité le conflit qui oppose mes sentiments à l'égard de

---

[33] Christopher Bollas, *Being a Character, Psychoanalysis and Self Experience* (London and New York: Routledge, 1992) 240-246.
[34] Bollas, *Being a Character* 242.
[35] Bollas, *Being a Character* 244.

Jean-Charles à ceux que j'éprouve pour mon père; il ne me déchire plus. Je
suis au net avec moi-même. (BI 59-60)[36]

Representing herself as formerly torn between her love for her father and
her husband in an arrested Electra scenario, Laurence explains away the
complexity of her mental breakdown with a glib psychic formula and
claims to have "moved on" at a psycho-affective level. Yet another reason
for her breakdown is intermittently suggested: that of being unable to rec-
oncile her acute moral consciousness and conscience (now articulated by
Catherine and Brigitte) with her passive, affluent existence amid the patriarchal technocratic bourgeoisie. Unable to read the newspapers for fear of
confronting "real" history (such as reports of women being tortured to
death), Laurence is nevertheless moved to respond somehow to Brigitte
and Catherine (BI 186-7). But the evidence suggests that Laurence is
silenced and more tangled than ever in the patriarchal web of the Symbolic
– be it manifest in her erasure in the family romance narrative of psychoanalysis, the "passéiste" humanistic discourse of her father or Jean-Charles's
narrative of capitalist technocracy and globalisation. The battle for her psychic equilibrium is not yet won for her voice is intermittently muted until
the end of the novel and she is scarcely able to act as an autonomous subject
within the patriarchal discursive grid of gender.

As her fractured narrative of third and first-person suggests, Laurence
is fighting to survive in language, to express a barely-glimpsed sense of self.
Her predicament is that Dominique's traumatising fashioning of her into a
"belle image" has forced her into an alienating identification with her
father, in which she is forever positioned as "jeune fille rangée" and unable
to represent her experience in her own authored narrative:

Je voudrais moi aussi revenir en arrière, déjouer les embûches, réussir ce que
j'ai manqué. Qu'ai je manqué? Je ne le sais même pas. Je n'ai pas de mots pour
me plaindre ou pour regretter. (BI 215)[37]

In a literal evocation of the Lacanian Symbolic, Laurence does not have the
words to express her lack ("manque") or her experience. Like Marguerite

---

[36] "I shall not relapse. Now I am quite aware of the real reasons for my breakdown and I have gone
beyond them: I have brought my conflict between my feelings for Jean-Charles and my feelings for my
father out into the open and it does not torment me any longer. I have settled accounts with myself."
(LBI 38)
[37] "I too should like to go back into the past, escape the traps and succeed in what I have failed in.
What have I failed in? I don't even know. My complaints or regrets do not form themselves into
words." (LBI 129)

Duras's Lol V. Stein, she is often quite simply not "there".[38] Like Lol, she exists beyond phallogocentric discourse, often speechless, her experience muted. However, it takes Laurence most of the text to understand the significance of her own silence. Early in the text, she depicts the silence she experiences in her relationship with Jean-Charles as a sign of the complicity and understanding "trop profond pour les mots" between them (BI 24).[39] Yet this is shown to be a delusionary and reactive interpretation of silence, triggered, as revealed later, by Laurence's traumatising childhood experiences of "de si lourds silences à la maison" (BI 48).[40] In this context, the "talking cure" of (a feminist) psychoanalytic treatment might prove valuable for Laurence, enabling her to objectify her experience in narrative. But in *Les Belles Images,* psychoanalysis and psychiatry more generally are represented as being of little use to girls and women. Psychiatry is represented as a simplistic mythologising discourse which is deployed by the régime of the patriarchal capitalist bourgeoisie to adapt "inappropriate" (because challenging) female responses to gendered alienation – as instanced by Catherine's "sensiblerie" or Laurence's breakdown. Psychoanalysis, in particular, is represented as being somewhat "passéiste" in the sense that it reads the present situation through the interpretative formulaic grid of past experience, thereby abnegating the contingent specificity of the present moment. Lacking the words and concepts to articulate her experience, past or present, Laurence finds an echo of her situation in an image from a story she remembers of a mole digging in the dark:

> Il fait nuit en elle; elle s'abandonne à la nuit. Elle pense à une histoire qu'elle a lue: une taupe tâtonne à travers des galeries souterraines, elle en sort et sent la fraîcheur de l'air; mais elle ne sait pas inventer d'ouvrir les yeux. Elle se la raconte autrement: la taupe dans son souterrain invente d'ouvrir les yeux, et elle voit que tout est noir. Ça n'a aucun sens. (BI 238)[41]

Laurence passes here from not being able to articulate her experience to not being able to see or understand her experience; either way, she is locked in a traumatised immanence.

---

[38] Marguerite Duras, *Le Ravissement de Lol V. Stein* (Paris: Gallimard, 1964).
[39] "[…] too deep for words." (LBI 18)
[40] "[…] such brooding silences at home." (LBI 31)
[41] "It was dark inside her; she gave herself up to the darkness. She thought about a story she had read: a mole felt its way through its underground tunnels; it came out and sensed the clean fresh air; but it could not find out how to open its eyes. She told herself the story another way: the mole in its underground dwelling found out how to open its eyes, and saw that everything was dark. None of it made sense." (LBI 142)

Frequently silenced by the phallogocentric mythologising order, Laurence speaks through her body in anorexia and through her daughter, Catherine. Indeed, food is a powerful political motif in *Les Belles Images* linking female subjectivity with an ethic of care in an increasingly globalised society which decrees "deux tiers du monde ont faim." To eat "les steaks épais, les salades, les fruits" is, as Laurence slowly realises, to be blind to the material reality evoked by the poster of the starving child, to the child labourers working in the Third World food factories, and to be force-fed the lies of the First World technocratic patriarchal bourgeoisie. Vomitting up her life at the end of the novel, Laurence finally articulates her fragile rebellion:

> Ils la forceront à manger, ils lui feront tout avaler; tout quoi? tout ce qu'elle vomit, sa vie, celle des autres avec leur fausses amours, leurs histoires d'argent, leurs mensonges. Ils la guériront de ses refus, de son désespoir. Non. [...] Et Catherine? lui clouer les paupières? "Non"; elle a crié tout haut. Pas Catherine. Je ne permettrai pas qu'on lui fasse ce qu'on m'a fait. Qu'a-t-on fait de moi? Cette femme qui n'aime personne, insensible aux beautés du monde, incapable même de pleurer, cette femme que je vomis. (BI 254)[42]

But Laurence cannot fully regurgitate this adapted self and its mythologising milieu, for she has nothing – no alternative narrative – to put in its place. Aware only dimly and intermittently of "what has been done to her", Laurence is anaesthetised, silenced and incapable of transcendence for most of the novel. Experiencing herself as torn between her discursively fabricated public self and an intermittent (and hence fragile) experiencing self, she is unable to challenge the discursive structures of gender, class and capitalist consumerism which have shaped her agential possibilities.

Towards the end of the novel, Laurence's trip to Greece with her father proves pivotal in her experience of filial and maternal love, enabling her to move from her position of childlike idealisation of her father to a more adult recognition of the ethical agency involved in parenting. Greece is, of course, the literal location of classical myth and the intellectual home of Laurence's passéiste father. Yet there are two versions of mythologised

---

[42] "They would force her to eat; they would make her swallow it all. All what? All that she vomited out, her life, the lives of others with their phony loves, their stories about money, their lies. They would cure her of her rejection and her despair. No. [...] And what about Catherine? Sew her eyes up? "No", she cries out loud. Not Catherine. I shan't let what has been done to me be done to her. What have they made of me? This woman who loves no one, who is indifferent to the beauties of the world, who cannot even weep – this woman that I vomit forth." (LBI 151-2)

Greece in *Les Belles Images:* the Greece of classical antiquity and the Greece that is a present-day consumer product, worthy of analysis in Barthes's discussion of "Le *Guide bleu*" in *Mythologies*. Here Barthes describes how this age-old institution of French tourist literature mythologises the countries which form the object of its touristic inventory, rendering them ahistorical repositories of monuments, peopled only by caricatural types:

> [...] l'humanité du pays disparaît au profit exclusif de ses monuments. Pour le *Guide bleu,* les hommes n'existent que comme "types" [...]. On retrouve ici ce virus de l'essence, qui est au fond de toute mythologie bourgeoise de l'homme. [...] La sélection des monuments supprime à la fois la réalité de la terre et celle des hommes, elle ne rend compte de rien de présent, c'est-à-dire d'historique, et par là, le monument lui-même devient indéchiffrable, donc stupide. Le spectacle est ainsi sans cesse en voie d'anéantissement, et le *Guide* devient, par une opération commune à toute mystification, le contraire même de son affiche, un instrument d'aveuglement.[43]

Similarly, according to Laurence's father's delusionary narrative of Greece, it is a country untouched by the corrupting forces of money or technology where communities of people enjoy an austere happiness, founded on "true" human values of dignity, brotherliness and generosity (BI 117). But once in Greece, Laurence recognises immediately, and reluctantly, that her father has mythologised the poverty and oppression in Greece, echoing Barthes's analysis of the *Guide bleu* touristic narratives. Again, it is specifically the effects of poverty and oppression on women which are identified: "Mais les villageois du Péloponnèse n'avaient pas l'air contents du tout, ni les femmes qui cassaient des cailloux sur les routes, ni les fillettes portant des seaux d'eau trop lourds" (BI 228).[44]

Unable to appreciate the rustic charm of the "pretty pictures" of contemporary tourist Greece or relate to the classical Greek myths and legends of her father's "musée intérieur," Laurence is faced with the "visages éteints" of the impoverished Greek populace, still suffering the effects of civil war.

---

[43] Barthes, *Mythologies* 122-3. "[...] the human life of a country disappears to the exclusive benefit of its monuments. For the *Blue Guide,* men exist only as 'types'. [...] We find again here this disease of thinking in essences, which is at the bottom of every bourgeois mythology of man. [...] To select only monuments suppresses at one stroke the reality of the land and that of its people, it accounts for nothing of its present, that is, nothing historical, and as a consequence, the monuments themselves become undecipherable, therefore senseless. What is to be seen is thus constantly in the process of vanishing, and the *Guide* becomes, through an operation common to all mystifications, the very opposite of what it advertises, an agent of blindness." (Barthes, *Mythologies* 74-6)

[44] "But the villagers of the Peloponnese did not look in the least happy, neither the women breaking stones on the roads nor the little girls carrying buckets of water too heavy for them." (LBI 136)

But it is her recognition of the effects of mythologising discourse on girls and women that will finally push Laurence into assuming her maternal agency by defending Catherine. Drinking in a taverne with her father, she watches with fascination the existential exuberance of a young Greek girl dancing juxtaposed with the dull, intermittent gaze of the girl's mother nearby:

> Une petite fille s'est mise à danser [...]; elle tournait sur elle-même, les bras soulevés, le visage noyé d'extase, l'air tout à fait folle. Transportée par la musique, éblouie, grisée, transfigurée, éperdue. Placide et grasse, sa mère bavardait avec une autre grosse femme tout en faisant aller et venir une voiture d'enfant avec un bébé dedans; insensible à la musique, à la nuit, elle jetait parfois un regard bovin sur la petite inspirée.
>
> – Tu as vu la gosse?
>
> – Charmante, a dit papa avec indifférence.
>
> Une charmante fillette qui deviendrait cette matrone. Non. Je ne voulais pas. [...] Je refusais qu'un jour elle ressemblât à sa mère, ne se rappelant même pas avoir été cette adorable ménade. Petite condamnée à mort, affreuse mort sans cadavre. La vie allait l'assassiner. Je pensai à Catherine qu'on était en train d'assassiner. (BI 222-3)[45]

In this instance, seeing the direct effects of gender oppression with her own eyes, Laurence realises the ethical importance of her maternal agency and that she has the power to "save" Catherine from the death-dealing patriarchal ideology of the technocratic bourgeoisie. An ideology to which her father is largely indifferent – because, as a bourgeois man, he is among its beneficiaries. Indeed, it is Laurence's slow recognition that her father is implicated in the perpetuation of the mythologising process in the guise of his patriarchal passéiste liberal humanism which will result in the final relinquishing of her paternal imago. Realising dimly the mystificatory power of this imago, Laurence attempts to assume an authentic maternal agency with regard to Catherine which incorporates a mutual respect between mother and daughter.

---

[45] "A little girl began to dance [...]; she spun, her arms in the air, her face aswim with ecstasy, quite beside herself, carried away by the music, dazzled, intoxicated, transfigured, rapt. Her calm, fat mother gossiped there with another heavy woman, and all the time she pushed a pram with a baby in it to and fro; she was wholly untouched by the music or the night, and from time to time she sent a cow-like gaze in the direction of her enraptured child.'
'Have you seen the little girl?'
'Charming,' said Papa, quite unmoved.
A charming little girl who would turn into that maternal figure. No. I would not have it. [...] I would not have it that one day she should look like her mother, not even remembering that she had ever been this enchanting maenad. Child condemned to death, to an appalling death with no corpse. Life was going to murder her. I thought of Catherine who they were murdering at that moment." (LBI 133)

Ultimately, then, in *Les Belles Images,* the future does belong to women and to the relationships between women – be they mother-daughter relationships as exemplified by Laurence and Catherine or relationships of friendship between (young) women such as Catherine and Brigitte – but only if they are relationships founded on reciprocity and respect. Throughout *Les Belles Images,* women are shown to be the prime casualties of patriarchal bourgeois mythology – sometimes through their own collusion with the system or through their ignorance or simply their fear. Although it may be too late for Dominique and even Laurence, for both are tangled to varying degrees in the discursive web of patriarchal myth, imago and image, Catherine and Brigitte incarnate a new generation of young women ready to speak out and to cast a critical and ethical gaze over patriarchy's "belles images" and, in so doing, they assume their future agential possibilities. This does not constitute a mythologisation of the future, à la Jean-Charles, for "les enfants auront leur chance. Quelle chance? Elle ne le sait même pas" (BI 258).[46] The future, then, is to be seized with respect for its unknown contingent possibilities.

In conclusion, Beauvoir's achievement in *Les Belles Images* is to have mythified myth by using semiology to expose ideology, thereby restoring female agency to make "histoire" in both its personal and collective sense.[47] For Catherine and Brigitte, the future is open – to contingency and praxis – and the value of history is affirmed.

---

[46] "The children will have their chance. What chance? She did not even know." (LBI 154)
[47] Barthes argues that the best weapon against myth is to mythify it, see *Mythologies* 135-7, 222-224.

Works Cited

Atack, Margaret. "Writing from the Centre: Ironies of Otherness and Marginality". In Ruth Evans, ed. *Simone de Beauvoir's The Second Sex, New Interdisciplinary Essays*. Manchester: MUP, 1998. 31-58.

Barthes, Roland. *Mythologies*. Paris: Seuil, 1970.

de Beauvoir, Simone. *Le Deuxième Sexe I, Les Faits et les mythes*. Paris: Gallimard, 1966.

_____. *The Second Sex*. London: Vintage, 1997.

_____. "Simone de Beauvoir présente *Les Belles Images:* An Interview with Jacqueline Piatier". In Blandine Stefanson, ed. "Introduction" to *Les Belles Images*. London: Heinemann Educational Books, 1980.

_____. *Les Belles Images* [1966]. Paris: Gallimard, 1967.

_____. *Les Belles Images*. Trans. Patrick O'Brian. London: Fontana Paperbacks, 1982.

_____. *Tout Compte fait*. Paris: Gallimard, 1989.

_____. *All Said and Done*. Harmondsworth: Penguin, 1977.

Bellos, David. *Georges Perec, A Life in Words*. London: The Harvill Press, 1999.

Bollas, Christopher. *Being a Character, Psychoanalysis and Self Experience*. London and New York: Routledge, 1992.

Duras, Marguerite. *Le Ravissement de Lol V. Stein*. Paris: Gallimard, 1964.

Flaubert, Gustave. *Correspondance*. Tome V. Paris: Editions Conard, 1933.

_____. *Madame Bovary* [1857]. Paris: Gallimard, 1981.

_____. *Madame Bovary*. Trans. Gerard Hopkins. Oxford: Oxford World's Classics: Oxford University Press, 1998.

Foucault, Michel. *Les Mots et les choses, une archéologie des sciences humaines*. Paris: Gallimard, 1966.

_____. *The Order of Things, an Archaeology of the Human Sciences*. London: Routledge, 1970.

Heath, Jane. *Simone de Beauvoir*. Hemel Hempstead: Harvester Wheatsheaf, 1989.

Ketler Penrod, Lynne. "Consuming Women Consumed: Images of Consumer Society in Simone de Beauvoir's *Les Belles Images* and Christiane Rochefort's *Les Stances à Sophie*". *Simone de Beauvoir Studies* 4 (1987): 160-175.

Lundgren-Gothlin, Eva. *Sex and Existence, Simone de Beauvoir's The Second Sex*. London: Athlone, 1996.

Perec, Georges. *Les Choses. Une Histoire des années soixante* [1965]. Paris: Julliard, 1988.

Ramazanoglu, Caroline, ed. *Up Against Foucault, Explorations of Some Tensions between Foucault and Feminism*. London and New York: Routledge, 1993.

7

The Rhetoric of Self-Deception: Conflicting Truths and the Undermining of Narratives in *La Femme rompue*

Annlaug Bjørsnøs

Simone de Beauvoir's last work of fiction, the short story collection *La Femme rompue,* was published in 1968. The main character in all three stories is a woman at a dramatic turning point in her life who, instead of adjusting to changing conditions, employs all her argumentative, emotional and psychic power to escape the inevitable. True to her feminist and existentialist position, and sharing Sartre's view on *la littérature engagée,* Beauvoir set out to write these stories with a specific mindset:

> Moi, je me proposais, dans *La Femme rompue,* de peindre les moments critiques de trois existences féminines, la rencontre avec la vieillesse; l'exaspération d'une solitude; la fin brutale d'un amour. Ce qui m'intéressait essentiellement dans ces histoires, c'était la mauvaise foi plus ou moins têtue avec laquelle mes héroïnes menaient leur combat.[1]

Clearly intending the three woman protagonists to be negative heroines, Beauvoir presents her short story project as a didactic one: "I am merely presenting the reality of what happens to women in our society. It is up to my readers to profit from their mistakes, to learn from their experiences and keep themselves free from situations that end the same way."[2] Bair additionally notes that the author was particularly engaged by the pertinence of the narrative form: "She decides to write about how women deceive themselves, using three different fictional techniques."[3]

Beauvoir's statements about this literary project demand the reader's critical awareness. Her desire to "merely [present] the reality" may intrigue the "post-modern" reader and require a different approach to the text. Sceptical about the representational function of narrative, the critical reader's attention is now drawn towards the way literary texts arrange or *construct* reality or a specific perspective on reality through the discursive strategies at work.

---

[1] Anne Ophir, *Regards féminins* (Paris: Denoël/Gonthier, 1976) preface by Beauvoir. "What I set out to do in *The Woman Destroyed* was to portray crucial moments in three women's lives, the coming to terms with old age, the exasperation of a lonely woman, the abrupt ending of a love story. What really interested me in these stories was the more or less stubborn bad faith of the heroines in their struggles." (my translation)

[2] Deirdre Bair, *Simone de Beauvoir. A Biography* (New York: Touchstone, 1990) 528.

[3] Bair 526.

I will focus in this essay on how the three women's realities are constructed and deconstructed through the specific discursive and narrative
practices deployed by Beauvoir, with an eye to the explicit authorial judge-
ments of the main characters as one of several dynamic functions in the texts.

"L'Age de discrétion"

The opening story, "L'Age de discrétion", is a first-person narrative,
where the character-narrator, a woman in her sixties whose name we never
discover, experiences a crisis in her relationship with her son and her husband, as well as difficulties in her professional life. The problem of ageing
and the shock of her son's unexpected resistance to the plans she has made
for his future seem to be the two pivotal axes of the narrative.

The retired but still highly active couple live in a flat in Paris, sur-
rounded by books and souvenirs from their many travels in Europe. Up
until recently, the woman has been teaching literature at the Sorbonne and
is about to publish a book on literary methodology. Her husband, a scien-
tist, is engaged with the world's sufferings, supporting freedom fighters
and political prisoners all over the world. Theirs is a meaningful, complete
life, where culture is highly valued. Their only son, Philippe, has been
brought up in this intellectual atmosphere, where high ideals, rooted in
left-wing values, are taken for granted. When the story begins, Philippe is
writing his thesis at the Sorbonne and thus seems to be following in his
parents' footsteps.

The opening sequence of the story, recounted in the present tense,
plunges the reader right into the middle of the character-narrator's
thoughts, as she impatiently waits for one of her son's rare visits:

> Ma montre est-elle arrêtée? Non. Mais les aiguilles n'ont pas l'air de tourner.
> Ne pas les regarder. Penser à autre chose, à n'importe quoi: à cette journée
> derrière moi, tranquille et quotidienne malgré l'agitation de l'attente. (FR 9)[4]

This first paragraph not only enables the reader to grasp the atmosphere of
anxiety and expectation and to become aware of the narrator's constant
striving towards self-control, but also foreshadows one of the main topics
of this story: the preoccupation with the nature and significance of time. I

---

[4] "Has my watch stopped? No. But its hands do not seem to be going around. Don't look at them.
Think of something else – anything else: think of yesterday, a calm, ordinary, easy-flowing day, in spite
of the nervous tension of waiting." (WD 11)

suggest that the narrative first deconstructs the main character's conception of temporal coherence, before finally opening up towards a more ambiguous position. As we shall see, her discourse is initially saturated with what we might term a highly modernist conception of time and historicity but, as I will demonstrate, the experiences she lives through as the story progresses serve to undermine this particular conceptual framework.

In the first pages, the character-narrator presents a seemingly detailed picture of herself, alternatively reporting her experiences in the present tense (in a series of interior monologues) and relating events in the past tense, as the plot smoothly unfolds. The narrative is dominantly recounted from her perspective, to the extent that other voices are barely audible.

The woman appears to be a reflective person, who has a tendency to problematise and analyze the various aspects of her life which preoccupy her from every possible angle. At the point the reader is about to enter into her world, she is leading a full and harmonious life, abounding in gentle happiness. For instance, she refers to "toutes ces rengaines sur la non-communication!" (FR 9)[5] in such a way as to suggest that this is not a problem that she can relate to. Furthermore, she describes her relation to her husband as being entirely open: "en gros nous n'ignorons rien l'un de l'autre." (FR 9).[6] Time has done nothing to change her feelings for him: "mon regard ne lui connaît pas d'âge. [...] Il semble parfois que le temps n'ait pas coulé. L'avenir s'étend encore à l'infini" (FR 10).[7] Her professional life also seems perfectly satisfactory – she is confident in her own abilities and is eagerly looking forward to the reception of her new book on literature.

At this stage she appears to have a concept of time that privileges its density, unity and permanence, and this is expressed on many occasions and in various ways as the story develops. Contemplating the little table in the library where the couple have been sitting together drinking tea over the years, she states: "Et de nouveau demain, dans un an, dans dix ans... Cet instant avait la douceur d'un souvenir et la gaieté d'une promesse" (FR 10).[8] Present, past and future all merge seamlessly in an image of everlasting marital harmony. The implication is that this state of affairs will last

---

5 "[...] all this going on about non-communication." (WD 11)
6 "[...] on the whole there is nothing we do not know about one another." (WD 11)
7 "[...] my eyes attribute no age to him. [...] Sometimes it seems that time has not moved by at all. The future still stretches out to infinity." (WD 12)
8 "[...] we should do so again tomorrow, and in a year's time, and in ten years' time. [...] That moment possessed the sweet gentleness of a memory and the gaiety of a promise." (WD 12)

forever, with the future envisioned as a stable linear progression ensuring the continuation of present security:

> J'ai suivi des yeux André. C'est peut-être dans ces instants où je le regarde s'éloigner qu'il existe pour moi avec la plus bouleversante évidence; la haute silhouette se rapetisse, dessinant à chaque pas le chemin de son retour; elle disparaît, la rue semble vide mais en vérité c'est un champ de forces qui le reconduira vers moi comme à son lieu naturel; cette certitude m'émeut plus encore que sa présence. (FR 10-11)[9]

She refers repeatedly to time as a comforting, organizing category with which she is perfectly at ease. Contemplating Paris from her balcony, she meditates on time and changing times, but these do not frighten her – on the contrary, she feels perfectly capable of mastering the constantly varying circumstances of life and this ability of hers is presented as a natural gift:

> La jeunesse de ce paysage me saute aux yeux: et pourtant je ne me rappelle pas l'avoir vu autre. J'aimerais contempler côte à côte les deux clichés: avant, après, et m'étonner de leurs différences. Mais non. Le monde se crée sous mes yeux dans un éternel présent; je m'habitue si vite à ses visages qu'il ne me paraît pas changer. (FR 11)[10]

She takes pleasure in imagining that she is part of a larger entity, of the totality of humankind in all its diversity, imagining herself at one with the world: "Comme je ne sors presque plus le matin, le marché me semblait exotique *(tant de marchés, le matin, sous tant de ciels)*" (FR 12).[11] Here, her unifying imagination even takes on a spatial dimension.

The style of her prose adds to the general impression of a strong belief in the meaningfulness of the world. In what Elizabeth Fallaize refers to as "highly polished mythical moments,"[12] the narrator's language swells with satisfaction as she relishes the idea of existence's historicity and its inner coherence:

> Reflets, échos, se renvoyant à l'infini: j'ai découvert la douceur d'avoir

---

[9] "My eyes followed André. Maybe it is during those moments, as I watch him disappear, that he exists for me with the most overwhelming clarity: his tall shape grows smaller, each pace marking out the path of his return; it vanishes and the street seems to be empty; but in fact it is a field of energy that will lead him back to me as to his natural habitat: I find this certainty even more moving than his presence." (WD 11-12)

[10] "I find the newness of the landscape stirringly obvious; yet I cannot remember having seen it look otherwise. I should like two photographs to set side by side, Before and After, so that I could be amazed by the differences. No; not really. The world brings itself into being before my eyes in an everlasting present: I grow used to its different aspects so quickly that it does not seem to me to change." (WD 13)

[11] "As I almost never go out in the morning anymore, the market had an exotic air for me *(so many morning markets, beneath so many skies)*." (WD 14, my emphasis).

[12] Elizabeth Fallaize, *The Novels of Simone de Beauvoir* (London and New York: Longman, 1981) 158.

derrière moi un long passé. Je n'ai pas le temps de me le raconter, mais souvent à l'improviste je l'aperçois en transparence au fond du moment présent; il lui donne sa couleur, sa lumière comme les roches ou les sables se reflètent dans le chatoiement de la mer. (FR 17)[13]

Although her lyrical outbursts may seem overblown, it is worth observing the metaphorical configuration of her euphoric vision of coherence. The rather trite imaginary scene pictured here, where time is captured in space, provides a foreground for the visual and emotive effects of the natural elements alluded to (light and space), each of which endows meaning to the other within an endlessly repeating, reverberating movement.

In her professional life, she directs her energies towards making conclusive statements, displaying an evident eagerness to achieve control within her area of research. Her new book aims at achieving mastery and precision in the field of literary analysis and she is in fact convinced that she has reached her goal:

– Vous savez ce que j'ai voulu faire: à partir d'une réflexion sur les œuvres critiques parues depuis la guerre, proposer une méthode nouvelle qui permette de pénétrer dans l'œuvre d'un auteur plus exactement qu'on ne l'a jamais fait. J'espère que j'ai réussi.

C'était plus qu'un espoir: une conviction. Elle m'ensoleillait le cœur. (FR 18-19)[14]

She believes firmly in the progress of science, and when her husband states that his younger collaborators are the only ones who come up with new ideas, she expresses her disagreement with this statement by quoting a verse from one of Valéry's poems: "Chaque atome de silence – Est la chance d'un fruit mûr" (FR 14). She comments on the verse in the following way: "De cette lente gestation, des fruits inespérés vont naître. Elle n'est pas terminée, cette aventure à laquelle j'ai passionnément participé" (FR 14).[15]

Even in her description of one of the pastimes which she enjoys (cross-

---

13 "Reflections, echoes, reverberating back and back to infinity: I have discovered the pleasure of having a long past behind me. I have not the leisure to tell it over to myself, but often, quite unexpectedly, I catch sight of it, a background to the diaphanous present; a background that gives it its color and its light, just as rocks or sand show through the shifting brilliance of the sea." (WD 19)
14 "You know what I wanted to do – to start off with a consideration of the critical works published since the war and then to go on to suggest a new method by which it is possible to make one's way into a writer's work, to see it in depth, more accurately than has ever been done before. I hope I have succeeded. It was more than a hope: it was a conviction. It filled my heart with sunlight." (WD 20-21)
15 "Unlooked-for fruit will come from this slow gestation. The adventure in which I have shared so passionately is not over." (WD 16)

word puzzles) the reader is once again struck by the way in which she takes delight in using her analytical mind to find the correct answers, to find meanings that she believes are simply waiting to be revealed:

> [...] j'ai lu les journaux et j'ai fait des mots croisés difficiles qui m'ont retenue trois quarts d'heure; quelquefois, ça m'amuse de rester longtemps penchée sur une grille où virtuellement les mots sont présents, bien qu'invisibles; pour les faire apparaître, j'use de mon cerveau comme d'un révélateur; il me semble les arracher à l'épaisseur du papier où ils seraient cachés. (FR 20)[16]

Our character-narrator expresses a supreme self-confidence in the superiority of her values in comparison with those of, for instance, her daughter-in-law Irène, whom she treats dismissively. One of the first indications of the fissures in this discourse of coherence and meaningfulness comes when Irène enters the fictional world. From the beginning, it is quite clear that she does not fit into the life that the mother has planned out for her son. With substantial arrogance, our heroine consciously ignores her daughter-in-law:

> Soudain il est apparu: [...]. Il m'a serrée très fort [...]. Je me suis dégagée pour embrasser Irène; [...]. Irène. Toujours je l'oublie; toujours elle est là. [...]. Je l'ai vite effacée. J'étais seule avec Philippe [...]. (FR 22)[17]

But it is not long before her well-organized world threatens to fall apart, as the truths she has constructed for herself are seriously challenged by others, although it does not have any immediate effect on her world view. During the dinner party she is so eagerly awaiting at the beginning of the story, Philippe (fearful of his mother's displeasure) reluctantly reveals his decision to abandon his thesis and to leave university in order to take up a new career with the help of his father-in-law. To justify his choice, Irène stands up, and in a somewhat provocative manner, tells the stunned parents that teaching and research are too poorly paid, that "enfin, c'est périmé, une thèse" (FR 25) and finally that "ce qui compte aussi c'est d'être dans le coup" (FR 25).[18]

The conflict that follows the inevitable (and violent) break up between

---

[16] "I read the papers and I did a difficult crossword puzzle that took me three-quarters of an hour: from time to time it is fun to concentrate for a long while upon a set of squares where the words are potentially there although they cannot be seen: I use my brain as a photographic developer to make them appear – I have the impression of drawing them up from their hiding places in the depth of the paper." (WD 22)

[17] "All at once he was there: [...] He hugged me very tight, [...]. I released myself so as to kiss Irène: [...] Irene. I always forget her: and she is always there. [...] Quickly I wiped her out. I was alone with Philippe [...]". (WD 24)

[18] "And then of course a thesis is utterly old hat"; "Being in the swim counts too." (WD 27)

mother and son after the dinner party, can be interpreted as an ordinary generational conflict where a range of arguments and emotions are expressed on
both sides. The younger generation is seen to embrace change, while the
older generation finds it hard to come to terms with new ideologies and
lifestyles. The conflict thus seems to follow an age-old pattern. André's view
is sceptical, but pragmatic about his son's decision, while his own mother
unexpectedly supports her grand-son. The implication of their attitude is
that parents must accept that each new generation must find new causes to
fight for (even if they are in opposition to their parents' wishes). Otherwise
humankind would come to a standstill, and not move forwards toward endlessly new horizons. As a part of the traditional narrative of human progress,
the dynamics of generational change conveys a highly modernist view of
time. As someone who holds to modernist views, our heroine should
embrace her son's courage and willingness to break away, but she is overcome by the loss of control that his decision implies. Her attitude towards
him (as opposed to her husband's more sympathetic view) is intransigent.

The rupture between mother and son draws increased attention to the
problems posed by temporality. Without leaving this conflict behind,[19] the
centre of narrative focus gradually shifts to the problem of ageing, and to
what our heroine sees as her husband's inability to deal with this problem.
Failing to control her son, she is all the more eager to rectify her husband's
attitudes. Or to put it another way: she now tries to re-establish meaningfulness by turning to another battlefield: the fight against what she sees as
clichéd views of old age.

She views her husband's attitude to ageing as pessimistic and defeatist
while the reader may simply conclude that he is trying to cope with the
natural process of ageing in a sensible way. She repeatedly underlines the
importance of being orientated towards the future, that is to say the importance of being committed to important causes, of having personal projects
and of staying young in mind. So, for example, on a particular sightseeing
trip, she states: "Mais en un sens, voir des choses, c'est oiseux. Il faut qu'un
projet ou une question vous attache à elles" (FR 52).[20] On many occasions,
she exhibits an extraordinarily strong belief in the individual's capacity to

---

[19] Since she still believes in historicity and its comforting, intrinsic power of arranging things the way
she wants, she tells herself: "Il va revenir. Il revenait toujours". (FR 56) "He will come back. He
always came back." (WD 58)
[20] "But in one way the mere sight of things is neither here nor there. You have to be linked to them
by some plan or some question." (WD 54)

mould his own existence according to his own principles, projects and goals.[21] She seems to think that you can make people into what you want them to be: "Un enfant, ça ne se constate pas. [...] Il devient ce que le font ses parents" (FR 44).[22]

But gradually her sense of wholeness and continuity is destabilized. In the beginning, the narrator has only a vague feeling that something is wrong. But she soon starts to have doubts about the feelings of historical continuity which she has always relied on, and her existence seems decentred:

> Les deux images que j'avais d'André au passé, au présent, ne s'ajustaient pas. Il y avait une erreur quelque part. Cet instant mentait: ce n'était pas lui, ce n'était pas moi, cette histoire se déroulait ailleurs. Ou alors le passé était un mirage. (FR 42)[23]

Still, she clings to her private, comforting truth as long as possible, in spite of her husband's gentle efforts to make her see things differently:

> – C'est agréable d'avoir derrière soi un long passé.
>
> – Tu crois que tu l'*as*? Pas moi le mien. Essaie donc de te le raconter.
>
> – Je sais qu'il est là. Il donne de l'épaisseur au présent. [...] Intellectuellement, on domine mieux les questions. (FR 49)[24]

Gradually she gains more insight and her vision of the world changes; she starts to acknowledge the inaccessibility of the past, as history and memory begin to lose their power to inspire completeness, leaving only questions and suppositions:

> Mon regard s'attardait avec surprise sur les objets que j'avais rapportés des quatre coins de l'Europe. Mes voyages, l'espace n'en a pas conservé la trace, ma mémoire néglige de les évoquer; et les poupées, les vases, les bibelots sont là. [...]   La terre est autour de moi comme une vaste hypothèse que plus jamais je ne vérifie. (FR 57-58)[25]

---

[21] One can very easily detect what can be called a "standard" existentialist discourse here.

[22] "A child is not something you can evaluate. [...] He turns into what his parents make him." (WD 46)

[23] "The two pictures I had, of the past André and the present André, did not coincide. There was an error somewhere. This present moment was a lie: it was not we who were concerned – not André, not I: the whole thing was happening in another place. Or else the past was an illusion." (WD 44-5)

[24] "'It's pleasant to have a long past behind one.' 'You think you *have* it? I don't, as far as mine is concerned. Just you try telling it over to yourself.' 'I know it's there. It gives depth to the present. [...] You have a much greater intellectual command of things.'" (WD 51)

[25] "My gaze lingered with astonishment upon the things I had brought back from every part of Europe. Space had retained no mark of my journeys, and my recollection would not trouble to call them to mind; and yet there they were, the dolls, the pots, the little ornaments. [...] All around me the world lies like an immense hypothesis that I no longer verify." (WD 59-60)

When her book becomes the target of negative criticism, she is forced to admit that her detractors are right, and that the book has nothing new to offer. There is a sudden reversal: rather than being extremely confident about her work, she becomes just as categorical in her disparaging attitude toward it:

> [...] ces pages étaient tout imprégnées de moi, c'était une intimité écœurante, comme l'odeur d'une chambre où on est resté confiné trop longtemps. [...] Pas un projet, pas un désir. [...] Quel vide en moi, autour de moi. Inutile. [...] Je me demandais comment on réussit encore à vivre quand on n'espère plus rien de soi. (FR 62-63)[26]

> Quelle duperie, ce progrès, cette ascension. [...] Et maintenant, ce serait très rapide et très lent: nous allions devenir de grands vieillards. [...] Moi, la vie allait peu à peu me reprendre tout ce qu'elle m'avait donné; elle avait déjà commencé. (FR 71-72) [27]

Devastated, she comes to understand that history and memory do not ensure predictability, and all at once her faith in linear temporality as the structuring framework for her existence loses its meaning. Far from providing the comforting backdrop to her life, time, she now realises, has the potential to break down into confusing, sometimes contradictory categories: "C'est terrible – j'ai envie de dire c'est injuste – qu'il puisse passer à la fois si vite et si lentement. [...] Tragiquement ma vie se précipite. Et cependant elle s'égoutte en ce moment avec quelle lenteur – heure par heure, minute par minute" (FR 64).[28] This breakdown of her conception of time leaves her confronted with space and its contingency. Art feels meaningless when devoid of its temporal dimension. Paintings, which she has loved, may very well become nothing but "des couleurs crachées par un tube et étalées par un pinceau" (FR 64).[29]

She desperately clings to the past, but when trying to recapture her and André's common history, she realizes that the past is not there for her to play with, it is no longer "un paysage dans lequel je pourrais me promener

---

26 "These pages were soaked through and through with my self – there was a sickening intimacy about it, like the smell of a bedroom in which one has been shut up too long. [...] Never a plan, never a wish. [...] What an emptiness within me – all around me. Useless. [...] I wondered how people managed to go on living when there was nothing to be hoped from within." (WD 64-65)

27 "What nonsense, this intoxicating notion of progress, of upward movement. [...] And now it would be very fast and very slow: we were going to turn into really old people. [...] As far as I was concerned life was gradually going to take back everything it had given me: it had already begun doing so." (WD 73-74)

28 "It is dreadful – I feel like saying it is unfair – that it should be able to go by both so quickly and so slowly. [...] My life was hurrying, racing tragically toward its end. And at the same time it was dripping so slowly, so very slowly now, hour by hour, minute by minute." (WD 66)

29 "[...] colors squeezed on from a tube and spread with a brush." (WD 66)

à ma guise" (FR 65).[30] Meaning can no longer be constructed from a perspective that can dominate past, present and future. Her depressed state of mind prevents her from regarding the future optimistically as a series of changes which she can easily adjust to, as long as she does not give in to the stereotypes of old age. The future is something that will happen to her, regardless of what she would will it to be.

The challenges this woman painfully faces do, in the end, have the effect of changing some of the entrenched attitudes she displayed at the beginning of the story. A solution to the conflict with Philippe is hinted at, and there is a new understanding between husband and wife, based on her coming to terms with ageing. Her "awakening" does not lead to a complete transformation of her *vision du monde,* as her stilted rhetoric, at times still suffused with emotion, demonstrates:

> Ils [les paroles d'un poème] m'unissaient aux siècles anciens où les astres brillaient exactement comme aujourd'hui. Et cette renaissance et cette permanence me donnaient une impression d'éternité. La terre me semblait fraîche comme aux premiers âges et cet instant se suffisait. (FR 80)[31]

However, the reader clearly witnesses a reorientation and a readjustment in her attitudes and in her language, which, as I see it, can be attributed to the destabilization of her sense of temporality. This reorientation makes her focus on the present time, with all its uncertainties. The final stage of the story thus suggests that she has attained a new openness and awareness of the unpredictable nature of life. This attitude stands in stark contrast to the rhetoric of stability and security typical of the beginning of the narrative. She now appears much less sure of herself, and her new openness is reflected in the simplicity and hesitancy of her language:

> Nous avions toujours regardé loin. Faudrait-il apprendre à vivre à la petite semaine ? […] Un instant le temps s'était arrêté. Il allait se remettre à couler. Et alors ? […]
>
> Ne pas regarder trop loin. […] Nous sommes ensemble, c'est notre chance. Nous nous aiderons à vivre cette dernière aventure dont nous ne reviendrons

---

[30] "[...] a landscape in which I could wander as I pleased [....]". (WD 67)
[31] "They [the words of a poem] were a link joining me to the past centuries, when the stars shone exactly as they do today. And this rebirth and this permanence gave me a feeling of eternity. The world seemed to me as fresh and new as it had been in the first ages, and this moment sufficed to itself." (WD 82)

pas. Cela nous la rendra-t-il tolérable? Je ne sais pas. Espérons. Nous n'avons
pas le choix. (FR 83-84)[32]

In my opinion, while the protagonist's egoistic and domineering behaviour may not inspire much sympathy in the reader, the text does not
endorse an altogether negative view of her, despite authorial intentions.
Although she initially displays an uncompromising attitude towards life,
expecting others and her son in particular to surrender unconditionally to
her *vision du monde,* her tireless self-analysis in the end contributes to the
final shift of perspective, in which she becomes more reconciled to the
unpredictability of existence.

Nevertheless the crisis she experiences entails a loss of meaning. The
world loses its depth and density as the coherent existence she has constructed for herself proves to be an illusion. She has no choice but to develop new thought patterns to cope with this new world.

"Monologue"

The title "Monologue" points to the narrative mode of this short story,
which immediately draws the reader in with its dramatic use of language,
as the first person narrator and sole actor of the piece, Murielle, gives
expression to her disturbed thoughts. The opening sequence succinctly
expresses her unbalanced state of mind, which finds its verbal corollary in
the crude and disjointed language she employs: "Les cons! J'ai tiré les
rideaux la lumière idiote des lampions et des arbres de Noël n'entre pas
dans l'appartement mais les bruits traversent les murs" (FR 87).[33]

As the story unfolds, the reader is able to reconstruct the main character's life story by extracting and connecting jigsaw-like bits and pieces from
her flow of words. Murielle, a woman in her forties, has lived alone since
her second husband Tristan left, taking with him their little son Francis, of
whom he has custody. Murielle also had a daughter, Sylvie, from her first
marriage to André, who continued to live with her after their divorce.
Sylvie's subsequent suicide (at the age of seventeen) leads the whole family

---

32 "We had always looked far ahead. Should we now have to learn to live a short-term life? [...] For a
moment time stopped still. It would soon start flowing again. What then? [...] Do not look too far
ahead. [...] We are together: that is our good fortune. We shall help one another to live through this
last adventure, this adventure from which we shall not come back. Will that make it bearable for us? I
do not know. Let us hope so. We have no choice in the matter." (WD 85)
33 "The silly bastards! I drew the curtains they keep the stupid colored lanterns and the fairy lights on
the Christmas trees out of the apartment but the noises come in through the walls." (WD 89)

to shun Murielle. Feeling misjudged and misunderstood, Murielle finds herself on the verge of hysteria. The monologue becomes a conduit for a myriad of emotions – frustration, hatred, resentment and self-pity. The vulgarity and harshness of her language betrays the overflow of uncontrolled emotions, expressed as venomous accusations and obscenities spat out at family members, neighbours, acquaintances and the world at large:

> Je ne suis pas raciste mais je m'en branle des Bicots des Juifs des Nègres juste comme je m'en branle des Chinetoques des Russes des Amerlos des Français. Je m'en branle de l'humanité qu'est-ce qu'elle a fait pour moi je me le demande. […] Un million d'enfants massacrés et après? les enfants ce n'est jamais que de la graine de salauds ça désencombre un peu la planète ils reconnaissent qu'elle est surpeuplée alors quoi? (FR 102-103)[34]

The story takes place over a very short time – just a few hours on New Year's Eve. Murielle is sitting alone, nervously preparing herself for the next day when Tristan and Francis are expected to come and see her. There is obviously much at stake in this visit:

> Il faut que je me repose c'est nécessaire je veux avoir ma chance demain avec Tristan; pas de larmes pas de cris. "C'est anormal cette situation. Même du point de vue fric quel gâchis ! Un enfant a besoin de sa mère." (FR 88)[35]

In her mind she runs through various arguments she intends to present to Tristan. She wants the three of them to live together again, but her motives are far from altruistic. Ultimately, she is concerned about the social stigma she suffers as an ageing single woman:

> Un homme sous mon toit. Le plombier serait venu le concierge me saluerait poliment les voisins mettraient une sourdine. Merde alors; je veux qu'on me respecte je veux mon mari mon fils mon foyer comme tout le monde. (FR 94)[36]

> Et puis ça serait la réhabilitation. (FR 114)[37]

---

[34] "I am not a racist but don't give a fuck for Algerian Jews Negroes in just the same way I don't give a fuck for Chinks Russians Yanks Frenchmen. I don't give a fuck for humanity what has it ever done for me I ask you. […] A million children have been massacred so what? Children are never anything but the seed of bastards it unclutters the planet a little they all admit it's overpopulated don't they?" (WD 105)

[35] "I've got to get some rest I have to I must be able to cope with Tristan tomorrow: no tears no shouting. This is an absurd position. A ghastly mess, even from the point of view of the dough! A child needs its mother." (WD 90)

[36] "A man under my roof. The plumber would have come the concierge would say good day politely the neighbors would turn the volume down. Bloody hell, I want to be treated with respect I want my husband my son my home like everybody else." (WD 96)

[37] "And then it would mean rehabilitation." (WD 117)

At this point, the reader can already discern the ways in which Murielle has internalised prevailing myths about femininity. Murielle is convinced that a woman's life cannot be fulfilled without a husband and child. Her desperate struggle to conform to this myth focuses the readers' attention on the issue of a woman's dependence on others for her happiness. Murielle's position as "victim" may of course initially predispose us in her favour. But we, as readers, are also aware that the narrative is a highly subjective one and that we cannot totally rely on the character-narrator's words to reconstruct the fabula.[38] Furthermore, Murielle's soliloquy implicitly opens up a space for other voices to be heard. In defending herself against the accusations of others, other perspectives are indirectly given voice and these in turn have the potential to influence the reader.

I would like to focus on the complex manner in which this narrative communicates with readers. Critics have already pointed out that as far as the stylistics of Beauvoir's fictional works are concerned, this short story breaks new ground. In my own reading, I draw on the title and therefore on the concept of the monologue to interpret both its narrative framework and its stylistic features. I suggest that an examination of the properties of the monological form reveal the extent to which its formal potentialities are fully exploited to serve Beauvoir's didactic aims.

Beauvoir herself comments on the title in the epigraph to the text, where she quotes Flaubert: "Elle se venge par le monologue" (FR 85).[39] Given Beauvoir's statements on the didactic function of *La Femme rompue* and her well-known assessment on the inferior position of women in society, the epigraph may be read as an indication to the reader that Murielle's unbalanced rage may well be justified. Even though the epigraph does not go so far as to completely exonerate Murielle, it at the very least suggests that her rage may be motivated by a desire to right wrongs committed against her, and that in some ways justice is at stake. "Accusations", "victim", "defence", "justice": – if I use these terms it is because Murielle, in a sense, is on trial, accused of being a bad mother and, as such, her monologue can be interpreted as the speech of a defendant.

As I have stated earlier, the female protagonists in *La Femme rompue* were

---

[38] When referring to the different elements of the narrative, I will use definitions from Mieke Bal, *Narratology. Introduction to the Theory of Narrative* (Toronto: University of Toronto Press, 1999) 5: "A story is a fabula that is presented in a certain manner. A fabula is a series of logically and chronologically related events that are caused or experienced by actors."

[39] "The monologue is her form of revenge." (WD 88)

destined to function as negative models of womanhood. This statement of intent immediately places the reader in a dual position. On the one hand, we are invited to understand Murielle and to find excuses for her: she does after all find herself in the position of a stereotypical female victim. On the other hand, we are supposed to reject her arguments and her life choices – since they are misguided – and to learn from her mistakes. In other words, Beauvoir's task is both to defend Murielle (to a point), and at the same time to show that her cause is in fact not defensible. As we shall see, this ambiguity is not only of thematic relevance; it also finds expression in the narrative form and stylistic expression of the story.

What are the formal characteristics of monological discourse? What kinds of rhetorical strategies are brought into play by the use of this particular form of literary composition? As there is only one speaker present, the form does not allow for any interchange of thoughts or opinions; there is a long message delivered and none received. The absence of interruptions from others, which would have the potential to provide corrective signals and allow the speaker to modify her/his perspective, defines the egocentric bias and consequent unreliability of the form. The monologue by its very nature monopolizes and fills up the shared space where speech interaction "normally" takes place. Whereas the logic of dialogue allows a multiplicity of potentially discordant voices, the logic of monologue favours absolute utterances that do not provide context or encourage discussion. The speaker, in the case of a monologue, tends to occupy a position of dominance, from which s/he aims to establish control by positioning the readers where s/he wants them to be. In other words, s/he manipulates the story so as to convince the readers that her/his version of events is a correct representation of the fabula.

Although powerful and potentially convincing through its effective silencing of contrasting opinions, the monologue thus undermines its own authority through a number of other effects, such as the abundant use of manipulative techniques and a fundamental lack of reliability. The monologue therefore favours ambiguity.

Let us look at the stylistic effects of Murielle's discourse. From the beginning of the short story, it is obvious that the structure of the sentences do not conform to norms of text production. Many syntactic sentences are contained in very long graphic units without punctuation. The lack of breaks in her speech produces a certain speed or nervousness in the text that grabs hold of the reader, obstructing her/his reflections. The relationship between sentences is confused – they are all, so to speak, on the same level, and the cohesion relies on implicit connection between fragments of meaning.

> Piquer une crise de nerfs devant le petit m'ouvrir les veines sur leur paillasson ça ou autre chose j'ai des armes je m'en servirai il me reviendra je ne pourrirai pas seule dans cette baraque avec ces gens là-haut qui me foulent aux pieds et les voisins qui me réveillent tous les matins avec leur radio et personne pour m'apporter à bouffer quand j'ai faim. (FR 93)[40]

This particular narrative technique gives the impression that the protagonist is speaking her thoughts spontaneously, as they occur to her, with no premeditated agenda. Drawn in by this apparently spontaneous flow, the reader is invited to follow the fluctuations of Murielle's mind and to accept her version of events at face value. To support this apparently transparent rhetoric, a series of statements, which reoccur like a refrain in the text, give the impression that Murielle considers herself to be a clear-sighted and neutral observer:

> J'étais propre pure intransigeante. (FR 89)

> Pas de concession pas de comédie: […] Je suis propre je suis vraie je ne joue pas le jeu […]. (FR 90)

> Lucide trop lucide. Ils n'aiment pas qu'on voie clair en eux; moi je suis vraie ne ne joue pas le jeu j'arrache les masques. (FR 97)

> Je suis restée cette petite bonne femme qui dit ce qu'elle pense qui ne triche pas. (FR 102)[41]

This rhetorical strategy of confusing relationships between sentences has yet another interesting effect. It soon appears that Murielle's monologue contains crucial, but hidden information needed to construct the fabula. Her incoherent flow of words disturbs the more logical ordering of foregrounding and backgrounding of information, and manipulates the reader to follow the narrator's own twisted logic. At other times, significant facts are put in between other more striking and colourful pieces of information that catch the reader's eye, as if the narrator hopes for the more important

---

[40] "Go into hysterics in front of the boy bleed to death on their doormat that or something else. I have weapons I'll use them he'll come back to me I shan't go on rotting all alone in this dump with those people on the next floor who trample me underfoot and the ones next door who wake me every morning with their radio and no one to bring me so much as a crust when I'm hungry." (WD 95; full stop added in translation)

[41] "I was clean straight uncompromising." (WD 91) "No compromise no act: […] I'm clean I'm straight I don't join in any act". (WD 92) "Clear-sighted too clear-sighted. They don't like being seen through: as for me I'm straight I don't join their act I tear masks off." (WD 99) "I'm still that proper little woman who says what she thinks and doesn't cheat." (WD 104)

information to pass unnoticed. For example, long before we discover that it was a mother-and-daughter conflict that led to Sylvie's suicide, Murielle talks about the problems that Sylvie's upbringing brought her ("dresser" – train – is the word Murielle uses throughout the story in this context). The narrative focus throughout the passage is on the difficulties that a mother experiences in bringing up a daughter and as such, the reader's attention may be deflected from crucial clues as to Murielle's maternal capacities, which are also contained in the passage:

> Sylvie n'était pas gentille j'en ai dégusté quand j'ai lu son journal; mais moi je regarde les choses en face. [...] Têtue comme une mule geignant des heures des jours pour un caprice il n'y avait aucune raison pour qu'elle revoie Tristan. (FR 94-95)[42]

The significant facts here are that Murielle reads her daughter's diary and prevents her from seeing a stepfather whom she apparently loves, both of which can be taken as strong evidence of maternal guilt.

A similar obfuscatory strategy is used in the following sequence, when Murielle describes the moment when she finds her daughter's dead body:

> Je la revois calme détendue et moi égarée et ce petit mot pour son père ca ne signifiait rien je l'ai déchiré il faisait partie de la mise en scène ce n'était qu'une mise en scène j'étais sûre je suis sûre – une mère connaît sa fille – qu'elle n'avait pas voulu mourir mais elle avait forcé la dose elle était morte quelle horreur! (FR 111-12)[43]

She may well be *égarée,* but she still has the presence of mind to tear up the suicide letter. This vicious act represents her last infringement on her daughter's integrity, and marks the end of years of abuse of maternal power. The casual way in which she refers to the suicide letter suggests that she is trying to make light of her act. She can therefore continue to believe in her self-image as a truthful woman.

The self-centeredness typical of monological discourse is reinforced by the narrator's extremely categorical view of the world. This is especially true of Murielle's aggressive attitude towards other people. This stance can be interpreted as the natural consequence of the position she finds herself

---

[42] "Sylvie was not a dear little anything I had a dose of that when I read her diary: but as for me I look things straight in the face. [...] Obstinate as a mule whining for hours on end days on end over a whim there wasn't the slightest reason for her to see Tristan again." (WD 96-97)

[43] "I can see her now calm relaxed and me out of my mind and the note for her father that didn't mean a thing I tore it up it was all part of the act it was only an act I was sure I am sure – a mother knows her own daughter – she had not meant to die but she had overdone the dose she was dead how appalling!" (WD 114)

in. In order to defend herself against others, she has to establish a clear distance between herself and them, lest they penetrate her consciousness and uncover her lies. But she has yet another enemy to fight – the enemy within. She is afraid that she will not be able to control her own feelings when seeing Tristan: "Ne pas l'engueuler ne pas commencer par l'engueuler ça ferait tout foirer. J'ai peur de demain" (FR 101).[44]

Embedded within the string of accusations and profanities uttered by Murielle are sudden flashes of lucidity mediated by short, clear-cut sentences, where naked pain breaks through:

> Sylvie est morte. Cinq ans déjà. Elle est morte. Pour toujours. Je ne le supporte pas. Au secours j'ai mal j'ai trop mal qu'on me sorte de là je ne veux pas que ça recommence la dégringolade non aidez-moi je n'en peux plus ne me laissez pas seule… Qui appeler? (FR 104)[45]

Her desperation leads her to make two phone calls during the evening/night, one to her mother, the other to Tristan. Despite the fact that this opens up to the possibility of dialogue, Murielle nevertheless continues her monologue, overriding the others' attempts to answer. Since she is not able to communicate, they both hang up on her.

We have seen that the monologue offers a narrative form in which the unmasking of the main character is effectually mediated. Murielle's efforts at dominating all those who surround her turn against her as her emotional and argumentative false play becomes clear to the reader, who is the ultimate judge of her credibility. As the story progresses and Murielle's narcissism and cruelty become more and more preposterous, it becomes increasingly difficult for the reader to identify with her.

Murielle's situation may of course be explained from more than one perspective. Genevieve Shepherd, in her psychoanalytical rereading of Beauvoir's fiction, diagnoses Murielle as paranoid neurotic, pointing to her obsessions about cleanliness, her delusions of jealousy and her erotomania (FR 223-31).[46] As Shepherd shows, there is more than enough textual evidence to support such assumptions. For instance, Murielle frequently

---

[44] "Don't bawl him out don't begin by bawling him out that would muck up everything. I dread tomorrow." (WD 103)

[45] "Sylvie is dead. Five years already. She is dead. Forever. I can't bear it. Help it hurts it hurts too much get me out of here I can't bear the breakdown to start again no help me I can't bear it any longer don't leave me alone. … Who to call?" (WD 106-07)

[46] Genevieve Shepherd, *Simone de Beauvoir's Fiction. A Psychoanalytic Reading* (New York: Peter Lang, 2003) 223-31. Terry Keefe also underlines how Murielle's self-deception is out of control, and that her behaviour indicates mental illness (paranoia), *Simone de Beauvoir* (New York: St. Martin's Press, 1998) 146-9.

returns to memories of a childhood and youth characterised by experiences of betrayal, unfaithfulness, lack of love and maternal abuse. In constructing her own adult life, Murielle has nevertheless blindly followed in her mother's footsteps and conformed to society's expectations by acquiring a husband and children.

In *Le Deuxième Sexe,* Beauvoir discusses the myths that motivate motherhood, this "suprême étape du développement de la femme" (DS II 329)[47] – myths that teach women how to become what she ironically calls a "complete individual". The story of Murielle and her difficult relationship with her daughter illustrates what can happen when such myths become the decisive parameters of an individual's life. When a woman who does not have the psychological or moral resources to take care of a child is seduced by the myth of the good mother, the results can be disastrous.

Murielle's relationship to motherhood is not least perceptible through her language. When it comes to talking about motherhood, the incongruous pomposity which her words take on serve only to emphasise the emptiness which underlies them: "un gosse privé de sa mère finit toujours par mal tourner" (FR 92), "un fils a besoin de sa mère une mère ne peut pas se passer de son enfant c'est tellement évident avec la pire mauvaise foi ça ne peut pas se nier" (FR 100).[48]

Murielle has used Sylvie to compensate for all the frustrations of her own childhood. According to Beauvoir: "Une mère qui fouette son enfant ne bat pas seulement l'enfant, en un sens elle ne le bat pas du tout; elle se venge d'un homme, du monde, ou d'elle-même; mais c'est bien l'enfant qui reçoit les coups" (DS II 373).[49] The relationship between a possessive mother and her child can be compared to that of a man and a woman: "elle [la mère] saisit en lui [l'enfant] ce que l'homme recherche dans la femme: un autre à la fois nature et conscience qui soit sa proie, son *double*" (DS II 370).[50] If the daughter wants to affirm her autonomy against her mother: "aux yeux de la mère,

---

[47] "[...] this supreme stage in woman's life history." (SS 501)
[48] "[…] a kid deprived of his mother always ends up by going to the bad." (WD 94-95) "[…] a boy needs his mother a mother can't do without her child it's so obvious that even the crookedest mind can't deny it." (WD 102)
[49] "A mother who punishes her child is not beating the child alone; in a sense she is not beating it at all: she is taking her vengeance on a man, on the world, or on herself." (SS 529)
[50] "she obtains in her child what man seeks in woman: an other, combining nature and mind, who is to be both prey and double." (SS 527)
[51] "This seems to the mother a mark of hateful ingratitude; she tries obstinately to checkmate the girl's will to escape; she cannot bear to have her double become an other." (SS 534)

c'est là un trait d'odieuse ingratitude; elle s'entête à 'mater' cette volonté qui se dérobe; elle n'accepte pas que son double devienne *une autre*" (DS II 381).[51] Murielle, whose whole existence has been justified through marriage and motherhood, has taken this argument to the bitter end. Her fight to preserve maternal power has literally resulted in the death of her daughter:

> Je la tenais oui j'étais ferme mais j'étais tendre toujours prête à bavarder avec elle je voulais être son amie et j'aurais baisé les mains de ma mère si elle s'était conduite comme ça avec moi. Mais quel caractère ingrat! Elle est morte et alors? Les morts ne sont pas des saints. Elle ne coopérait pas elle ne me confiait rien. (FR 97)[52]

Elizabeth Fallaize points to the link between language and violence in this short story, showing how Murielle uses words to create herself and to impose herself on others.[53] Language and violence also seem integrated in another way. Murielle's apartment is not the only spatial sign of her imprisonment. The narrative creates a textual space where there is no possible exit for Murielle. Feeling suffocated by her loneliness, she tries to reach out to the outside world, but her efforts are aborted by her self-centeredness and she is drawn further and further into herself. She is no longer in any position to inflict pain on anybody but herself, her power over others has vanished. Just as her paranoid fear of contamination severs relations with others, her self-directed words cut her message off from any potential addressee. Words represent her only means of defending herself, but in the end they work against her. Her defence speech mimes prevalent myths about women, and as such is prone to simplistic argumentation and inane statements. For, as Roland Barthes states, language that is impregnated with mythological assumptions is necessarily prone to simplification, since myths themselves are by their very nature reductive – they cannot take account of the complex interplay of human behaviour:

> En passant de l'histoire à la nature, le mythe fait une économie: il abolit la complexité des actes humains, leur donne la simplicité des essences, il supprime toute dialectique, toute remontée au-delà du visible immédiat, il organise un monde sans contradictions parce que sans profondeur, un monde étalé dans l'évidence, il fonde une clarté heureuse: les choses ont l'air de signifier toutes seules.[54]

---

52 "I had her under control yes I was firm but I was always affectionate always ready to talk I wanted to be a friend to her and I would have kissed my mother's hands if she had behaved like that to me. But what a thankless heart. She's dead and so all right what of it? The dead are not saints. She wouldn't cooperate she never confided in me at all." (WD 99)

53 Fallaize, *Novels* 160-5.

54 Barthes 230-1.

Psychologically realistic, "Monologue" offers a sophisticated representation of an interior life marked by great distress. Through the tight structure of her text, Beauvoir manages to show the destructive power of mythological language, when embodied in a person who is not capable of engaging in communicative discourse. A prisoner of her own monologue, Murielle will never be able to gain any insight into herself, others or the world around her, and on this symbolically significant New Year's Eve, she fully acquires the status Beauvoir intended for her – that of a truly negative heroine.

"La Femme rompue"

The last and longest story in the collection is the title story, "La Femme rompue", which has received by far the most attention from critics. The story was born out of Beauvoir's engagement in the lives of her woman compatriots. She had received many letters from women who had lived through the fairly commonplace, but painful experiences of their husbands leaving them for another woman, and their stories inspired Beauvoir to "donner à voir leur nuit", as she puts it in *Tout Compte fait* (175).[55] The story was first serialised in the women's magazine *Elle* some few months before it was published in the short story collection in 1968. Reactions to the story, however, both shocked and disappointed the author, since readers did not come away with the interpretation that Beauvoir had planned. In her view: "Leurs réactions reposaient sur un énorme contresens" (TCF 178).[56] To her, the protagonist and destroyed woman, Monique, is a negative heroine, in the sense that she clings to myths and high ideals, refusing to recognise her individual freedom and responsibility. Beauvoir clearly intended for her heroine to be the guilty one, whereas the public identified with the heroine's situation and blamed her unfaithful husband: "J'aurais voulu que le lecteur lût ce récit comme un roman policier; j'ai semé de-ci de-là des indices qui permettent de trouver la clé du mystère: mais à condition qu'on dépiste Monique comme on dépiste un coupable" (TCF 175-76).[57] Before I return to this question, which will be the main focus of this essay, I will provide a brief summary of the story.

---

[55] "[…] speaking about their darkness and making it evident." (ASD 140)

[56] "Their reactions were based upon an immense incomprehension." (ADS 142)

[57] "I hoped that people would read the book as a detective story; here and there I scattered clues that would allow the reader to find the key to the mystery – but only if he tracked Monique as one tracks down the guilty character." (ASD 140)

"La Femme rompue" takes the form of a diary, where Monique, the character-narrator and writer, sets out to describe and analyse her thoughts and experiences. The motive for her writing (although it takes some time before she admits this to herself) is the change in her husband Maurice's attitude – a change that makes her suspect he is seeing somebody else. The diary entries span six-and-a-half months, with the first entry on September 13th, and the last on March 24th. During this time, Monique goes through a painful process that starts with her suspicions about her husband's unfaithfulness and ends with his leaving her for another woman, terminating their 22-year-long marriage. The setting is commonplace, although dramatic for Monique. The real dynamic tension in the story results from Monique's way of handling the crisis, which takes on an existential dimension and becomes a fight to survive. The text explores in detail the literary *topos* of "the jealous wife" as Monique experiences it, and as she plays out, or so it seems, every stage a jealous person in her situation might be expected to go through.

Having initially overlooked the first signals of her husband's dalliances, Monique ultimately cannot ignore her lingering suspicions. She forces Maurice to admit his adultery. She then goes on to convince herself that his affair is not to be taken seriously. Deciding to play the tolerant wife, she accordingly adopts a detached, "civilised" attitude: "j'avais adopté sans peine la tactique du sourire car je suis convaincue qu'en effet cette histoire ne compte pas tant pour Maurice" (FR 137);[58] "j'ai adopté une attitude compréhensive, conciliante, je dois m'y tenir" (FR 140).[59] She soon realizes, however, that his affair is not just a trifling matter, and this painful comprehension alters her behaviour so she can react to the multiple threats she now feels.

Her changing interpretation of the facts, along with the growing intensity of her own emotions, results in a range of corresponding tactics or responses. Her focus turns alternately inwards and outwards, and she is alternately hoping and despairing. Feeling her own virtues as a mother and wife lessened by her rival's supposedly outstanding qualities, she tries to bolster her damaged ego by depicting herself a martyr, sacrificed when her husband abandons his moral values. In her own eyes, she is defending the just cause of truth and authenticity against intrusion from a false and super-

---

[58] "I had easily adopted the tactics of the smile because I was sure that in fact this affair had not much importance for Maurice." (WD 139)
[59] "Since I have adopted an understanding, kindly attitude I must stick to it." (WD 142)

ficial rival. "Authentique: c'était un mot à la mode, à l'époque. Il disait que j'étais authentique. [...] Il se laisse prendre aux fausses valeurs que nous méprisions. [...] Je voudrais que ses yeux se dessillent vite" (FR 157).[60]

As time passes, however, she turns a lucid eye on herself, almost obsessively scrutinizing her own erroneous behaviours and shortcomings; at times she is amazingly frank in her self-criticism: "Ne pas tomber dans les pièges du dévouement: je sais très bien que les mots donner et recevoir sont interchangeables et combien j'avais besoin du besoin que mes filles avaient de moi" (FR 143).[61]

But her reactions will soon reach far beyond the "civilized" response she had initially planned. Monique humiliates herself with "uncivilised" actions and reactions, living up to each and every cliché we know of the desperate, deceived wife. For example, after failing to bring down Noëllie in Maurice's eyes, she tries to imitate what she takes to be her rival's values and interests. Her excessive curiosity makes her childish and mean; she shouts, she cries, she pleads – further demeaning herself in self-destruction. She becomes physically ill and apathetic with suicidal thoughts; shutting herself up in the apartment, she lets herself go completely.

Beauvoir's choice of the diary as the narrative structure for this work signals a follow-up of the discursive intimacy presented in the two previous texts. The reader is given a close-up of the character-narrator as she relates her activities and reflections through a particularly dramatic period of her life. The immediacy inherent in the diary style gives us the impression of direct access to the interior world of the protagonist, and makes us feel as if we are confronted with a particularly private document, of a true story, of non-fiction, so to speak. But already by the 4th entry the reader is disabused of this illusion of truth and transparency, as Monique parenthetically notes: "(Curieuse chose qu'un journal: ce qu'on y tait est plus important que ce qu'on y note)" (FR 128).[62] Her distressing discovery of the diary's deceiving character is written out clearly long before the end of the story: "Il n'y a pas une ligne de ce journal qui n'appelle une correction

---

[60] "Authentic: that was the word everyone was using in those days. He said I was authentic. [...] He lets himself be taken in by false values that we used to despise. [...] I wish the scales would drop from his eyes soon." (WD 158)

[61] "I must not plunge into the pitfall of devotion – I know very well that the words give and receive are interchangeable, and I know very well how much I needed the need my daughters had of me." (WD 145)

[62] "(What an odd thing a diary is: the things you omit are more important than those you put in.)" (WD 130)

ou un démenti. [...] Il y a des phrases qui me font rougir de honte... [...].
Je me mentais. Comme je me suis menti!" (FR 222-23).[63] Monique proves
unreliable even for herself, leading the reader to wonder, at least at this
stage of the story: Does she really want to tell the truth?

With the title story of the collection, the readers are once again invited into a fictional world where the question of "truth" – that is, the
detection of lies and the search for an honest meaning – is a main focus.
To emphasise the importance of this topic, Beauvoir employs rhetoric
from the semantic field of law and morality: we are constantly returned to
the issues of guilt, responsibility, judgement, proof, etc. The contrasting
signals about the question of truth, which never result in any clear
answers, make us return with a new awareness to the questions concerning what Beauvoir called the *misreadings* of her text. The discrepancy in the
interpretations signalled by the author invites scrutiny of the levels of
meaning embedded in the text. In her analysis, Toril Moi discusses why
Beauvoir's clearly feminist authorial interpretation, which faulted
Monique for the marriage's failure, failed to convince her target group,
women in Monique's situation:

> For most readers, whether or not they otherwise agree with the author, the fact
> that Maurice has managed to lie to Monique about his affairs with other
> women for over eight years makes this interpretation somewhat uncomfortable.
> [...] It is no wonder that a reading which tends to exonerate philandering hus-
> bands and instead blame their unsuspecting wives for not being interesting
> enough failed to appeal to the readers of *Elle*.[64]

Terry Keefe signals a similar understanding of the spectrum of interpretations when he states that "no careful interpretation of "La Femme
rompue" could fail to take account of Beauvoir's point that Monique is,
and has long been, self-deceived."[65] However, he emphasises that it is only
upon second reading that the text opens itself up to such an interpretation,
since a first reading automatically focuses on Maurice's bad treatment of
Monique.

I would like to suggest that the authorial denunciation of the character-
narrator in this narrative is articulated through an *ironic* discourse, a discourse

---

63 "There is not a single line in this diary that does not call for a correction or a denial. [...] There are some
remarks that make me blush for shame... [...]. I was lying to myself. How I lied to myself!" (WD 224)
64 Toril Moi, "Intentions and Effects" Rhetoric and Identification in Simone de Beauvoir's 'The Woman
Destroyed.'" *What is a Woman? And Other Essays.* (Oxford: Oxford University Press, 1999) 458, 461.
65 Keefe 150.

that failed to be apprehended by the readers who "misunderstood". The use of irony is a risky game. To be effective, that is, to be understood by the reader, the ironic device must be forceful enough to give an indication of the author's intention. If not, the ironic effect simply fails, and the reader understands the text in a literal fashion. Furthermore, irony does not only function as a one-way instrument solely at the author's disposal. It is a particular form of construction that allows the interpreter to read irony where it was not intended – and vice versa.

I think there are a number of reasons why Beauvoir's ironic tone remained unperceived. The explanations I will put forward to account for this will also serve to illustrate other forceful dynamics in the text that cast light on readers' "misinterpretations".

A short definition of irony tells us simply that it is "a double significance which arises from the contrast in values associated with two different points of view."[66] However, as Linda Hutcheon points out:

> With irony, there are [...] dynamic and plural relations among the text or utterance (and its context), the so-called ironist, the interpreter, and the circumstances surrounding the discursive situation; it is these that mess up neat theories of irony that see the task of the interpreter simply as one of decoding or reconstructing some "real" meaning [...], a meaning that is hidden, but deemed accessible, behind the stated one.[67]

Hence, the use of such a writing technique requires a complex discursive strategy and extra-textual factors that need to function together to make up the ironic effect. The authorial use of irony implies a tacit appeal for a reading pact between the author and the reader – similar to Lejeune's "autobiographical pact"[68] – along with an unwritten assumption of what is taken for granted or understood as shared knowledge and/or values. But Beauvoir was unquestionably part of a different experiential and intellectual world than the intended readers of the text. In retrospect, one might argue that the ideological conditioning of the average woman reader in French society in the 1960s had not come as far as Beauvoir had thought, and that full identification with her implicit existentialist and feminist argumentation ought not to be expected. At best, women readers perceived "Beauvoir" as an author who stood up for women's rights; therefore it was to be expected

---

[66] Geoffrey N. Leech and Michael H. Short, *Style in Fiction* (London and New York: Longman, 1981) 278.
[67] Linda Hutcheon, *Irony's Edge: The Theory and Politics of Irony* (London and New York: Routledge, 1995) 11.
[68] Philippe Lejeune, *Le Pacte autobiographique* (Paris: Seuil, 1975).

that she would side with the woman in a marital conflict where the husband cheats on his wife. According to L. Hutcheon, "to read ironically is also to read with suspicion."[69] Beauvoir had planned for a critical – or ironical – reading of her text, suggesting the detective story as an interpretative pattern. However, even if the readers understood that their role was to track down a suspect, their identification with Monique is not surprising. Sympathetic identification thus overrules the power of irony.

If we look at the diarist's use of language to find evidence for Beauvoir's ironic intention, we may easily see clues left for the reader about Monique's problematic complacency. Glorifying her own virtues, especially those who imply selfless devotion to others, Monique's immodest, boastful assertions work against her to reveal an unsympathetic side of her character:

> Je supporterais mal de n'être pas totalement à la disposition des gens qui ont besoin de moi. (FR125)[70]

> J'attends beaucoup des gens que j'aime – trop peut-être. J'attends et même je demande. Mais je ne sais pas exiger. (FR 149)[71]

> Je suis sûre que je vaux mieux qu'elle. (FR 196)[72]

Hélène de Beauvoir (the author's sister) had the following to say about the book's different interpretations and its audiences: "Il y a deux catégories de gens qui l'aiment: les gens simples qui sont touchés par le drame de Monique; les intellectuels qui saisissent les intentions du livre" (TCF 180).[73] Although the irony in this statement is evident enough for the second category of readers, it is apparently insufficient for the first group to condemn Monique altogether. Her somewhat pretentious statements here seem counterbalanced by her honest reflections on other occasions, where she has no problems admitting faults and selfish behaviour. It appears as though the author has too effectually disguised her judgement of Monique for her irony to be clear, and/or readers, given their shared responsibility for making the irony in the story work, have simply closed their eyes to the implicit critique of the character-narrator.

The author states in *Tout Compte fait* that her intention was to "montrer

---

[69] Hutcheon 125.
[70] "I should find it hard to bear if I were not entirely free to help the people who need me." (WD 127)
[71] "I expect a lot of the people I love – too much, perhaps. I expect a lot, and I even ask for it. But I do not know how to insist." (WD 151)
[72] "I am certain that I am worth more than she is." (WD 197)
[73] "There are two sorts of people who like it – simple people who are moved by Monique's tragedy, and intellectuals who grasp what it is all about." (ASD 144)

[…] comment la *victime* essayait d'en fuir la vérité" (TCF 175; my emphasis).[74] However, to Beauvoir, the "truth" about Monique is only to be found when all the evidence is assembled: "Aucune phrase n'a en soi son sens, aucun détail n'a de valeur sinon replacé dans l'ensemble du journal" (TCF 176).[75] Seen as a whole, there is no doubt that Monique in her diary attempts to protect herself from truths she does not want to face.[76] The depiction of her lies and her silences, her suppressions and her concealments do not, however alter her status as a victim – Beauvoir herself uses the word in her otherwise critical remarks about Monique. Even for the ("second") category of readers, who are presumably acquainted with the significant intertext *Le Deuxième Sexe,* Beauvoir's irony may not be univocally directed towards the female party:

> Et le pire est que son dévouement même apparaît comme importun; il se convertit aux yeux du mari en une tyrannie à laquelle il essaie de se soustraire; et cependant, c'est lui qui l'impose à la femme comme sa suprême, son unique justification; [...] C'est la duplicité du mari qui voue la femme à un malheur dont il se plaint ensuite d'être lui-même victime. […] Elle passe son existence à mesurer l'étendue de cette trahison. (DS II 323-24)[77]

So if the readers have closed their eyes to Monique, it may be because they have been too focused on her husband's duplicity. Maurice's behaviour is perhaps the single most important factor that undermines the effect of irony used to depict Monique. His love affair has gone on for eighteen months by the time Monique pushes him to admit it. Although he also appears to be sorry for what he is doing to his wife, there is textual evidence enough to support the suggestion that a calculating mind, well aware of his male privileges, is lurking behind his mask of compassion. Concurrently with his occasional empathy, he closely observes his wife's reactions so as to take advantage of the liberty they allow him, as seen in the scene immediately following Monique's adoption of "the tactics of the smile":

> En prenant le petit déjeuner, Maurice m'a dit que désormais quand il sortirait

---

[74] "[...] show how the victim tries to escape from the truth." (ASD 140)

[75] "No words have their real meaning, no details their true validity unless they are reset in the context of the diary as a whole." (ASD 140-1)

[76] See for example Fallaize, *Novels* 165-72.

[77] "And the worst of it is that her very devotion often seems annoying, importunate; it is transformed for the husband into a tyranny from which he tries to escape; and yet he it is who imposes it upon his wife as her supreme, her unique justification. [...] It is the duplicity of the husband that dooms the wife to a misfortune of which he complains later that he is himself the victim. [...] Her life through, she measures the extent of that betrayal." (SS 496-497)

le soir avec Noëllie, il resterait toute la nuit chez elle. C'est plus décent pour elle comme pour moi, prétend-il. – Puisque tu acceptes que j'aie cette histoire, laisse-moi la vivre correctement. (FR 139-40)[78]

Maurice is waiting – that is, he refuses to take responsibility for his actions and make the necessary choice. When Monique asks him how he sees their future, he answers: "Je ne veux pas te perdre. Je ne veux pas non plus renoncer à Noëllie. Pour le reste, je nage…" (FR 208).[79] On another occasion, in response to a direct question from Monique, Maurice hesitantly makes a move towards freeing himself from her: "Ce dont j'aurais envie – je ne lui en ai pas parlé, c'est toi que ça concerne – c'est de vivre seul pendant quelque temps. Il y a une tension entre nous qui disparaîtrait si nous cessions – oh! provisoirement – d'habiter ensemble" (FR 234).[80] His discourse here is drenched with insincerity. There is evidence that Maurice had hoped he could get away with his double-dealing: "J'espérais me débrouiller entre Noëllie et toi" (FR 243).[81] Eager to purchase some time with Noëllie, Maurice tries to make a distasteful deal with his wife:

> [...] Il souhaite partir en week-end avec Noëllie. En compensation, il s'arrangera pour ne plus travailler ces soirs-ci, nous aurons beaucoup de temps à nous. J'ai eu un sursaut de révolte. Son visage s'est durci: 'N'en parlons plus'. Il est redevenu aimable mais j'étais bouleversée de lui avoir refusé quelque chose. Il me jugeait mesquine ou du moins inamicale. Il n'hésiterait pas à me mentir la semaine suivante: la séparation serait consommée entre nous. (FR 148-49)[82]

Monique's reaction shows that there is really no correct way for her to handle the situation, since she is caught up in a destructive vicious circle for which she shares equal blame.

---

78 "During breakfast Maurice told me that from now on, when he goes with Noëllie in the evening, he is going to spend the whole night at her place. It is more seemly for her, just as it is for me, he says. 'Since you acquiesce in my having this affair, let me live it decently.'" (WD 141-42)
79 "'I don't want to lose you. I don't want to give up Noëllie, either. As for everything else, I just don't know where I am…'" (WD 209-10)
80 "'What I should like – I have not spoken of it to her: you are the one it concerns – is to live by myself for a certain time. There is a tension between us that would vanish if – just for the time being, of course – we were to give up living together.'" (WD 235-36)
81 "I hoped I should manage somehow with Noëllie and you." (WD 244)
82 "[...] He would like to go off for the weekend with Noëllie. By way of compensation he would arrange not to work these coming evenings so that we should have plenty of time to ourselves. I showed that my mind revolted against it. His face hardened. 'Let's not talk about it anymore.' He grew amiable again, but having refused him something quite overwhelmed me. He was thinking of me mean-minded, or at least unfriendly. He would not hesitate to lie to me the following week: the separation between us would be fully accomplished." (WD 150)

The text clearly portrays conflicting images when it comes to the questions of truth, guilt and bad faith in the case of Monique versus Maurice. Hence the reader is faced with a textual ambiguity – and no clearly delineated object of negative evaluation.

In "Monologue", I pointed out the ways in which the very mode of the narration gives clues to direct readers' interpretation. In "La Femme rompue", I would argue, the narrative form of the diary contributes to reinforce the effect of familiarity and close contact with the protagonist. In the event that the reader initially responds sympathetically to the implicit invitation to intimacy and emotional involvement that the form implies, that sympathy is likely to be strengthened as the story moves on. Hence, the form itself might work against an ironic interpretation. According to Hutcheon: "From the point of view of the *interpreter,* irony is [...] the making or inferring of **meaning** in addition to and different from what is stated, together with an attitude toward both the said and the unsaid."[83] Ironic discourse thus seems to require evaluative *distance,* asking for the interpreter to discriminate between several layers of meaning-making. However, the implicit textual request for this need for distancing may be blurred if it is counterbalanced by positive evidence that favours the subject of the irony – which is, as I have tried to show, exactly the case here. Monique acknowledges her own *mauvaise foi.* The apparent sincerity of her account of the sufferings she is going through, along with her restless and fervent self-examination cannot help but move the reader and predispose him/her in her favour – especially when seen in the light of the futility of her actions and reactions: "Je me tourmente. Comment les gens me voient-ils? En toute objectivité, qui suis-je?" (FR 201)[84] "Comme je voudrais me voir avec d'autres yeux que les miens!" (FR 216)[85] Her seemingly contradictory statements and shifting mind may also be accorded a sympathetic interpretation, since this is a way of sorting out her thoughts, constantly having to reposition herself to meet shifting realities.

In fact, Monique's reactions to her husband's affair are an exact illustration of Beauvoir's own description in *Le Deuxième Sexe* of the trapped position the betrayed married woman finds herself in:

> Trop complaisante, la femme voit son mari lui échapper [...]. Cependant, si

---

[83] Hutcheon 11.
[84] "I am torturing myself. What is the general opinion of me? Quite objectively, who am I?" (WD 202)
[85] "How I should like to see myself as others see me!" (WD 217)

elle lui interdit toute aventure, si elle l'excède par sa surveillance, ses scènes, ses exigences, elle peut l'indisposer contre elle gravement. [...] Dissimuler, ruser, haïr et craindre en silence, miser sur la vanité et les faiblesses d'un homme, apprendre à le déjouer, à le jouer, à le manoeuvrer, c'est une bien triste science. (DS II 305)[86]

Beauvoir's prime target for criticism is the *institution of marriage* – she is not exclusively aiming at a married woman's self-deception. By making use of an ironic discourse that has not been "correctly" comprehended, Beauvoir has unintentionally added to the complexity of the text, increasing its potentialities of meaning. To a modern reader, more inclined to accept and even to appreciate such textual qualities, the deplorable destiny of *both* Maurice and Monique is more likely to come clear, and therefore, Beauvoir's critical view of the institution as such becomes all the more visible.

Conclusion

In his discussion of the waning of the modern movement in western culture at the end of the 1950s and early 1960s, and the subsequent coming of post-modernism, Fredric Jameson considers existentialism in philosophy (along with other artistic and philosophical "movements") to be "the final, extraordinary flowing of a high-modernist impulse which is spent and exhausted by them."[87] There is no doubt about Beauvoir's commitment to existentialist philosophy, which is also the underpinning for her views on women's liberation and hence her didactical intentions with *La Femme rompue*. However, in my view, this short story collection also reveals some interesting features that to a certain extent, allow for readings more in line with a "post-modern" perception of narratives.

We have seen that the three stories, through their narrative and discursive modes and the revelation of the protagonists' self-delusion, constantly examine the problems around the idea of truth and true meaning. Although the three women come from different social classes, they share a feeling that situations that they believed to be fundamental and immutable have fallen

---

[86] "If she is too obliging, a wife finds her husband escaping her, [...]. But if she denies him any adventures whatever, if she annoys him with her watchfulness, her scenes, her demands, she is likely to turn him definitely against her. [...] This is indeed a melancholy science – to dissimulate, to use trickery, to hate and fear in silence, to play on the vanity and the weaknesses of a man, to learn to thwart him, to deceive him, to "manage" him." (SS 487)

[87] Fredric Jameson, *Postmodernism, or the Cultural Logic of Late Capitalism* (London and New York: Verso, 1993) 1.

apart. The texts also express an ambivalence about the future as a possible organizing horizon. The strategies in the text that aim at deconstructing the protagonist's dominant discourse may also (as with the title story) become the object of deconstruction, and as such, end up illustrating the ambiguous character of language. Beauvoir's last work of fiction thus in many ways also conveys meanings and forms of expression that are likely to find resonance with contemporary readers.

Works Cited

Bair, Deirdre. *Simone de Beauvoir. A Biography*. New York: Touchstone, 1990.

Bal, Mieke. *Narratology. Introduction to the Theory of Narrative*. Toronto: University of Toronto Press, 1999.

Barthes, Roland. *Mythologies*. Paris: Éditions du Seuil, 1957.

_____. *Mythologies*. Selected and translated by Annette Lavers, St Albans, Herts: Paladin, 1973.

Beauvoir, Simone de. *La Femme rompue*. Paris: Gallimard, 1967.

_____. *The Woman Destroyed*. Translated by P. O'Brian, New York: Pantheon Books, 1987.

_____. *Le Deuxième Sexe*. Vol I & II. Paris: Gallimard 1976.

_____. *The Second Sex*. Translated and edited by H.M. Parshley, Harmondsworth: Penguin Books, 1976.

_____. *Tout Compte fait*. Paris: Gallimard, 1972.

_____. *All Said and Done*. Translated by P. O'Brian, Harmondsworth: Penguin Books, 1977.

Fallaize, Elizabeth. *The Novels of Simone de Beauvoir*. London and New York: Routledge, 1990.

_____. (ed.). Simone de Beauvoir. *A Critical Reader*. London and New York: Routledge, 1998.

Hutcheon, Linda. *Irony's Edge: The Theory and Politics of Irony*. London and New York: Routledge, 1995.

Jameson, Fredric. *Postmodernism, or the Cultural Logic of Late Capitalism*. London and New York: Verso, 1993.

Keefe, Terry. *Simone de Beauvoir*. New York: St. Martins Press, 1998.

Leech, Geoffrey N. & Michael H. Short. *Style in Fiction*. London and New York: Longman, 1981.

Moi, Toril. "Intentions and Effects: Rhetoric and Identification in Simone de Beauvoir's 'The Woman Destroyed.'" *What is a Woman? And Other Essays*. Oxford: Oxford University Press, 1999. 451-97.

Ophir, Anne. *Regards féminins*. Paris: Denoël/Gonthier, 1976.

Schoentjes, Pierre. *Poétique de l'ironie*. Paris: Éditions du Seuil, 2001.

Shepherd, Genevieve. *Simone de Beauvoir's Fiction. A Psychoanalytic Rereading*. New York: Peter Lang, 2003.

CONTRIBUTORS

Susan Bainbrigge is a Lecturer in French at the University of Edinburgh. Her research focuses on 20th century and contemporary French literature and Autobiography studies, and she has published *Writing against Death: the Autobiographies of Simone de Beauvoir* (2005) and articles on Beauvoir, Suzanne Lilar, Jean-Paul Sartre and Serge Doubrovsky in the context of writing the self. More recent research has taken her into the field of Belgian francophone literature and she has edited, with Jeanette den Toonder, a book on Amélie Nothomb entitled *Amélie Nothomb: Authorship, Identity and Narrative Practice* (2003), and is currently working on Belgian francophone cultural and literary identity.

Annlaug Bjørsnøs is an Assistant Professor in the Romance Section of the Department of Modern Languages at the University of Trondheim, NTNU, specializing in surrealism, literary theory, French feminist theory, existentialism and Simone de Beauvoir. Her research interests included individuality in literature, with reference to Rousseau's fiction, modern literature, and in particular Simone de Beauvoir. Her publications include *Jumelés par l'angoisse, séparés par l'extase. Une analyse de l'oeuvre poétique de Joyce Mansour* (Solum Forag/Didier Érudition, 1998), "Le 'moi relatif' et l'individuation dans *Julie, ou la Nouvelle Héloïse* de Rousseau," *Romansk Forum* 16 (2002), and "Assuming Ambiguity, Embracing Lack: Simone de Beauvoir and the Postmodern Subject", *Simone de Beauvoir Studies* 18 (2002).

Sarah Fishwick is a full-time tutor in the Department of French Studies, University of Birmingham, where she teaches and lectures on numerous French language and culture modules. She is the author of the study of corporeality in Beauvoir's writings entitled *The Body in the Work of Simone de Beauvoir* (Peter Lang, 2002) and has published several other articles on Beauvoir's work. Her current research project takes the fiction of the French writer and playwright Marie Redonnet as its focus. Her article, "Encounters with Matisse: Space, Art and Intertextuality in A.S. Byatt's *The Matisse Stories* and Marie Redonnet's *Villa Rosa*" was published in 2004.

Alison T. Holland lectures in French at Northumbria University where she is Head of Modern Foreign Languages. Her research focuses on the textual strategies that Simone de Beauvoir uses in her fiction. She is a member of the Simone de Beauvoir Society and her work has appeared in *Simone de Beauvoir Studies*. Her articles on Beauvoir's fiction include "Identity in Crisis: The Gothic Textual Space in *L'Invitée*," *Modern Language Review* (2003). Her book, *Simone de Beauvoir: A Beginner's Guide* was published by Hodder and Stoughton in December 2002. Her publications also include "The Quest for Identity in the Later Fiction of Simone de Beauvoir" in *Women in Contemporary Culture: Roles and Identities in France and Spain,* ed. Lesley Twomey (Intellect, 2000).

Louise Renée is Associate Professor of French literature at the University of Manitoba in Winnipeg, Canada. Her areas of interest include Simone de Beauvoir, feminist theory, women's writing, the 20th century novel in France, francophone literature and authors from Manitoba. She has given public lectures on Simone de Beauvoir, including "Simone de Beauvoir: A Feminist Thinker for Morally Corrupt Times," Centre for Professional and Applied Ethics, 2003. Her publications in *Simone de Beauvoir Studies* include: "The Gendering of Melancholia in Beauvoir's Fictional Works" (2000-1), "Orange Blossoms and Roses: Love Imagery in the First Chapter of *Les Mandarins*" (1994), and "'Les Mythes' de Simone de Beauvoir: Subtile Déconstruction de *La Nausée* de Jean-Paul Sartre" (2003-4).

Elizabeth Richardson Viti is Professor of French at Gettysburg College where she teaches in the Department of French and Italian and on the Women's Studies Program. Her book, *Mothers, Madams and "Lady-like" Men: Proust and the Maternal* (Summa, 1994), combines her interest in the novel and feminist literary theory. This interest has also led to the publication of articles on pedagogy: "He Said, She Said: a Feminist Approach to Teaching the Twentieth-Century Novel in the Twenty-First Century," *The French Review* (2000). She has also written on women writers: "Passion simple and Madame, c'est à vous que j'écris: That's MY Desire," *Studies in 20th Century Literature* (2001).

Ursula Tidd teaches in the Department of French Studies at the University of Manchester, UK. Her research interests are the literature and philosophy of Simone de Beauvoir, post-war French literature and thought, especially autobiography, ethics and French Holocaust literature. Her recent University Press publications include *Simone de Beauvoir, Gender and Testimony* (Cambridge, 1999), "For the Time Being: the Representation of Temporality in Simone de Beauvoir's Autobiography," in *The Existential Phenomenology of Simone de Beauvoir,* ed. Lester Embree and Wendy O'Brien (Kluwer, 2001), "Simone de Beauvoir: The Subject in Question," *Nottingham French Studies* (2003), and *An Introduction to Beauvoir's Thought* in the "Critical Thinkers" series (Routledge 2004).

INDEX